NIGHT+DAY
SAN FRANCISCO

By Julianne Balmain
with Kate Chynoweth

PULSE GUIDES

Pulse Guides' Night+Day San Francisco is an independent guide. We do not accept payment of any kind from events or establishments for inclusion in this book. We welcome your views on our selections. Please email us: **feedback@pulseguides.com**.

The information contained in this book was checked as rigorously as possible before going to press. The publisher accepts no responsibility for any changes that may have occurred since, or for any other variance of fact from that recorded here in good faith.

No part of this book may be reproduced in any form without permission in writing from the publisher, except by a reviewer who wishes to quote brief passages for a published review. This publication is a creative work fully protected by all applicable copyright laws, as well as by misappropriation, trade secrets, unfair competition, and all other applicable laws. The authors and editors of this work have added value to the underlying factual material herein through one or more of the following: unique and original selection, coordination, expression, arrangement, and classification (including the itineraries) of the information.

Distributed in the United States and Canada by National Book Network (NBN).
First Edition. Printed in the United States. 30% postconsumer content.
Copyright © 2006 ASDavis Media Group, Inc. All rights reserved.
ISBN-10:0-9759022-9-6; ISBN-13:978-0-9759022-9-5

Credits

Executive Editor	Alan S. Davis
Editor	Christina Henry de Tessan
Author	Julianne Balmain
Contributor	Kate Chynoweth
Copy Editors	Gail Nelson-Bonebrake, Elizabeth Stroud
Maps	Chris Gillis
Production	Jo Farrell, Samia Afra
Cover Design	Wil Klass, Clara Teufel

Photo Credits: (Front cover, left to right) Les Byerley, Getty Images, Alex Hong; (Back cover, left to right) David Phelps, Christopher Inch, Getty Images, and Ben Renard-Wiart; (Inside cover, top) Ruby Skye; (Inside cover, middle and bottom; back cover left) courtesy of The Kimpton Group; (Julianne Balmain, p.8) Christopher Irion.

Special Sales

For information about bulk purchases of Pulse Guides (ten copies or more), email us at bookorders@pulseguides.com. Special bulk rates are available for charities, corporations, institutions, and online and mail-order catalogs, and our books can be customized to suit your company's needs.

NIGHT+DAY
The Cool Cities Series from PULSE GUIDES

P.O. Box 590780, San Francisco, CA 94159
pulseguides.com

Pulse Guides is an imprint of ASDavis Media Group, Inc.

The Night+Day Difference

Pulse of the City

Our job is to point you to all of the city's peak experiences: amazing museums, unique spas, and spectacular views. But the complete *urbanista* experience is more than just impressions—it is grownup fun, the kind that thrives by night as well as by day. Urban fun is a hip nightclub or a trendy restaurant. It is people-watching and people-meeting. Lonely planet? We don't think so. Night+Day celebrates our lively planet.

The Right Place. The Right Time. It matters.

A Night+Day city must have exemplary restaurants, a vibrant nightlife scene, and enough attractions to keep a visitor busy for six days without having to do the same thing twice. In selecting restaurants, food is important, but so is the scene. Our hotels, most of which are 4- and 5-star properties, are rated for the quality of the concierge staff (can they get you into a hot restaurant?) as well as the rooms. You won't find kids with fake IDs at our nightlife choices. And the attractions must be truly worthy of your time. But experienced travelers know that timing is almost everything. Going to a restaurant at 7pm can be a very different experience (and probably less fun) than at 9pm; a champagne boat cruise might be ordinary in the morning but spectacular at sunset. We believe providing the reader with this level of detail makes the difference between a good experience and a great one.

The Bottom Line

Your time is precious. Our guide must be easy to use and dead-on accurate. That is why our executive editor, editors, and writers (locals who are in touch with what is great—and what is not) spend hundreds of hours researching, writing, and debating selections for each guide. The results are presented in four unique ways: The *99 Best* with our top three choices in 33 categories that highlight what is great about the city; the *Experience* chapters, in which our selections are organized by distinct themes or personalities (Hot & Cool, Hip, and Classic); a *Perfect Plan* (Three Days and Nights) for each theme, showing how to get the most out of the city in a short period of time; and the *San Francisco Black Book*, listing all the hotels, restaurants, nightlife, and attractions, with key details, contact information, and page references.

Our bottom line is this: If you find our guide easy to use and enjoyable to read, and with our help you have an extraordinary time, we have succeeded. We review and value all feedback from our readers, so please contact us at **feedback@pulseguides.com**.

From the Publisher:

I've had the travel bug ever since my first summer job during college—escorting tour groups around Europe to evaluate them for my parents' travel company. When I retired from the paper business ten years ago I set out on a journey to find the 100 most fun places to be in the world at the right time. The challenge of unearthing the world's greatest events—from the Opera Ball in Vienna to the Calgary Stampede—led me to write a guidebook.

The success of *The Fun Also Rises*, named after Ernest Hemingway's *The Sun Also Rises*, which helped popularize what has become perhaps the most thrilling party on earth (Pamplona's Fiesta de San Fermín, also known as the Running of the Bulls), persuaded me that there were others who shared my interest in a different approach to travel. Guidebooks were neither informative nor exciting enough to capture peak experiences— whether for world-class events or just a night on the town.

My goal is to publish *extraordinary guides for extraordinary travelers.* **Night+Day**, the first series from Pulse Guides, is for Gen-Xers to Zoomers (Boomers with a zest for life), who know that if one wants to truly experience a city, the night is as important as the day. **Night+Day** guides present the best that a city has to offer—hotels, restaurants, nightlife, and attractions that are exciting without being stuffy—in a totally new format.

Pulse Guides abides by one guiding principle: Never settle for the ordinary. We hope that a willingness to explore new approaches to guidebooks, combined with meticulous research, provides you with unique and significant experiences.

After spending a major portion of every year on the road, I get to return home to one of the great cities in the world, San Francisco. I'm excited to be launching Pulse Guides' **Night+Day** series with the San Francisco guide—it has given me an opportunity to know my city even better, and along with our writers and editors, to show its fun side to you.

Wishing you extraordinary times,

Alan S. Davis, Publisher and Executive Editor
Pulse Guides

P.S. To contact me, or for updated information on all of our Night+Day guides, please visit our website at **pulseguides.com**.

TOC

INTRODUCTION 9
   Night+Day's San Francisco Urbie 12

THE 99 BEST OF SAN FRANCISCO 15
   Always-Hot Restaurants 16
   Brunches 17
   Chic Asian Restaurants 18
   Club Scenes 19
   Dim Sum 20
   DJ Bars 21
   Fine Dining 22
   Gay Bars and Clubs 23
   Historic San Francisco 24
   Late-Night Eats 25
   Late-Night Hangouts 26
   Latin Restaurants 27
   Live Music Venues 28
   Lounges with a View 29
   Neighborhood Bars 30
   Only-in-San Francisco Experiences 31
   Outdoor Activities 32
   Power Lunch Spots 33
   Restaurants with a View 34
   Restaurants with Bars 35
   Romantic Dining 36
   Scene Bars 37
   Seafood Restaurants 38
   Sex in the City 39
   Sexy Lounges 40
   Spas 41
   Sushi Restaurants 42
   Tiki Bars 43
   Trendy Hangouts 44
   Trendy Tables 45
   Wine Bars 46
   Wine Lists 47
   Workouts 48

EXPERIENCE SAN FRANCISCO ...49
Hot & Cool San Francisco ...50
- The Perfect Plan (3 Days and Nights) ...51
- The Key Neighborhoods ...55
- The Shopping Blocks ...56
- The Hotels ...58
- The Restaurants ...62
- The Nightlife ...72
- The Attractions ...82

Hip San Francisco ...88
- The Perfect Plan (3 Days and Nights) ...89
- The Key Neighborhoods ...93
- The Shopping Blocks ...94
- The Hotels ...95
- The Restaurants ...98
- The Nightlife ...108
- The Attractions ...118

Classic San Francisco ...122
- The Perfect Plan (3 Days and Nights) ...123
- The Key Neighborhoods ...127
- The Shopping Blocks ...128
- The Hotels ...129
- The Restaurants ...132
- The Nightlife ...146
- The Attractions ...152

PRIME TIME SAN FRANCISCO ...157
- Prime Time Basics ...158
  - Eating and Drinking ...158
  - Weather and Tourism ...158
  - National Holidays ...159
- The Best Events Calendar ...160
- The Best Events ...161

HIT THE GROUND RUNNING ...167
- City Essentials ...168
  - Getting to San Francisco: By Air ...168
  - Getting to San Francisco: By Land ...172
  - San Francisco: Lay of the Land ...173

Getting Around San Francisco 173
Other Practical Information (Money Matters; Metric Conversion; Safety; Numbers to Know; Gay and Lesbian Travel; Traveling with Disabilities; Print Media; Radio Stations; Shopping Hours; Attire; Size Conversion; Drinking; Smoking; Drugs; Time Zone; Additional Resources for Visitors) 175
Party Conversation—A Few Surprising Facts 180
The Cheat Sheet (The Very Least You Ought to Know About San Francisco) (Neighborhoods, Landmarks, Great Parks, Hills, Party Zones, Big Museums, Linguistic Mistakes to Avoid, Performing Arts Centers, Sports Teams, Cardinal Rule, and Coffee) 181
Just for Business & Conventions 188

San Francisco Region Map 190

LEAVING SAN FRANCISCO 191
Overnight Trips
Mendocino 192
Monterey and Carmel 194
Napa Valley 196
Sonoma Valley and Healdsburg 198
Day Trips
Big Sur 200
East Bay 201
Muir Woods, Muir Beach, Stinson Beach 202
Point Reyes 203
Santa Cruz 204
Sausalito and the Marin Headlands 205
Tiburon and Angel Island 206

SAN FRANCISCO BLACK BOOK 207
San Francisco Black Book by Neighborhood 208
San Francisco Black Book 212
San Francisco Unique Shopping Index 230

Heart of San Francisco Map 231
San Francisco Neighborhoods Map 232

About the Authors

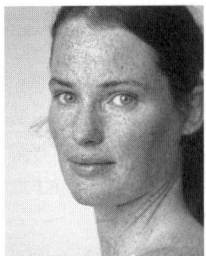

Julianne Balmain is the author of numerous books having to do with seeking fun of one sort or another, including the *Kama Sutra Deck* and *Office Kama Sutra*. A consummate diner who is excessively fond of night spots, she is also the author, writing as Nadia Gordon, of three mystery novels set in the Napa Valley wine country and steeped in the culinary life. Find out more at nadiagordon.com.

Kate Chynoweth's books include *The Risks of Sunbathing Topless*, an anthology of women's travel essays, and several travel guides, including *The Best Places to Kiss: Northern California*. Her writing on travel, food, and lifestyle appears in *Real Simple, Seattle,* and *Sunset.*

Acknowledgments

Thank you to all the party people and hearty eaters who helped make this book possible. Without you, I might still be at home, wondering where the action is. Thanks especially to Altura, discerning master of the San Francisco scene. And finally, a tip of the hat to young Ivan, who bravely ventured where few babies dare to go. To Alan, Christina, and Kate, your many valuable insights and contributions made all the difference.
Julianne Balmain

Gratitude, as ever, to my in-house San Francisco native, Dave Griffith, who was even more indispensible than usual while I was working on this book. Thanks also goes to Christina Henry for being the best-informed editor any travel writer could wish for—and not just because she was raised in Cow Hollow.
Kate Chynoweth

Introduction

San Francisco: What It Was

Welcome to San Francisco, otherwise known as the City by the Bay! Set on the edge of the Pacific Ocean, this beautiful metropolis is world-famous for its steep, scenic hills, picturesque coastline, and freewheeling West Coast character. Since it exploded into prominence with the Gold Rush, San Francisco has drawn visionaries of every stripe, from the notoriously materialistic (gold-digging 49ers, 1990s dot-commers) to the famously radical (Summer of Love hippies, gay activists). But whether you think of it as a stylish mecca for the rich and ambitious, or an anything-goes party town, a few days here will show you why the phrase "I left my heart in San Francisco" has become the city's unofficial motto.

The area's history begins 4,000 to 5,000 years ago with a tribal group known as the Ohlone whose likely reasons for settling here—mild weather, fresh water, and abundant seafood—sound pretty familiar today. Archaeological excavation of giant shell mounds, many of which were 20 or 30 feet high and 600 feet long and 200 feet wide, show the massive amounts of mollusk shells the group discarded (you're not the only one who loves Northern California for the oysters!). The tribe's migratory and peaceful way of life was interrupted during the era of European exploration and colonialism, however, and declined as the strength and control of the Spanish increased in the later part of the 18th century. The Spanish established their most northerly outpost in San Francisco at Mission Dolores in 1776.

But it wasn't merely the Spanish who wanted a piece of this promising and beautiful peninsula; and as Russian, English, and French explorers all made their way here, the shipping trade increased, centering on what was called Yerba Buena Cove. (Today, plaques at the corners of Market and First and Bush and Market Streets mark the cove's original shoreline; the Financial District is on landfill.) The town, then called Yerba Buena, was a tiny and dusty village with a population of 459, plus a constant ebb and flow of military and naval personnel. Even when it became part of the United States in July 1846, little Yerba Buena hardly

> **From the moment that an enterprising local paraded down a main street with a vial of gold dust and proclaimed, "Gold on the American River!" San Francisco was the place everyone wanted to be.**

seemed destined for greatness—until gold was found in the nearby Sierra foothills in 1848.

The Gold Rush opened the floodgates, and during its first three years, more than 200,000 people arrived in California, in a completely unique peaceful mass migration. From the moment that an enterprising local named Sam Brannan—the same one who'd insisted on renaming the village San Francisco in 1847 in the hope of luring ship captains familiar with San Francisco Bay—paraded down a main street with a vial of gold dust and proclaimed "Gold! Gold! Gold on the American River!" San Francisco was the place that everyone wanted to be.

The city became a boom town, with the newly minted rich gambling in the big saloons and rubbing shoulders with scruffy new arrivals on the crowded streets. Just a decade after the Gold Rush began, the population of San Francisco was well over 50,000, and the city's well-lit streets were lined with posh hotels and storehouses. Growth continued by leaps and bounds, and between the 1870s and 1900 the endless rows of Victorian houses that San Francisco is so famous for today started springing up. This was also the era of the cable car, a new form of transportation that made the city's steepest hilltops accessible; on Nob Hill, the city's millionaires competed over who could build the most ornate mansion. At the same time, the city's have-nots and ne'er-do-wells found their own neighborhoods; the most criminal congregated in a notoriously dangerous part of town near the waterfront known as the Barbary Coast.

The famous earthquake of 1906 struck on April 18, with a magnitude of 8.25, and lasted 49 seconds; but it was the great fire that followed that caused the most damage, destroying about 28,000 buildings. More than half of the city's estimated 400,000 residents were left homeless. The rebuilding pushed the limits of the city outward, and new neighborhoods were settled; downtown was constructed anew. Suddenly, the Seal of the City and County of San Francisco, which shows a phoenix, the legendary Greek bird, arising from burning fire, seemed even more apropos than when it had been adopted in 1852 after the great fires of the 1840s.

A measure of just how spectacularly the city rebuilt itself was evidenced by the Panama-Pacific International Exposition of 1915, one of the most splendid of the world's fairs. The centerpiece building, the Palace of Fine Arts, a neoclassical rotunda, still stands proudly today in the city's Marina District. Eighteen years later, construction began on the Golden Gate Bridge, the city's most famous landmark, and for years after its completion in 1937 it ranked as the longest suspension bridge in the world.

In the mid-1950s, writers like Jack Kerouac and Allen Ginsberg gathered around the fulcrum of poet Lawrence Ferlinghetti's City Lights bookstore (which still stands today on Columbus Avenue) in North Beach, typifying the "Beat Generation" with their nonconformist beliefs and wild Bacchanalian parties. When the hippie revolution exploded in the 1960s, playing out on the psychedelic stage of Haight-Ashbury, it seemed the Beats had paved the way. San Francisco became headquarters for groovy "acid test" parties and for bands like Jefferson Airplane, the Grateful Dead, and Big Brother and the Holding Company, led by Janis Joplin. In 1967, the "Human Be-In" happened in Golden Gate Park, and the following summer, Haight-Ashbury was home to the world-famous Summer of Love. It was an inevitable comedown when the 1970s ushered in a new era; but even after the hippies departed, San Francisco remained inextricably linked to the legacy of the 1960s, characterized by a tolerance for alternative lifestyles and diversity.

San Francisco's now-famous gay community came out extravagantly in the 1970s, and charged into triumph with the 1977 election of gay activist Harvey Milk to the city's Board of Supervisors. But tragedy struck the next year, when Dan White, an outspoken antigay former police officer and former city supervisor, assassinated Milk as well as George Moscone, the mayor of San Francisco. The entire city went up in arms when White received a lesser charge after his defense attorneys used what became referred to as the "Twinkie defense," in which they argued that he was suffering from "diminished capacity" worsened by eating too much sugary junk food. In the early 1980s, the first cases of the as-yet-undiagnosed AIDS emerged, and by mid-decade it had started taking its deadly toll. But the city's resilient gay community, still proudly identified with the rainbow flag, has recovered and the Castro remains one of the city's most vibrant and fun neighborhoods.

Key Dates

1770s	Spanish take control of this area, then called Yerba Buena Cove.
1776	Mission Dolores is built.
1848	Gold is discovered on the American River.
1849	The Gold Rush draws tens of thousands to the area.
1906	The earthquake strikes April 18. Fire rages through the city.
1915	Panama-Pacific Int'l Exposition
1937	Golden Gate Bridge is completed.
1950s	The Beat Generation arrives.
1968	Haight-Ashbury's Summer of Love.
1990s	The dot-com boom draws tens of thousands who come seeking to make their fortune.

Night+Day's San Francisco Urbie

Night+Day cities are chosen because they have a vibrant nightlife scene, standard-setting and innovative restaurants, cutting-edge hotels, and enough attractions to keep one busy for six days without doing the same thing twice. In short, they are fun. They represent the quintessential *urbanista* experience. This wouldn't exist but for the creativity and talents of many people and organizations. In honor of all who have played a role in making San Francisco one of the world's coolest cities, Pulse Guides is pleased to give special recognition, and our Urbie Award, to an individual or organization whose contribution is exemplary.

The San Francisco Urbie: Kimpton Hotel Group

When Bill Kimpton opened his first boutique hotel in San Francisco in 1981, he launched a trend that has changed the way visitors stay in the City by the Bay, and in fact, around the world.

Kimpton Hotel Group is known for its commitment to rejuvenating older properties and turning them into stylish, contemporary haunts for sophisticated travelers. "Our guests are as individual in personality and style as our hotels," explains Kimpton CEO Tom LaTour. "In the past, most travelers were either on the road for business or pleasure. Today, however, many guests want to combine diverse elements of work and play into a single visit."

Kimpton boutiques share five elements—care, comfort, style, flavor, and fun—recognizable by public spaces that encourage guests to socialize, nightly wine and cheese gatherings, destination restaurants, and even a pet goldfish to keep you company for the duration of your stay. They take the "home away from home" philosophy to heart by emphasizing comfort and convenience—yoga accessories, deluxe pillows, exercise equipment in the room, and extra-long beds for tall guests. "We build strong emotional connections with our guests one interaction at a time," says Latour. Although Kimpton himself passed away, the boutique concept he pioneered continues to grow, and there are now 39 Kimpton properties in the United States and Canada.

(In San Francisco we recommend these Kimpton hotels: Harbor Court Hotel, Hotel Monaco, Hotel Palomar, Hotel Triton and Prescott Hotel.)

Cultural revolutions weren't the only things happening in San Francisco in the '60s and '70s—the city was also emerging as a forerunner in celluloid and in conservation. The groundbreaking movies filmed here in the 1960s include *Guess Who's Coming to Dinner* and *The Graduate*, and two Alfred Hitchcock films, *Vertigo* and *The Birds*. In 1968, the movie *Bullitt* used San Francisco's steep, mean streets to great effect with car chases; other movie producers took note, and even in recent years movies such as *The Rock* have showcased the city's dramatic terrain. Meanwhile, powerful environmental organizations like the Sierra Club successfully lobbied the city to create the Golden Gate National Recreation Area (GGNRA) in 1973; one of the largest urban national parks in the world, it protects some 75,000 acres of land and water from the Marin Headlands and Muir Woods to the Presidio.

Given the proximity of its southern neighbor, Silicon Valley, it was inevitable that San Francisco would get caught up in the dot-com boom of the 1990s. And indeed, the city had a renaissance that recalled the Gold Rush. Industry visionaries arrived in droves and transformed SoMa's warehouses into sleek office space, while the newly rich and brash (and young) spent their thousands at the city's of-the-moment bars and restaurants. Millions changed hands as fortunes were made on ephemeral ideas linked to good domain names, and the cost of living soared. When the boom went bust in the late '90s, most of the fortunes were lost—although San Francisco did not become a less expensive place to live as a result. Today, its housing prices rank among the highest in the nation.

San Francisco: What It Is

Today's San Francisco is a cultural melting pot of more than 750,000 people, a city of vibrant neighborhoods that attracts visitors from around the globe. From the Latino-influenced Mission, which has become a mecca for hipsters, lined with legendary taquerias, packed bars, and vintage shops, to the bustling streets of the city's famous Chinatown; from the splendid mansions of Pacific Heights to the scenester nightclubs of SoMa (South of Market); from the shops of Union Square to the charmingly chaotic Italian coffee shops in North Beach, there is virtually no part of San Francisco that doesn't engage all the senses at once. And if culture is what you're after, the city has it in spades, from the gleaming SFMoMA to the ornate and historic Opera House.

"The City by the Bay" is an apt nickname for San Francisco. Beautiful views of the sparkling bay and urban landscape are everywhere, whether you're cresting Nob Hill on the cable car or strolling across the Golden Gate Bridge. And then there are the city's beautiful people, whom you'll spot everywhere from the San Francisco Opera to the exclusive bars. This is also a town filled with hot restaurants, and the "food mafia"—the city's chic restauranteurs, food critics, and die-hard restaurant patrons—are a force of their own. In addition, get to know the city's hip intelligentsia, led by nationally known writers like Dave Eggers and Po Bronson, or its outrageous politicians, like the infamous former mayor Willie Brown and controversial current mayor Gavin Newsom, and it's clear to see that San Franciscans have as much style and personality as the city they live in.

> **Today's San Francisco is a cultural melting pot of more than 750,000 people. From the Latino-influenced Mission to bustling Chinatown; from splendid mansions in Pacific Heights to SoMa nightclubs, there is virtually no part of the city where all of the senses aren't engaged at once.**

You're here to have fun, and with our help, you will have no trouble finding it!

Welcome to fabulous San Francisco ...

THE 99 BEST of SAN FRANCISCO

Who needs another "Best" list? You do—if it comes with details and insider tips that make the difference between a good experience and a great one. We've pinpointed the 33 categories that make San Francisco exciting, magnetic, and unforgettable, and picked the absolute three best places to go for each. Whether you live in San Francisco or are just visiting, this is the way to play in the City by the Bay.

 ## Always-Hot Restaurants

#1–3: San Francisco's reputation before the dot-com boom was anti-fashion, anti-scene—in fact, anti just about everything. But then the nightlife scene changed when cutting-edge restaurants tapped into a clientele eager to enjoy dining with a buzz and homegrown style.

Foreign Cinema
2534 Mission St., Mission, 415-648-7600 • Hot & Cool

The Draw: A reliable treat that makes any night feel like a special occasion, Foreign Cinema delivers rock-solid Mediterranean cuisine to a well-heeled clientele in an inspiringly modern yet comfortable atmosphere.

The Scene: While movies play in the courtyard, a central fireplace warms a spacious dining room with an industrial edge. The crowd, from young hotties to expense account executives, is uniformly fashionable. *Mon-Thu 6-10pm, Fri 6-11:30pm, Sat 11am-11:30pm, Sun 11am-10pm. $$*

Hot Tip: Migrate to Laszlo Bar—especially nice on a Saturday night—after dessert for a cocktail with the beautiful people and the DJs that move them.

Garibaldi's
347 Presidio Ave., Pacific Heights, 415-563-8841 • Classic

The Draw: Sophisticated yet comfortable, Garibaldi's has a New York vibe and consistently good food.

The Scene: A favorite hangout of the stylish Pacific Heights set, Garibaldi's is lively yet intimate, both casual and elegant. *Mon-Thu 11:30am-2:30pm and 5:30-10pm, Fri 11:30am-2:30pm and 5:30-10:30pm, Sat 5:30-10:30pm, Sun 5:30-9pm. $$*

Hot Tip: Ask for a table in the front room, preferably by the window, and order the chicken Milanese.

Zuni Café
1658 Market St., Hayes Valley, 415-552-2522 • Hip

The Draw: Whether you stop in for a weekday lunch, a weekend brunch, an evening cocktail at the copper-topped bar, or one of the finest Mediterranean dinners you're likely to find anywhere, you'll always find a relaxed but sophisticated crowd in high spirits at this local institution.

The Scene: Most nights a smart-looking crowd gathers at the bar and around the cocktail tables, while couples and groups fill the labyrinthine dining areas, where some tables are so close you'll get to know your neighbors. *Tue-Sat 11:30am-midnight, Sun 11am-11pm. $$*

Hot Tip: Sample the oysters, then settle in for the house specialty, roasted chicken from the wood fired oven with bread salad, for two.

Brunches

#4–6: San Francisco is a brunch town. On Sundays, favorite spots spill over with packs of friends. Although there's no shortage of great places, these more than deserve their reputation as the perfect way to ease into a Sunday.

Ella's
500 Presidio Ave., Pacific Heights, 415-441-5669 • Classic

The Draw: Ella's always attracts a Pacific Heights crowd for its classic take on weekend brunch, with a line trailing out the door.

The Scene: Albeit a low-key setting, this is the home of the $150 T-shirt. Guys roll out of bed into their most comfortable Gucci sandals, ready to enjoy freshly squeezed OJ, homemade breads, pancakes, and hearty eggs among their peers. *Mon-Fri 7am-9pm, Sat-Sun 8:30am-2pm. $*

Hot Tip: Drag yourself out of bed an hour or two before ten and you'll be in good shape to avoid the crowd. Otherwise, pick up a newspaper, ask for a cup of coffee to keep you company, and enjoy the wait.

The Terrace
Ritz-Carlton Hotel, 600 Stockton St., Downtown, 415-773-6198 • Classic

The Draw: Sunday Jazz Brunch in the Terrace's courtyard is the crème de la crème of Sunday morning dining. The Ritz has it all: a beautiful garden setting, masterful service, an excellent buffet, and live jazz.

The Scene: Life is all sunshine and roses at the Terrace, where grandmothers and hipsters alike feel quite at home—that is, if home were terribly, terribly grand. The extensive buffet includes everything from fresh fruit and eggs to sushi, oysters, and more. *Mon 6-11am, 11:30am-2:30pm, and 6-9:30pm, Tue-Sat 6:30-11am and 11:30am-2:30pm, Sun 6-10am, 10:30am-2:30pm, and 6-9:30pm. $$$*

Hot Tip: Much the same routine applies Monday through Saturday, sans jazz. Lingering over a cappuccino feels even more decadent on a Tuesday.

Universal Cafe
2814 19th St., Mission, 415-821-4608 • Hip

The Draw: Consistently great food, a menu that changes weekly based on what's in season, and friendly service make this a favorite spot to linger.

The Scene: It seems like the weather is always fine, the day lazy, and the crowd handsome at this chic and compact Mission cafe. Grab your shades and make like one of the beautiful people. *Tue-Thu 5:30-9:30pm, Fri 11:30am-2:30pm and 5:30-10:30pm, Sat 9am-2:30pm and 5:30-10:30pm, Sun 9am-2:30pm and 5:30-9:30pm. $*

Hot Tip: There are no reservations for brunch. Either show up early (before 10:30) or call ahead to scope out how long a wait you're in for.

Chic Asian Restaurants

#7–9: The Asian fusion cuisine explosion that rocked the city in the '80s and '90s has settled into a crackling blaze of ongoing ingenuity and impeccable execution. In addition to offering a dazzling array of flavors, these places dish up a lively scene peopled by a stylish crowd in its Thursday-night best.

Ana Mandara
891 Beach St., Fisherman's Wharf, 415-771-6800 • Classic

The Draw: Locals come here for the magical blend of fantasy ambiance and excellent modern Vietnamese cuisine. Co-owned by *Nash Bridges* stars Don Johnson and Cheech Marin, Ana Mandara has Hollywood flair, with a lavish interior that evokes the tropical splendor of Vietnam.

The Scene: Decadent Ana Mandara caters to the expense account crew, highbrow visitors, and special-occasion diners. The look is high romance, making it an imaginative choice for a grand night out. *Sun-Thu 5:30-9:30pm, Fri-Sat 5:30-10:30pm, Mon-Fri 11:30am-2pm.* $$

Hot Tip: You can get the full menu in the beautiful Cham Bar, where they also have a great selection of wines and proprietary cocktails.

Betelnut
2030 Union St., Marina, 415-929-8855 • Hot & Cool

The Draw: Exotic cocktails, impeccably flavorful seafood dishes prepared with Shanghai flair, a buzzing crowd, and a posh neighborhood.

The Scene: The Marina District's best—young, well-heeled, and ready to party—are here all evening and into the night. Manolo Blahniks optional but strongly encouraged. *Sun-Thu 5-11pm, Fri-Sat 5pm-midnight, daily 11:30am-5pm.* $

Hot Tip: Get a side of the Szechuan green beans for the table to share. Follow the crowd to nearby watering holes such as MatrixFillmore.

Slanted Door
One Ferry Building, Embarcadero, 415-861-8032 • Hot & Cool

The Draw: Slanted Door serves delicious modern Vietnamese cuisine in an equally modernist setting, to be consumed elbow to elbow with other well-groomed, festive, fashionably modern people. Its location, perched on the bay, affords beautiful natural light and a pretty view.

The Scene: Everybody loves Slanted Door. Despite a heavy flow of tourists, the place manages to sustain a thoroughly chic vibe. Especially mid-week, you'll find creative professionals taking up every seat at the bar. *Sun-Thu 5:30-10pm, Fri-Sat 5:30-10:30pm, daily 11:30am-2:30pm.* $$

Hot Tip: Reserve early. And bring your horn, it's noisy in there.

Best

Club Scenes

#10–12: Thanks to a rich vein of local DJ talent and a surge in the population of young and affluent residents, San Francisco's once-sleepy nightlife has received a jolt of fresh energy in recent years.

Loft 11
316 11th St., SoMa, 415-701-8111 • Hot & Cool

The Draw: Sleek and modern, the beautiful setting at Loft 11 makes it one of the city's most exciting weekend hangouts.

The Scene: Liquid walls contribute to the ambiance, while Asian-influenced small plates keep hunger at bay. The young, hip, urban crowd comes out in its Saturday best, looking to show some skin in style. Leave the navy blazer and khakis at home. *Thu-Sat 6:30pm-2am.*

Hot Tip: For those in the market for a little sweet talk and dirty dancing, Loft 11 is a good place to start shopping. If you've got a posse, grab a private booth with bottle service to feel like a VIP.

Mezzanine
444 Jessie St., SoMa, 415-625-8880 • Hot & Cool

The Draw: Gritty, ultra-urban Mezzanine is a 12,000-square-foot slice of the promised land for the serious, no-bridge-and-tunnel-folk-allowed dance crowd, boasting one of the best sound systems in the city and attracting A-list DJs spinning underground house music and break beats.

The Scene: You may wonder where you are going when you duck into the seedy alley Mezzanine calls home. Inside, multiple rooms offer plenty of space to explore, as well as extensive wall space for the latest work by featured artists. *Hours vary. For details on events, check mezzaninesf.com.*

Hot Tip: Hit Mezzanine at midnight or later for an after-hours session to rival any club scene anywhere. Beware, the 'tude runneth over.

Ruby Skye
420 Mason St., Downtown, 415-693-0777 • Hot & Cool

The Draw: The grand opulence of the space, situated in the theater district, sets the stage for a night of high decadence. A cutting-edge sound system and sophisticated lighting make star DJs like Mark Farina and Frenchy Le Freak, feel right at home.

The Scene: Only a handful of places command full nightlife regalia in San Francisco. Ruby Skye is certainly one of them. The (mostly) young and (mostly) hetero crowd dons its sexy best for this top-of-the-food-chain venue. *Thu 9pm-2am, Fri 9pm-3am, Sat 8pm-4am.*

Hot Tip: Ruby Skye is the city's big gun, ideal for high-caliber holidays and Saturday nights. Arrive before eleven to avoid a nasty line.

Best Dim Sum

#13–15: In a city with a bustling Chinatown, a thriving Chinese community, and a long history of Asian influence, dim sum is lingua franca. Don't fret if you let the sautéed asparagus go by. It won't be long before carts loaded with seafood dumplings, silver wrapped chicken, and stuffed lotus leaves roll by.

City View
662 Commercial St., Financial District, 415-355-9991

The Draw: Although the setting is plain, City View consistently draws crowds for its impeccable dumplings and other tantalizing dishes, all served from carts circulating between tables.

The Scene: A block from the Transamerica building, bustling City View attracts a devoted crew of rosy-cheeked suits and suitlets from the Financial District in addition to its core clientele of Chinatown regulars. *Mon-Fri 11am-2:30pm, Sat-Sun 10am-2:30pm.* $–

Hot Tip: Keep an eye out for the glazed walnut prawns, spicy salted prawns, and shrimp dumplings. Follow up with one of the deliciously crunchy steamed vegetable dishes.

Ton Kiang
5821 Geary Blvd., Richmond, 415-387-8273 • Classic

The Draw: Ton Kiang not only serves some of the best dim sum in town at very affordable prices, but does it all day long—including dinner.

The Scene: What the place lacks in ambiance it more than makes up in flavor. Located in the Richmond District where fog is plentiful and tourists are not, the dining room is packed with regulars who flock here from all over town. *Mon-Thu 10am-10pm, Fri 10am-10:30pm, Sat 9:30am-10:30pm, Sun 9am-10pm.* $

Hot Tip: Warm up with one of the clay pot dishes, the perfect complement to a chilly July or August day in Fog City.

Yank Sing
One Rincon Center, 101 Spear St., SoMa, 415-957-9300,
49 Stevenson St., SoMa, 415-541-4949 • Classic

The Draw: Terrific dim sum in a bright, elegant setting that is hard to beat.

The Scene: Pace yourself. The carts never stop coming by with the next delectable treat. Financial District suits pack both locations at lunchtime. On weekends, it's largely families and groups. *Rincon: Mon-Fri 11am-3pm, Sat-Sun 10am-4pm. Stevenson: Daily 11am-3pm.* $

Hot Tip: At Rincon Center, try for a table on the lovely atrium court.

DJ Bars

#16–18: The DJ is to the new millennium what the fashion photographer was to the '60s. If you're young, artistic, and unspeakably hip, you become a DJ. And if you are very, very good at keeping the crowd energized, you spin at these local outlets of international beat chic.

Milk
1840 Haight St., Haight, 415-387-6455 • Hip

The Draw: Located in the heart of the Haight, Milk covers the DJ experience from a different perspective, specializing in dance-ready hip-hop, soul, and funk—as opposed to the more Euro-centric spin that's dished up at places like Pink and Sublounge.

The Scene: Expect strong drinks, a low-frills ambiance, and plenty of lively, twenty-something hipsters getting way funky. *Mon-Fri 7pm-2am, Sat-Sun 2pm-2am.*

Hot Tip: Tuesdays and Thursdays are great nights at Milk. Check the website for Sunday special events, which can attract a hip local crowd.

Pink
2925 16th St., Mission, 415-431-8889 • Hip

The Draw: A fresh face in the scruffy Mission District, Pink is a tiny space that's big on both style and substance, namely in the form of consistently great DJs from around the world spinning consistently great music.

The Scene: High heels, slick ensembles, lipstick, and expensive drinks set the tone at this glittery new favorite. Arrive ready to flaunt what you've got. *Fri-Sat 9pm-3am, Sun and Tue-Thu 9pm-2am.*

Hot Tip: Pink can be happening just about any night of the week, but the later, the better. Stop by mid-week and you never know which celebrity DJ you might find at the turntables.

Sublounge
628 20th St., Potrero Hill, 415-552-3603 • Hip

The Draw: Savor some of the best dance music the city has to offer at this unpretentious art gallery cum quirky secret spot populated by locals who know a good dance scene when they see it.

The Scene: Part Jetsons, part retro jet set, heavy on the red lights, the interior is amusingly original. Sit in a salvaged airline seat, pull down controls for your very own PlayStation from the overhead compartment, and settle your martini in the cup holder. At the glowing bar, hipsters gather to fuel up before heading downstairs to work it out. *Wed-Fri 6pm-2am; Sat 7pm-2am.*

Hot Tip: Check out happy hour for a 21st-century bohemian experience.

Fine Dining

#19–21: In the culinary Mecca that is the Bay Area, certain temples of worship stand out. These are the places where the roasted Maine lobster is a work of art, the caviar is Beluga, and even a sauté of vegetables is mouthwatering.

Fifth Floor

Hotel Palomar, 12 Fourth St., SoMa, 415-348-1111 • Hot & Cool

The Draw: Perhaps the most elegant restaurant in town, Fifth Floor rules the day when it comes to romance, French cuisine prepared to perfection, and a dining experience worthy of the pampered elite.

The Scene: Four is a large party at Fifth Floor, where you are apt to find mostly couples of a certain distinction tucked in among the dark woods, cream linens, and zebra-print accents. Ladies, pearls and gemstones, please. Gentlemen, this night calls for your best suit. *Mon-Fri 7-10am and 5:30-10pm, Sat 8-11am and 5:30-11pm, Sun 8-11am.* $$$

Hot Tip: If dinner sounds too rich, get a taste of Fifth Floor in the lounge outside the dining room. You can order gourmet snacks, enjoy the fantastic wine list, and consort with others there to schmooze and sample.

Gary Danko

800 North Point St., Fisherman's Wharf, 415-749-2060 • Classic

The Draw: Chef Gary Danko's three-, four-, and five-course prix fixe menus are the gold standard of fine dining in the city. The menu offers an exuberant array of dishes in French-influenced California style.

The Scene: Light woods, showpiece floral arrangements, and seating in muted butterscotch tones create a refined setting in which to enjoy a five-star meal. *Daily 5:30-10pm. Bar open 5pm-midnight.* $$$

Hot Tip: Chocolate lovers must have the baked soufflé with two sauces. Others should try the world-class cheese cart.

Michael Mina

Westin St. Francis, 335 Powell St., Downtown, 415-397-9222 • Hot & Cool

The Draw: Pure elegance. Chef Michael Mina's eponymous restaurant is a graceful masterpiece where the food is a perfectionist's dream.

The Scene: Mina works his magic in signature flavor suites (everything arrives in three versions) served in a dining room as crisp, light, and modern as it is grand. The air crackles with culinary anticipation. Patrons run to the upper crust, from ladies in Chanel suits to visiting jet-setters. *Mon-Sat 5:30-10pm, Sun 5:30-9:30pm.* $$$

Hot Tip: Be ready for gustatory adventure—and by all means have the lobster pot pie. Why not go big and splurge on the seven-course classic tasting menu? The calories? The cost? This is not a place to consider either.

THE 99 BEST OF SAN FRANCISCO

Gay Bars and Clubs

#22–24: San Francisco's long history as the center of the gay pride movement means that there are as many gay bars here as there are colors in the rainbow. Whether you're cruising the talent or just taking in the scene, you won't lack for options. These three spots are perennial favorites.

Lexington Club
3464 19th St., Mission, 415-863-2052 • Hip

The Draw: Billed as "Your friendly neighborhood dyke bar," the Lexington is a surprisingly rare breed in San Francisco. They just don't make dyke bars the way they used to, or at least not as plentifully, but this one is the genuine article with plenty of ambiance.

The Scene: Butch and femme out of central casting mingle and drink in this low-key neighborhood bar where 20-something lesbians come to meet each other and play pool. *Mon-Thu 5pm-2am, Fri-Sat 3pm-2am.*

Hot Tip: Don't miss the rather remarkable graffiti and other embellishments in the bathrooms.

Pilsner Inn
225 Church St., Castro, 415-621-7058 • Hip

The Draw: The outdoor garden provides a perfect setting for the reasonably attractive twenties and thirties crowd to gather.

The Scene: Pilsner mixes up all kinds of people, from the Castro gay crowd to people of all sexualities looking for a comfortable bar to drink a beer, play some pool, and give the pinball machine a workout. That said, if you are looking to meet women, this is not your place. *Daily 10am-2am.*

Hot Tip: Time to light up? In smoke-free California, the outdoor garden at Pilsner is a place to bond with fellow die-hards.

SF Badlands
4121 18th St., Castro, 415-626-9320 • Hip

The Draw: This gay dance club comes complete with mirrored disco ball, dance music, and plenty of hunky men to pick up.

The Scene: The aforementioned hunky gay men, those who love them, and a few adventurous others come here to dance the night away. *Daily 2pm-2am.*

Hot Tip: Sunday afternoon is the best time to drop by, sip a beer, cruise the talent, and dance to a Madonna video.

Historic San Francisco

#25–27: A century and a half ago, San Francisco was just a collection of waterfront warehouses and a few saloons. Then the Gold Rush hit, bringing the world's masses, eager to make their fortune. It's been a wild ride since, with stops for jazz, Beat poetry, free love, and the Internet along the way.

Broadway

The Draw: A collision of cultures takes place daily along Broadway in North Beach. Part old-country Italian holdout, part Chinatown, part beatnik paradise, packed with strip clubs and lounges, Broadway has every delight a pleasure-seeker could wish for.

The Scene: Bohemian days started on Broadway, where jazz, poetry, rustic Italian food, and marijuana combined to fuel the '50s Beat Generation. The artsy types still drink at Tosca, Vesuvio, and Specks. Today the scene also includes upscale lounges, excellent restaurants, and several establishments purveying bare booty.

Hot Tip: Get your literature on at City Lights, the landmark bookstore operated by Beat poet Lawrence Ferlinghetti.

Haight-Ashbury

The Draw: Everybody should stand at the corner of Haight and Ashbury, ground zero for the Summer of Love, once in their lives.

The Scene: A kaleidoscopic blend of aging and nouveau hippies, fashionistas, drag queens, and street urchins crowds the sidewalks in this district that wears its history on its sleeve. There was a time when the Haight was the land that time forgot. Today it boasts fashionable shopping at its edgy best and the confident air of the deeply cool.

Hot Tip: When was the last time you smoked a hookah? Stop by Kan Zaman (1793 Haight St.) to fire up a bowl of apricot tobacco, sip sweet mint tea, and muse upon the gyrations of the passing belly dancer. For more subdued refreshment, turn down Cole Street and pay a visit to the Eos Wine Bar.

Valencia Street

The Draw: Funky Valencia Street has gone upscale, almost. It makes a colorful stroll, especially between 16th and 21st Streets. Dive bars, vintage and contemporary furniture and clothing shops, bookstores, cafes, and restaurants occupy every available inch of retail space.

The Scene: *Vanity Fair* recently named the Mission District the "Hippest Neighborhood in America," officially marking its moment of gentrification. And yet layers of working-class immigrant populations—first Irish, German, and Italian; later Latin American of every stripe—are still vibrantly present.

Hot Tip: Walk west two blocks on 16th Street to visit Mission Dolores, the city's oldest building, completed in 1791.

THE 99 BEST OF SAN FRANCISCO

Late-Night Eats

#28–30: That quick drink before dinner turned into a three-hour minglefest. Now it's midnight and all you've had to eat since lunch is six gin-infused olives and a handful of cashews. Where can you get a meal that doesn't come wrapped in foil and surrounded by tortilla chips? Fret not, famished traveler.

Bagdad Café
2295 Market St., Castro, 415-621-4434 • Hip

The Draw: Occupying prime corner real estate in the Castro District, unofficial people-watching capital of the world, the Bagdad Café beckons with its big windows and classic diner food all day and all night, every day.

The Scene: This is the place to indulge in a juicy cheeseburger at 4am among the post–after party crowd. *24 hours.* $–

Hot Tip: Surprise, the wine list is quite good.

Globe
290 Pacific Ave., Financial District, 415-391-4132 • Hot & Cool

The Draw: Simple, flawless food served in the cozy restaurant cum bar, which maintains a perpetual buzz, even after most other restaurants have closed.

The Scene: The city's chefs tend to hang out after work in this chic warehouse space. They'll be sitting next to grownups who stay up late and eat downtown, meaning hipsters with good jobs at ad agencies and the like. *Mon-Fri 11:30am-3pm and 6pm-1am, Sat 6pm-1am, Sun 6-11:30pm.* $$

Hot Tip: The rotisserie chicken is the best in town.

Oola
860 Folsom St., SoMa, 415-995-2061 • Hot & Cool

The Draw: Chef Ola Fendert serves his inventive take on Mediterranean cuisine late into the night, making this a buzzing and welcome new option for midnight feasting.

The Scene: A young, stylish crowd packs the narrow, industrial-chic space to nosh on spiced ahi tuna, baby back ribs, rack of lamb, and other savory delights. *Mon 6pm-midnight, Tue-Sat 6pm-1am, Sun 6-11pm.* $$

Hot Tip: Shoot for a table at ten or eleven to be part of the night's liveliest moment. Or drop by after dinner elsewhere for a nightcap at the bar.

25

 # Late-Night Hangouts

#31–33: It's not over till it's over, and if you've got stamina, that may not be until really, really late. If midnight has long passed and your groove is still going strong, here's where to hook up with other hearty revelers. A couple of these spots will take you into the sunrise and beyond.

DNA Lounge
375 11th St., Mission, 415-626-1409 • Hot & Cool

The Draw: A wicked sound system, an energetic crowd, and great music make this one of the best places in town to dance into the wee hours.

The Scene: Party people, go-go dancers, and other mainstays of the urban dance tribe hit DNA Lounge ready to get down to some serious booty shaking. *Check website (dnalounge.com) for hours, which vary depending on event.*

Hot Tip: On Friday nights and many Saturdays, they keep things moving until 5am, so if you get a late start on the night, this is your ticket.

The EndUp
401 Sixth St., SoMa, 415-646-0999 • Hip

The Draw: Fag Friday segues early Saturday morning into a mixed party that lasts until 4pm. Or arrive as late as you want on Saturday night and stay until Sunday. You can even round out the weekend with the notorious Sunday night dance party, starting at 9pm and continuing into the commute hours.

The Scene: You name it, you'll find it here. Drag queens, Gucci boys, slaves to the new economy, party promoters, and girlie girls. When other venues shut down, people end up at the EndUp. *Thu 10:30pm-4:30am, Fri 10pm-6am, Sat 6am-1pm and 10pm-6am, Sun 6am-4am.*

Hot Tip: If you missed Burning Man, head for the patio and squint a little. You'd swear you were on the Playa.

Le Duplex
1525 Mission St., SoMa, 415-355-1525 • Hot & Cool

The Draw: San Francisco's first self-proclaimed boîte (short for *boîte de nuit*, French for nightclub) opened in mid-2005, offering a dramatic, elegant setting in which to dance and romance. Part dance club, part Euro-lounge, it makes for an ideal late-night hybrid scene.

The Scene: The city's A- to B+ list of beautiful people and high-rolling night-lifers love this slick spot, with its VIP areas upstairs, complete with curtains for privacy and a catwalk for a bird's-eye view of the talent downstairs. *Tue-Wed, Sat 9pm-2am, Thu-Fri 4pm-2am.*

Hot Tip: The beloved DJ Frenchy Le Freak spins every Friday night.

THE 99 BEST OF SAN FRANCISCO

Latin Restaurants

#34–36: If you just want a taco, there are plenty of choices in the Mission District. But the Latin influence extends throughout the city and is highlighted by fashionable restaurants serving high-end cuisine.

Andalu
3198 16th St., Mission, 415-621-2211 • Hip

The Draw: An early trendsetter in the tapas scene, Andalu has perfected the art of small plates with major flavor, including polenta fries, Coca-Cola–braised short ribs, and teensy little ahi tuna tacos with salsa.

The Scene: Expect your typical well-dressed, slightly subdued urbanite crowd roughly between the ages of thirty and fifty at this richly hued oasis. *Sun-Tue 5:30-10pm, Wed-Thu 5:30-11pm, Fri-Sat 5:30-11:30pm.* $$

Hot Tip: Have the white sangria. To make a night of it, take in the latest art-house flick, a brainy documentary, or a cinematic classic across the street at the Roxie Cinema, a San Francisco icon of independent film.

Limón
524 Valencia St., Mission, 415-252-0918 • Hip

The Draw: A tiny nook in 2003, Limón quickly expanded to meet the demand for its refreshing array of Peruvian flavors, from piquant marinated chicken to succulent calamari and savory paella.

The Scene: Most nights find Limón busy with urbanites getting their supper on. Loft-style with a split level and orange and lime splashes of color, the aesthetic is enthusiastically modern yet casual. *Mon-Thu 11:30am-3pm and 5-10:30pm, Fri 11:30am-3pm and 5-11pm, Sat noon-11pm, Sun noon-10pm.* $$

Hot Tip: Don't miss the lomo saltado, a favorite Peruvian mix of top sirloin, tomatoes, onions, and French fries.

Tres Agaves
130 Townsend St., SoMa, 415-227-0500 • Hot & Cool

The Draw: Tequila at its best and dressed-up Mexican fare are served in the city's most stylish Mexican restaurant.

The Scene: A stylish young crowd gathers to sample tequilas and dig into spicy shrimp, shredded beef, and chunky guacamole in this cavernous, industrial-chic space just around the corner from SBC Park. *Mon-Thu 11am-1am, Fri-Sat 11am-2am, Sun 10am-3pm.* $

Hot Tip: Order a margarita. The limes are imported from Mexico, and the owners are tequila experts.

Best Live Music Venues

#37–39: You missed the '60s, '70s, and '80s? Not to worry. Music has played a significant role in San Francisco's recent history and a good deal of it has been preserved, largely thanks to the staying power of these legendary clubs.

Bimbo's 365 Club
1025 Columbus Ave., North Beach, 415-474-0365

The Draw: Bimbo's seldom disappoints. Steeped in the era of big bands and old-school Italian pleasures, today it's a plush setting for slick dance bands and nouveau burlesque.

The Scene: Back in the day, you could have found a young Rita Cansino, later Rita Hayworth, kicking up her heels in the chorus line. The decadent spirit of San Francisco in the '30s lingers in the ambiance, but these days the crowd is young partiers of varying degrees of hipness looking to dance the night away. C≡

Hot Tip: Watch for one of the showy, choreographed cover bands such as Superbooty doing funk, soul, or rock for a night sure to work up a sweat.

The Fillmore Auditorium
1805 Geary Blvd., Pacific Heights, 415-346-6000

The Draw: It's the Fillmore, man. This place is a rock institution. Who's on hand depends on the act, but this red-velvet–clad venue is always a classic.

The Scene: Raise your glass to the memory of promoter Bill Graham. The Fillmore has a long history, but it really came into its own in the psychedelic '60s, when bands like Jefferson Airplane, Santana, and the Grateful Dead ruled the stage. Today you can soak up the legendary vibe while seeing anyone from Los Lobos to Ani DiFranco. CB≡

Hot Tip: It's almost all standing room, so wear comfortable shoes. Bring your earplugs in case you end up next to a speaker.

Slim's
333 11th St., SoMa, 415-255-0333

The Draw: Slim's has been a great, intimate place to see live rock 'n' roll since Boz Scaggs opened it in the late '80s.

The Scene: It's standing room only except for a few tables upstairs. Everybody crowds the stage and dances up a storm. CF≡

Hot Tip: It's located in the heart of the nightclub district, which has been updated with some very fresh lounges, so you're in good shape for a nightcap after the show. Start the evening with a nearby cocktail at Wish (see p.117) or carry on the action at Loft 11 (see p.76).

Best — Lounges with a View

#40–42: Where is Tony Bennett when we need him? You'll just have to settle for the incredible views as the backdrop to a first sip of an icy martini or a sugary cosmo.

Harry Denton's Starlight Room
Sir Francis Drake Hotel, 21st Fl., 450 Powell St., Downtown, 415-395-8595 • Classic

> The Draw: Drenched in red velvet and Liberace pomp, the chandelier-lit Starlight Room serves those looking for romance and a spectacular view.
>
> The Scene: If there's not a frosty martini or a flute of champagne in your hand shortly after you arrive, something's wrong. An older (forty-something), more subdued, and yet still well-dressed crowd hits the Starlight Room. Look for more suits than tattoos, more couples than singles. *Daily 5pm-2am.* C
>
> Hot Tip: To do it right, be there with cocktail in hand in time for the sunset. On Wednesdays, illustrious promoter Sebastian presents a late-night party that's routinely wall-to-wall with the hot young nightclub crowd.

Top of the Mark
InterContinental Mark Hopkins, 999 California St., Nob Hill, 415-392-3434 • Classic

> The Draw: The summit of refinement, the Top of the Mark sits on the 19th floor atop Nob Hill, offering a near–360 degree view.
>
> The Scene: If it's Sunday night, it's sultry jazz. Tuesday is jazz piano. Wednesday is Latin jazz, and on weekends it's the jazz orchestra. And every night, pearls and dinner jackets are entirely appropriate. *Mon-Thu 6:30-11am, noon-2:30pm, and 5pm-midnight, Fri-Sat 6:30-11am, noon-2:30pm, 4pm-1am, Sun 10am-2:30pm and 5pm-midnight.* C
>
> Hot Tip: The menu lists 100 different martinis. Order a Blue Velvet Martini and hum the theme song as you dance cheek to cheek.

View Lounge
San Francisco Marriott Hotel, 39th Fl., 55 Fourth St., SoMa, 415-896-1600 • Classic

> The Draw: The Marriott's architecture has endured its share of ridicule, but the three-story windows in its skyscraper bar provide incomparable vistas.
>
> The Scene: Catering to the expense account and convention crowd, this isn't the place to use up your nightlife tickets. That said, it's a great place to unwind before dinner. *Sun-Thu 4pm-midnight, Fri-Sat 4pm-2am.* B
>
> Hot Tip: Arrive early to watch the wall of fog rise up and roll over Twin Peaks.

Neighborhood Bars

#43–45: Next to cafes and Internet startups, San Francisco excels best at the neighborhood bar, of which there are literally dozens worth visiting. They run the gamut from scruffy to slick to Irish to hipster hangout. These are great places to observe—and mingle with—locals in their natural habitat.

El Rio
3158 Mission St., Mission, 415-282-3325 • Hip

The Draw: El Rio is eclectic San Francisco at its most diverse and funky. Where else can you hear live flamenco and dance to Afro beat, salsa, reggae, and DJs spinning funk, punk, and soul—all in one night? The patio is also a big plus.

The Scene: Young, hip locals, musically savvy Gen-Xers, Gen-Yers thirsty for a cheap beer on the patio—they're all here, just about any night of the week. *Mon-Thu 5pm-2am, Fri-Sun 3pm-2am from March–November. In winter, open at 3pm Fri only, 5pm all other days.*

Hot Tip: In town on Sunday? Swing by for live salsa in the afternoon.

Harvey's
500 Castro St., Castro, 415-431-4278

The Draw: Named after Harvey Milk, Harvey's is a celebration of the city's rainbow culture. Drop by for your slice of local history, a cold beer, and some tasty pub food.

The Scene: Expect plenty of locals who come to enjoy the relaxed atmosphere, tourists who come to observe the locals while pretending not to, and fans of the curly fries who come to indulge their habit. *Mon-Fri 11am-midnight, Sat-Sun 9am-2am.*

Hot Tip: Is that Greg Louganis's Speedo displayed on the wall? Why, yes, it is. Don't miss the excellent collection of Castro-themed memorabilia.

Jade Bar
650 Gough St., Hayes Valley, 415-869-1900 • Hot & Cool

The Draw: A sexy setting for a happy-hour cocktail and a snack. Do you fantasize about sipping a cosmo while you dip your chicken skewer in a coconut-peanut sauce and kick back in a lounge straight out of *Wallpaper?* Welcome to Jade Bar.

The Scene: At happy hour, the after-work crowd arrives—young suits and suitlets. Late night, the same crowd shows up in club attire, taking turns smoking outside. *Mon-Sat 5pm-2am, Sun 8pm-2am.*

Hot Tip: This is an excellent first-date spot. Take that recent acquisition upstairs, where it's sometimes quiet and always intimate, to get down to some serious chitchat.

THE 99 BEST OF SAN FRANCISCO

Only-in-San Francisco Experiences

#46–48: Alcatraz Island and the Golden Gate Bridge are unique, but there are other quintessentially San Franciscan activities that most visitors miss.

AsiaSF
201 Ninth St., SoMa, 415-255-2742 • Classic

The Draw: California-Asian cuisine, a sublevel dance floor, Asian fantasy décor, and a crew of "gender illusionists" doubling as servers combine for a night's experience none soon forget.

The Scene: The dining room features bamboo-clad walls, shoji screens, paper lanterns, and a Chinese-red central runway where the gorgeous talent kicks out show tunes. Tourists and groups of locals celebrating special occasions populate many of the tables. This is a good place to take a date, but not a good place to find one. *Mon-Wed 6:30pm-2am, Thu 6pm-2am, Fri 5:30pm-2am, Sat 5pm-2am, Sun 6pm-2am.* $$

Hot Tip: After 11pm, the spacious downstairs club plays hip-hop and house, and hosts regular parties such as Love Underground, an erotically charged gathering that takes place every fourth Friday.

Audium
1616 Bush St., Pacific Heights, 415-771-1616 • Classic

The Draw: If you've always wondered what psychoactive drugs are like, just say yes to the Audium and you will get a pretty good idea.

The Scene: The circular listening room has 169 strategically shaped and situated speakers for a sensual experience nonpareil. In a darkened room sounds move past, over, and under the 49 seats, literally bathing listeners in sound. *Performances every Fri and Sat at 8:30pm (arrive early).* $$

Hot Tip: There is an escape path in case you feel too disoriented.

Glide Memorial United Methodist Church
330 Ellis St., Downtown, 415-674-6000 • Hip

The Draw: A cornerstone of the community, Glide has been inspiring visitors with its phenomenal choir and tireless charitable efforts for 40 years. The philosophy is acceptance. It's an unconditional love thing.

The Scene: A cross-section of the city, and the world, fills the pews to celebrate the heavens and everything under them with glorious song. The Glide Ensemble belts out jazz, blues, gospel, and spirituals while the diverse crowd produces cheers, tears, and spontaneous outbursts of faith. *Services every Sunday at 9am and 11am.*

Hot Tip: Arrive half an hour early to be assured of getting a seat.

Outdoor Activities

#49–51: San Francisco is one of the most beautiful places in the world. Even if you're not normally the outdoorsy type, it's worth shaking off that hangover and heading out to get some fresh air in one of these sublime settings.

Angel Island
Between Alcatraz Island and Tiburon

The Draw: The ride across the bay on a Blue and Gold Ferry from Fisherman's Wharf would be a worthy outing in itself. Once you're on the island, miles of paths lead to picnic spots and spectacular views at every turn.

The Scene: Services have been kept to a minimum in order to preserve the natural beauty of the island, though there is a cafe, bike rental, and tram tour April through September. You can even reserve a day of sea kayaking. *Daily 8am to sundown year-round.*

Hot Tip: Ferries leave from Tiburon as well. Drive across the Golden Gate and have lunch at Sam's Anchor Café before going for a hike on the island for an exhilarating day.

Golden Gate Bridge
North end of Presidio, Hwy. 101 heading north out of the city, 415-921-5858 • Classic

The Draw: A sublime marriage of form and function, the Golden Gate Bridge is a wonder from all perspectives. It's beautiful to look at from afar, beautiful to walk or bike across, beautiful to drive over.

The Scene: On a sunny day, the view from the bridge is genuinely breathtaking, encompassing everything from the gateway to the open ocean to the city's skyscrapers and the dramatic green hillsides of Marin. *Bridge sidewalk open to bikes and pedestrians during daylight hours.*

Hot Tip: The far side is further across than it looks—1.7 miles. Even on warm days, a walk across the bridge will get chilly. Wear a windbreaker.

Golden Gate Park
Bounded by Stanyan, Fulton, Lincoln, and the Great Highway, Richmond, 415-831-2700 • Classic

The Draw: San Francisco's central green space—three miles long and larger than New York's Central Park—offers everything from a Japanese tea garden to French lawn bowling.

The Scene: Lush gardens, vast lawns, concerts, dreamy picnic spots, paddle boats, in-line skating—whatever the outdoor pastime, it's very likely taking place here.

Hot Tip: The park is closed to automobile traffic on Sundays, making walking, biking and skating a treat. The sportier set can rent skates or bikes at 3038 Fulton St., 415-668-1117.

Power Lunch Spots

#52–54: The Financial District and the adjoining area South of Market are a culinary paradise. The toughest part of your meeting may be deciding on a restaurant. At these stellar spots, you're assured of an inviting ambiance that will help seal the deal.

Hawthorne Lane
22 Hawthorne Ln., SoMa, 415-777-9779 • Classic

The Draw: Near Moscone Center, Hawthorne Lane has East-meets-West Cali-Asian cuisine with tables spaced far apart.

The Scene: Tucked away in an ivy-clad brick building that exudes secret-garden appeal, if not exclusivity, this sophisticated restaurant has a perfect mix of white linen, floral arrangements, and modern art. Jackets predominate, although casual foodies who come for the lower-priced lunch menu may be sitting next to you. *Mon-Fri 11:30am-1:30pm and 5:30-9pm, Fri-Sat 5:30-10pm. Hors d'oeuvres at the bar Mon-Fri 3pm-midnight, Sat-Sun 5pm-midnight.* $$$

Hot Tip: Start your three-martini lunch, or sample from the top-rate wine list, at the small but beautiful bar, complete with savvy bartenders.

One Market
One Market St., Embarcadero, 415-777-5577 • Hot & Cool

The Draw: In a contemporary, airy setting you can seal the deal over an American menu comprised of seasonal ingredients sourced locally.

The Scene: Tall, arched windows open up the dining room to the view of the palm-lined Embarcadero waterfront. Expect the tables to be packed with Financial District types enjoying a long lunch. *Mon-Thu 11:30am-2pm and 5:30-9pm, Fri 11:30am-2pm and 5:30-9pm, Sat 5:30-9pm.* $$

Hot Tip: To avoid the distraction of scenery and the bustle of the open kitchen, ask for a table in the raised seating area.

Town Hall
342 Howard St., SoMa, 415-908-3900 • Hot & Cool

The Draw: The Old World (by California standards) atmosphere provides a warm, comfortable setting for conducting business.

The Scene: In a handsome old building with plenty of exposed brick, Town Hall serves reliably good Cali-Med-American food—sophisticated comfort food to suit the surroundings. *Mon-Thu 11:30am-2:30pm and 5:30-10pm, Fri 11:30am-2:30pm and 5:30-11pm, Sat 5:30-11pm, Sun 5:30-10pm.* $$

Hot Tip: At lunch, nothing beats the burger, one of the best in town.

Best Restaurants with a View

#55–57: One of San Francisco's draws is its breathtaking beauty. The city, the bay, the bridges, the Pacific, and the Marin Headlands are a feast for the eyes, one that you can combine with a literal feast at these great restaurants.

Greens Restaurant
Fort Mason Center, Bldg. A, Marina Blvd., Marina, 415-771-6222 • Classic

The Draw: Where else can you have all-vegetarian food in an airy dining room and look straight out at Marina sailboats, the great ocher towers of the Golden Gate Bridge, and the lush hillsides of the Marin Headlands?

The Scene: Greens has taken vegetarian cookery to new levels. Expect a crowd that loves to eat its vegetables and knows how to appreciate organic produce, as well as the handcrafted wood interior. *Mon 5:30-9pm, Tue-Fri noon-2:30pm and 5:30-9pm, Sat noon-2:30pm and 5:30-9pm (prix fixe dinner), Sun 10:30am-2pm. $$*

Hot Tip: Reserve for lunch or Sunday brunch to make the most of the view. You'll be well situated for a walk along the Marina Green afterward.

Julius' Castle
1541 Montgomery St., North Beach, 415-392-2222 • Classic

The Draw: To say that Julius' Castle has a dramatic, panoramic, spectacular view is an understatement. It has the view of all views, spanning almost the entire bay, picture-perfect from nearly every seat in all four levels of this landmark establishment.

The Scene: Like an Old West saloon, Julius' Castle is steeped in carved dark woods and original Victorian-era details dating back to its Gold Rush beginnings. The classic cuisine, duck breast, steak, and fish, while good, is not the main attraction here. *Daily 5-9:30pm. $$$*

Hot Tip: Turn up the romance with a sunset walk. Start in North Beach and make your way to Coit Tower. From there, find the light pole at the head of the Greenwich steps, 187 of which will land you at the Castle.

Sutro's at the Cliff House
1090 Point Lobos Ave., Richmond, 415-386-3330 • Classic

The Draw: Situated on a rocky point at the north end of Ocean Beach, the sleek, contemporary Sutro Wing of the Cliff House has floor-to-ceiling windows facing the Pacific and the Marin coastline.

The Scene: A modernist setting and dazzling ocean views combine with fine Californian cuisine for big romance, big style. *Daily 11:30am-3:30pm and 5-9:30pm. $$*

Hot Tip: It's all about the view, so go on a sunny day or at sunset (you can't see much at night). Or skip the food and stop in the Zinc Bar for a drink.

THE 99 BEST OF SAN FRANCISCO

Restaurants with Bars

#58–60: Used to be the bar at a restaurant was a place to wait for your table. These days, hot restaurants are adding chic destination bars to draw the right kind of dinner crowd and create a buzz.

Circolo
500 Florida St., Potrero Hill, 415-553-8560 • Hot & Cool

The Draw: Circolo serves a menu of Latino-Asian dishes. A sleek lounge in the signature white of our times beckons before and after dinner.

The Scene: Multimedia businesspeople and fans of "intelligent nightlife" populate the restaurant and lounge, which have a decidedly boom-time luxury feel. *Sun-Thu 5-10pm, Fri-Sat 5pm-2:30am.* $$

Hot Tip: If cocktails after dinner did more to rev you up than cool you down, cross the street to Whisper, the huge after-hours mega-club that gets moving fast on the weekends after midnight.

Frisson
244 Jackson St., Financial District, 415-956-3004 • Hot & Cool

The Draw: Take the TWA terminal at JFK, cross it with a Denny's circa 1970, throw in a dash of *2001: A Space Odyssey,* and add contemporary lounge sounds from Europe's capitals, and you've got Frisson.

The Scene: The fashionable crowd looks right at home in this beautiful, contemporary space, where the cocktails come mixed with fresh fruit juices and the dinners feature artistic combinations. *Tue-Fri 5pm-2am, Sat 6pm-2am, Sun 11am-5pm.* $$

Hot Tip: Don't miss the lounge downstairs, and be sure to visit the facilities, an intriguing affair complete with a co-ed island for washing up.

Levende Lounge
1710 Mission St., Mission, 415-864-5585 • Hot & Cool

The Draw: It offers a winning combination of excellent food in a very hip setting, complete with good house music after dinner and Sunday brunch with a DJ.

The Scene: New in 2004, Levende has swiftly taken a solid place in San Francisco's entertainment repertoire. The diverse crowd ranges from alternative Mission District types to adventurous suits. A robust calendar of guest DJs and party events keeps things interesting. *Dinner Tue-Fri 5-11pm, Sat 6-11pm, Sun 6-11pm. Bar Tue-Sat until 2am. Sun brunch 11 am-4pm.* $$

Hot Tip: Had dinner elsewhere? This place goes late, so stop in to sip, chat, and step to the DJ beat. Also a great choice for Sunday brunch (until 4pm!), when you can make your own Bloody Mary.

35

 # Romantic Dining

#61–63: Intimate dinners are about more than food, of course. They're about lighting, ambiance, service, and wine, not to mention that nameless special something that gets your mojo humming.

Boulevard
One Mission St., Embarcadero, 415-543-6084 • Classic

The Draw: Haute cuisine in the French–New American style is rarely done better. Add in views of the water, excellent service, and an extensive wine list, and you have a winner.

The Scene: Parisian bistro managers might visit Boulevard to see how it's done. Housed in the historic Audiffred Building, the interior is all dark woods, Belle Epoque details, tulip-shaped lamps, and floral motifs. There is even a mosaic floor representing a peacock. *Mon-Thu 11:30am-2pm and 5:30-10pm, Fri 11:30am-2pm and 5:30-10:30pm, Sat 5:30-10:30pm, Sun 5:30-10pm.* $$$

Hot Tip: Take a stroll along the nearby waterfront to put you in the mood.

Café Jacqueline
1454 Grant Ave., North Beach, 415-981-5565 • Classic

The Draw: You say you want romance? Chef Jacqueline Margulis is ready to romance you right down to your toes. Her tiny, country-French restaurant serves almost nothing but soufflés, each lovingly prepared by Jacqueline herself and sized to share.

The Scene: It is tempting to call the simple, quiet setting quaint, but that would diminish the gravity of what Jacqueline accomplishes with her airy creations. The ambiance is heavy with anticipation, both of soufflés and of passion. *Wed-Sun 5:30-11pm.* $$

Hot Tip: The place fills up quickly, so call ahead to reserve a table. And for the love of God, order the Grand Marnier soufflé for dessert.

Fleur de Lys
777 Sutter St., Downtown, 415-673-7779 • Classic

The Draw: Let a flicker of hesitation or displeasure cross your brow and a jacketed server will be at your side an instant later. Fleur de Lys is like being royalty for an evening.

The Scene: When it's time for a fine French meal in an intimate setting and price is no object, there is no better choice than Fleur de Lys. A subdued setting lends itself to tender conversation and romance. The coat rack is more likely to hold last year's Brioni cashmere than this year's Gucci. *Mon-Thu 6-9:30pm, Fri 5:30-10:30pm, Sat 5-10:30pm.* $$$

Hot Tip: Take her here on a first date and she'll know you mean business. Same goes for that important anniversary or birthday

Best Scene Bars

#64–66: Sexy is the word for it. A slew of designer night spots has sprung up around town, decked out in ultramodern décor and the perfect backdrop to a night of refined debauchery. Dress the part and get ready to strike a pose.

Fluid Ultra Lounge
662 Mission St., SoMa, 415-615-6888 • Hot & Cool

The Draw: From the austere exterior—the name is featured only in the artful arrangement of the door handles—to the minimalist, high-tech interior dominated by Miami white and a bar that changes color Jetsons-style, Fluid offers a chic, futuristic spot to drink, dance, and mingle.

The Scene: Expect young ladies in their best sexy gear and guys trying not to look too eager. The space is so elegant, you almost wish for a red rope policy. *Wed-Fri 5pm-2am, Sat 10pm-after hours.*

Hot Tip: Roll by dressed to impress on a Friday or Saturday night. Try the mojito or the lemony-sweet Fluid martini.

MatrixFillmore
3138 Fillmore St., Marina, 415-563-4180 • Hot & Cool

The Draw: A yuppie power center, the place fills to capacity and spills out the door with pleasure-seeking post-sorority girls and the thirty-something businessmen who love them.

The Scene: In the '60s, the MatrixFillmore was the place to see local bands like Jefferson Airplane. It reopened almost 30 years later, made over as a futuristic lounge with a centerpiece fireplace and other artful touches. The party takes off on Thursday nights and flies high into the small hours of Sunday morning. This is a great place to meet people. *Daily 5:30pm-2am.*

Hot Tip: Dine at the Balboa Cafe to make the after-dinner commute a snap.

Redwood Room
Clift Hotel, 495 Geary St., Downtown, 415-929-2372 • Hot & Cool

The Draw: Ian Schrager knows how to throw a party and how to pick a venue. Having endured an edgy revamp, the historic Redwood Room retains much of its dignity while boasting a good deal of new energy.

The Scene: The dramatic Philippe Starck–designed setting attracts a consistently glamorous crowd of the Southern California ilk. Expect out-of-town visitors dolled up in their sexiest nightlife finery, a few of the glitzier locals, men with money eager to valet their hot rides out front, and troupes of girls sending off the bride-to-be with a few rounds of cosmopolitans. *Sun-Thu 5pm-2am, Fri-Sat 5pm-2am.*

Hot Tip: If you are trying to look your best, do not lean over the translucent tables lit from below.

Best | Seafood Restaurants

#67–69: Take the cable car to Fisherman's Wharf for seafood? Not a bad idea, but for truly memorable seafood, visit one of these upscale establishments where the fish is king.

Aqua
252 California St., Financial District, 415-956-9662 • Classic

The Draw: Aqua means artfully presented seafood and desserts in a suitably sophisticated setting.

The Scene: The picture of refinement, Aqua brings out the inner duke or duchess. Soft lighting, muted colors, and high ceilings help complete a luxuriously relaxing mood. A long, dimly lit bar invites you to linger over one of more than 300 wines on offer. *Mon-Fri 11:30am-2pm and 5:30-9:30pm, Sat-Sun 5:30-9:30pm.* $$$

Hot Tip: If you've had a good day in the stock market, spring for the Chef's Tasting Menu with wine pairings—it will be an evening to remember.

Farallon
450 Post St., Downtown, 415-956-6969 • Hot & Cool

The Draw: Step into Farallon and enter a deep-sea fantasy, with chandeliers like elaborate jellyfish, a spiral-shaped Nautilus Room, vaulted ceilings resembling an undersea cave, and kelp-covered columns lit from within.

The Scene: With its 300 seats and location near Union Square, Farallon attracts the steady stream of tourists it was designed to accommodate, without feeling overly touristy. With such a fun ambiance, even the locals turn up when it's time for a fancy seafood dinner. *Mon 5:30-10pm, Tue-Thu 11:30am-10pm, Fri-Sat 11:30am-11pm, Sun 5-10pm.* $$$

Hot Tip: Odd hours can be best at this tourist-heavy spot. If you have theater plans nearby, sneak in at 5:30-6pm for a three-course prix fixe.

Hayes Street Grill
320 Hayes St., Hayes Valley, 415-863-5545 • Classic

The Draw: Opened in 1979 by famed chef and co-owner Patricia Unterman, the Hayes Street Grill has been serving excellent seafood and other dishes based on fresh, seasonal ingredients ever since.

The Scene: Traditional and low-key, it's nevertheless a destination restaurant fit for special nights. Diners are often on their way to the opera or symphony around the corner. *Mon-Thu 11:30am-2pm and 5-9:30pm, Fri 11:30am-2pm and 5-10:30pm, Sat 5:30-10:30pm, Sun 5-8:30pm.* $$

Hot Tip: Lunch is worth the trip as much as dinner. Stroll Hayes Street afterward for a chic array of boutiques catering to design and fashion aficionados.

Best — Sex in the City

#70–72: Every city has its own take on sexuality. In San Francisco, it's about being open-minded (no surprise here). Whatever your kink, as long as everyone involved is of age and willing, welcome to the party.

Baker Beach
Presidio National Park • Hip

The Draw: Get naked in the sun (or chilling fog) in sight of the glorious Golden Gate Bridge and Marin Headlands.

The Scene: Everything goes at the north end of Baker Beach, where revelers do naked yoga, sunbathe naked, and play naked Frisbee. It's not about pecs and implants. The full range of human form is unapologetically unveiled.

Hot Tip: Bring extra sunscreen for those hard-to-reach spots. The water is cold and treacherous. It's best for splashing and wading, not swimming.

Good Vibrations
603 Valencia St., Mission, 415-522-5460 • Hip

The Draw: Sex shops don't get friendlier or more inviting than Good Vibes, a San Francisco fixture since 1977. Where else can you peruse a complete selection of dildos, vibrators, erotica, and mild S&M gear in a clean, well-lighted space?

The Scene: Shoppers include the same crowd you might expect at the local supermarket, including couples feeling adventurous and women of all ages testing new battery-powered companions. *Sun-Wed 11am-7pm, Thu-Sat 11am-8pm.*

Hot Tip: The staff is helpful, knowledgeable, and professional. If you have questions, they have snicker-free answers.

Power Exchange
74 Otis St., Mission, 415-487-9944

The Draw: Like the unicorn, sex clubs are that mythical creature so many people wonder about. Wonder no more. The Power Exchange is an authentic sex club where actual sex acts among strangers occur. Voyeurs and exhibitionists, step right up to the head of the line.

The Scene: The underbelly crowd of San Francisco turns up for the various theme nights. Expect plenty of dudes mixed in with ladies of all shapes and sizes, multiple piercings, hair dyed every color under the rainbow, mild to extra-spicy S&M scenarios, and more. Don't be surprised if you're asked to do something scandalous. *Mon-Thu 9pm-4am, Sat 9pm-6am, Sun 9pm-4am.*

Hot Tip: Men interested in women would be wise to bring a date, an open-minded date, that is.

Best — Sexy Lounges

#73–75: The Italian furniture and minimalist aesthetic have arrived, bringing with them a chance to drape yourself across a classic of modern design while you sip your sidecar and scrutinize the newcomers. The mood is European elegance mixed with late-night decadence. Gentlemen, start your engines.

Dolce
440 Broadway, North Beach, 415-989-3434 • Hot & Cool

The Draw: Billed as a "high-concept DJ lounge" and "an oasis from the ordinary," Dolce is decidedly upscale, complete with a VIP lounge, bottle service, and all the Las Vegas–style trimmings.

The Scene: New in 2005, Dolce is all dressed up in the latest white-on-white fashions, with fancy furniture to loll around on and end tables in modernist shapes. The crowd is equally dolled up and ready to party. *Wed-Sat 9pm-2am.* C=

Hot Tip: Go early (around 10pm) on weekends to avoid the line, or try Thursday night for a great local crowd.

Suede
383 Bay St., Fisherman's Wharf, 415-399-9555 • Hot & Cool

The Draw: This sophisticated and even exotic take on the living room is filled with rich textures and earth tones. The large space is divided into two areas; one for dancing, one for relaxing. When you spot the candles, secluded booths, and luxurious pavilions, you'll know it's time to relax.

The Scene: It can get crowded, both with troupes of girls (girls' night out) and guys (testosterone overload). The vibe is aggressive and sexy. These are the people who take their Saturday nightlife seriously. *Fri-Sat 9pm-2am, plus special events.* C=

Hot Tip: Dress your best to pass the scrutiny of the door folk.

Suite one8one
181 Eddy St., Downtown, 415-345-9900 • Hot & Cool

The Draw: Perhaps the best of the many sophisticated new lounges around town, Suite one8one looks like a chic hotel suite expanded to include a dance floor and complete with white cubes, candles, beds, and elegant areas to stretch out and strike a pose.

The Scene: The very young and hip dance club crowd comes out in its finest. Have your favorite Gucci-Prada-Dolce and Gabbana cleaned and pressed if you want to make an impression on the door keepers, not to mention the clientele. *Thu-Sat 9pm-4am.* C=

Hot Tip: If you want to lounge on those long Italian sofas and vie for a spot on the big bed between dances, reserve a VIP table with bottle service.

Best Spas

#76–78: When the going gets tough, the tough get exfoliated, massaged, and anointed with essential oils. Whether your idea of a soothing ambiance is timeless grandeur or futuristic minimalism, San Francisco offers a wide range of options for spa indulgence.

International Orange Day Spa
2044 Fillmore St., Pacific Heights, 888-894-8811 • Hot & Cool

The Draw: If frou-frou New Age spa décor gives you hives, you'll love the minimal chic of International Orange. The yoga lounge is one of the prettiest places you'll ever do a downward dog.

The Scene: Yoga babes and Pacific Heights society girls pack the white-on-white rooms daily, cultivating their bliss in any number of ways. *Mon-Fri 11am-9pm, Sat-Sun 9am-7pm.* $$$

Hot Tip: The spa's luxury products are available online, so you can continue to indulge in its fabulous selection even after you get home.

Nob Hill Spa
Huntington Hotel, 1075 California St., Nob Hill, 415-474-5400 • Classic

The Draw: The indoor infinity pool with a view of downtown definitely puts the *ahh* in spa. As posh and opulent as spas in San Francisco get, the NHS offers a full range of treatments, many of an Ayurvedic persuasion.

The Scene: Facials, massages, scrubs, and body wraps are the stock-in-trade in the ten private treatment rooms, where the privileged and temporarily privileged come to be rubbed and anointed. You can relax knowing a feng-shui expert was consulted in the spa's construction to ensure a serene and harmonious setting. *Daily 8am-8pm.* $$$$

Hot Tip: NASA has been busy developing ways to keep you from aging, including photomodulation, a kind of LED light therapy on offer here.

Tru Spa
750 Kearny St., Financial District, 415-399-9700 • Hot & Cool

The Draw: Not necessarily a place to lounge the day away, Tru is where you go to get groomed, chill out, and get back in the action. There is no apricot flouncing and no Enya here. Suitably modern music accompanies the ultramodern décor.

The Scene: Tru attracts an upscale crew looking for the better massage, the progressive facial, and the Moji-Toe pedicure. *Mon, Tue, Thu, Fri 9am-9pm, Wed noon-8pm, Sat 10am-8pm, Sun 11am-6pm.* $$$$

Hot Tip: Do not miss the Tropical Rainforest Room. Splurge on that extra half-hour of massage, as Tru donates a portion of its proceeds to various environmental organizations.

Best Sushi Restaurants

#79–81: Sushi took the city by storm a few years ago, and its popularity never abated. Although there's plenty of choice these days, when you want to have it just right, roll to one of the mighty triad below.

Kyo-Ya
Palace Hotel, Two New Montgomery St., SoMa, 415-546-5090 • Classic

The Draw: It's not about ambiance. The Kyo-Ya space is quiet, serene, almost plain. Serving traditional Japanese cuisine by the book, it's known for excellent and fresh sushi and sashimi prepared to camera-ready perfection.

The Scene: Japanese businessmen make Kyo-Ya their home away from home, knowing the prices keep casual sushi fans at bay and the décor prevents hipsters from lingering. Only serious sushi connoisseurs need apply. *Tue-Fri 11:30am-2pm and 6-10pm, Sat 6-10pm.* $$

Hot Tip: Challenge your palate with the kaiseki dinner menu, a six-course "odyssey of flavors, textures, and colors" that changes monthly.

Ozumo
161 Steuart St., SoMa, 415-882-1333 • Hot & Cool

The Draw: The Japanese-inspired cuisine is some of the best in the city. The Zen-modernist setting is spectacular, complete with a sushi bar with a million-dollar bay view.

The Scene: A crowd of the upscale cool culled from the Financial District professionals frequents both the restaurant and the equally inviting sake lounge, a supremely tasteful space with a decidedly sexy feel. *Mon-Wed 11:30am-2pm and 5:30-10pm, Thu-Fri 11:30am-2pm and 5:30-10:30pm, Sat 5:30-10:30pm, Sun 5:30-10pm, lounge until closing.* $$

Hot Tip: Friday night after work can be quite a scene. The jam-packed bar is a good place to meet people.

Sushi Groove South
1516 Folsom St., SoMa, 415-503-1950 • Hip

The Draw: South of Market hipsters converge on this dark ultramodern space where the music is fresh, the sushi is fresher, and the beautiful people check you out at the door.

The Scene: Techno hip, but surprisingly light on the attitude, this is the place to bust out that vinyl miniskirt (ladies) or overengineered Puma street shoes (gents). *Mon-Tue 6-10pm, Wed-Thu 6-10:30pm, Fri-Sat 6-11:30pm.* $$

Hot Tip: If you like Sushi Groove South, try the equally hip original Sushi Groove at 1916 Hyde on Russian Hill.

Best Tiki Bars

#82–84: Sitting on the edge of the Pacific has its advantages, such as the inevitable presence of that most exotic of species, the tiki bar. When you long for the rustle of grass skirts, try one of these instant tropical paradises.

Sneaky Tiki
1582 Folsom St., SoMa, 415-701-8454 • Hip

The Draw: Good pan-Asian food, sweet drinks, and an appealingly modernist yet tongue-in-cheek interpretation of the tiki motif combine for good plain fun.

The Scene: This stretch of Folsom is still gritty enough to scare off the oldsters and tourists. Inside you'll find hipsters and coolios and dot-com second-wavers sucking on rum punch and dipping sweet potato straws in mango ketchup. *Mon-Fri 11am-4pm and 5-10pm, Sat-Sun 5-10pm.*

Hot Tip: Things get happy from 4:30 to 7:30pm daily when a drink order earns you a free pupu platter.

Tonga Room
Fairmont Hotel, 950 Mason St., Nob Hill, 415-772-5278 • Classic

The Draw: The Tonga Room boasts thatched-roof huts, fake palm trees, and plenty of festive, campy fun.

The Scene: Groups of FiDi revelers trudge up the big hill to hoist blender drinks at the happy hour discount while they eat their fill from the $7 Pacific Rim buffet and stand in awe of the indoor hurricane—complete with rain and thunder! *Sun-Thu 6-10pm, Fri-Sat 6-11pm.*

Hot Tip: Happy hour is 5 to 7pm weekdays. If you can't make that, hit the T-Room early or late on Saturday night to mix with troupes of young revelers.

Trader Vic's
555 Golden Gate Ave., Hayes Valley, 415-775-6300 • Classic

The Draw: If the birthplace of the Mai Tai isn't worth honoring, what is?

The Scene: This longstanding kitschy haunt closed in 1995 only to reopen in a new location in 2005. The crowd hasn't changed: indigenous backslappers and pedigreed socialites of all ages. *Restaurant Mon-Fri 11:30am-2:30pm and 5-10pm, Sat 5-10pm, Sun 4-10pm. Bar daily 11:30am-12:30am.*

Hot Tip: Near the symphony and opera houses, Trader Vic's offers an oasis where you can have dinner or sip a fruity cocktail from a mug shaped like a shrunken head while you kill time before a performance.

Best Trendy Hangouts

#85–87: You want to be in the center, where everyone who's anyone wants to be. You want to be cool and hang with the in crowd, not that you would admit it or even use the word *cool*. You want to wear your new Prada shirt with the Italian detailing and have it be no big thing. You can.

Bambuddha Lounge
Phoenix Hotel, 601 Eddy St., Downtown, 415-885-5088 • Hot & Cool

The Draw: Crowds line up every weekend to work it in the Asian fantasy décor of this landmark bar located in the retro-hip Phoenix Hotel. Dinner features quite good Southeast Asian cuisine.

The Scene: The closest thing San Francisco has to a night out in Hollywood, Bambuddha has a rock-and-roll feel, as though Keith Richards might saunter down to the pool in his dressing gown at any moment. If you're looking for the Skybar of San Francisco, this is the place. *Tue-Thu 5:30-10:30pm, Fri-Sat 5pm-2am.* C F ≡

Hot Tip: Weekends draw a packed house. During the week, there is often an event or party to crash. Order the Lychee-tini for a sweet sensation.

Mr. Smith's
34 Seventh St., SoMa, 415-355-9991 • Hot & Cool

The Draw: Three levels of dancing, drinking, and mingling with a glossy crew of twenty-, thirty-, and, yes, even forty-somethings can't be wrong. Mr. Smith's captures that elusive perfect balance of glam and grit that spells success for a nighttime hangout.

The Scene: Victorian touches lend this modern setting a note of fantasy that inspires a mood of debauchery, conveniently served in three flavors: drinking and schmoozing (main floor), lounging and nuzzling (upstairs), moving and grooving (basement). *Wed-Fri 6pm-2am, Sat 8pm-2am.* ≡

Hot Tip: On Wednesdays, five clams buys a martini made with any vodka or gin in the house.

111 Minna Gallery
111 Minna St., SoMa, 415-974-1719 • Hot & Cool

The Draw: Without a doubt, this is the place for a downtown drink among the young, trendy, and gainfully employed after work. Art openings and special events are frequent.

The Scene: Live music is a definite possibility when the DJ isn't spinning. Expect the eclectic, from surf rock to skate punk. Beware the giant metal fly overhead. *Tue 5-10pm, Wed 5-11pm, Thu-Sat 5pm-2am.* C ≡

Hot Tip: Minna is especially fun on Wednesday nights, when Qool, a long-running after-work party, brings in the best and brightest.

Best — Trendy Tables

#88–90: In a city where eating out is sport, science, art, theater, and the local obsession all rolled into one, choosing the top three must-have tables is a tall order. New places spring up, flower, and close their doors before you can get a reservation. For the moment, these are the hot plates du jour.

A16
2355 Chestnut St., Marina, 415-771-2216 • Hot & Cool

The Draw: Simple is the toughest game of all, and both the food and the atmosphere succeed with classic simplicity at A16, a newcomer that quickly endeared itself to every food critic in the Western world.

The Scene: The young, trendy Marina District crowd gathers in this narrow contemporary space nightly, and increasingly competes with the magazine review set (older, not local) for reservations. Southern Italian cuisine with pizzas, pasta, and meat prepared alla Napoli is matched by one of the city's most Italian and best wine lists. *Sun-Tue 5-10pm, Wed-Thu 11:30am-2:30pm and 5-10pm, Fri 11:30am-2:30pm and 5-11pm, Sat 5-11pm.* $$

Hot Tip: Go mid-week when the crowd is mostly locals, meaning younger and more fashionable than the weekenders. Sunday and Monday nights you may find the place peppered with local chefs on their night off.

RNM Restaurant
598 Haight St., Haight, 415-551-7900 • Hip

The Draw: A sultry, ruby-lit, forward-thinking spot that isn't South of Market, offers a great wine list, and serves impeccable food.

The Scene: The décor is modern, sexy design at its best, complete with chain-mail curtains and a futuristic puffball of a chandelier. The crowd is mixed but stylish. *Tue-Thu 5:30-10pm, Fri-Sat 5:30-11pm.* $$

Hot Tip: The grilled hearts of romaine with blue cheese gets high marks.

supperclub San Francisco
657 Harrison St., SoMa, 415-348-0900 • Hot & Cool

The Draw: It's sort of like ordering room service and eating in bed, only there are lots of other people there and instead of pay per view you get to watch a trapeze artist.

The Scene: The two-tier theater-like setting is done in white on white, making it easy to see your five-course set meal. Sexy people lounge on beds, and later do their sexy-people dance late into the night. *Bar open Tue-Sun 6:30pm-2am. Dinner at 7:30pm.* $$

Hot Tip: Don't mess up the décor with your khakis and Reeboks. This is theater for people who take their pleasure seriously. Play the part in your most outrageously sexy attire. Think Bond, James Bond. Or else Prada, Miuccia Prada.

Best Wine Bars

#91–93: With Napa and Sonoma just around the corner, you'd think that wine bars would be as ubiquitous as Starbucks in San Francisco. Although that's not quite the case, the choices for fun places to sample excellent wines in a pleasant setting is growing.

CAV
1666 Market St., Hayes Valley, 415-437-1770 • Hot & Cool

The Draw: CAV draws a sophisticated local crowd enjoying the choice of some 300 wines from around the world, including 40 served by the glass, in a sleek, cosmopolitan setting.

The Scene: In a long narrow room with a minimalist, almost stark, décor, a lively crowd gathers to dabble in tastes, flights, and glasses from the dazzling selection of wines, and choose fine accompaniments from an eclectic small- and large-plates menu. *Mon-Thu 5:30-11pm, Fri-Sat 5:30pm-midnight.*

Hot Tip: Co-owner Tadd and bartender Gus have been on the SF restaurant scene for more than a decade and know their stuff—trust their recommendations.

First Crush
101 Cyril Magnin St., Downtown, 415-982-7874 • Hot & Cool

The Draw: The massive wine list is especially fun because it features only California wines. Sample the heavy hitters, discover up-and-comers, and discover hard-to-find wines by short-run artisan producers.

The Scene: The after-work crowd turns up for drinks and dinner. The mood is friendly and casual, with the focus on exploring new wines and sampling the California-style menu replete with fresh ingredients, seafood, grilled meats, and a quite respectable cheese plate. *Sun-Wed 5-11pm, Thu-Sat 5pm-midnight.*

Hot Tip: Scope out both upstairs and downstairs seating options before accepting a table—both are excellent, but the atmosphere in each area is very different.

Nectar
3330 Steiner St., Marina, 415-345-1377 • Hot & Cool

The Draw: Nectar is a sweet little spot for getting the evening started. The look is chic and the list is international, described in over-the-top, glorious detail.

The Scene: Young upper-crust types feeling sophisticated trickle in after work and fill the place by dinnertime. The seats at the bar invite solos to saddle up and work their wine speak on whoever lands nearby. *Mon-Thu 5:30-10:30pm, Fri-Sat 5:30pm-midnight, Sun 2-9pm.*

Hot Tip: Save your appetite for greener pastures. The emphasis here is on the wine and the chance to mingle in a civilized setting.

Best Wine Lists

#94–96: A wine list is like an art collection. You can throw all the money at it you want, but only good taste will make it great. Bacar wins for volume, Masa's for taste, and Rubicon for that magic combination of the two.

Bacar
448 Brannan St., SoMa, 415-904-4100 • Hot & Cool

The Draw: Born at the peak of the dot-com boom, Bacar is big, slick, and ambitious. Its wine list is rumored to include more than 1,300 selections, covering terroirs from Napa Valley to Cape Town.

The Scene: The young, the stylish, and the stock-optioned gather to listen to live jazz and hoist the tome of a wine list over what the owners call "modern brasserie" cuisine. *Mon-Thu 5:30-11pm, Fri 11:30am-midnight, Sat 5:30pm-midnight, Sun 5:30-10pm.* $$$

Hot Tip: Downstairs and the main floor can be very noisy. If you want to converse, get a table upstairs. Arrive early to sample one of the carefully crafted flights in the downstairs lounge.

Masa's
648 Bush St., Downtown, 415-989-7154 • Classic

The Draw: With serious art on the chocolate-brown walls, serious white linen on the tables, and serious French food on the menu, Masa's is a heavy hitter. The wine collection harbors rare treasures.

The Scene: The quiet, minimalist dining room invites concentration. Don't be surprised if the chef sends out a few amuse-bouches to, well, amuse your mouth. *Tue-Sat 5:30-9:30pm.* $$$

Hot Tip: On a wine list with more than 1,000 selections, there's room for all kinds of specialties, but the focus here is on local Cabernet Sauvignons and white Burgundies. For dessert, order a glass of 20-year-old Chateau d'Yquem, simply because you can.

Rubicon
558 Sacramento St., Financial District, 415-434-4100 • Classic

The Draw: Still waters run deep. From an unassuming exterior, Rubicon opens up to a lovely dining room that has endured at the top of the local food chain for more than a decade. Beneath lies a wine collection to make the most sturdy oenophile swoon.

The Scene: If it were legal to smoke cigars, the FiDi suits that populate Rubicon weeknights would surely be lighting up. Expect a middle-aged crowd on weekends. *Mon-Sat 5:30-10:30pm, Wed 11:30am-2pm.* $$

Hot Tip: The extensive, even awe-inspiring wine list is packed with well-aged, small-production, and hard-to-find gems.

Best Workouts

#97–99: Yoga is the unofficial workout of choice in San Francisco. Every neighborhood has its yoga studio and troop of devotees. When they're not doing yoga, sporty locals can be found mountain biking or surfing. And when they're getting their sweat on indoors, you'll find them at the places below.

It's Yoga
848 Folsom St., SoMa, 415-543-1970

The Draw: While a beautiful open space, a terrific vibe, and an om-riffic sitting area where you can whisper-mingle with others while you wait for your class to begin are all great assets, the real appeal is the teaching.

The Scene: Regulars fill the place for the early afternoon classes, including girls with upper body tone to make Jennifer Garner envious and he-yogis who can hold a perfect headstand and sit in full lotus. *Mon-Fri 7:30am-7:30pm, Sat 8:30am-noon, Sun 9:30am-4:30pm.* $

Hot Tip: For a truly uplifting session, check the schedule at itsyoga.com for a class taught by founder Larry Schultz.

Mission Cliffs
2295 Harrison St., Mission, 415-550-0515 • Hip

The Draw: With 50-foot climbing walls and more than 80 routes, Mission Cliffs is a rare indoor climbing experience. Even if you've never climbed, you can take a brief safety class and head for the ropes your first time.

The Scene: Think brainy granola types with six-packs and dreadlocks—and we're talking about the girls. This is the Burning Man crowd and a few tech executives with an itch for adventure. *Mon-Fri 6:30am-10pm, Sat-Sun 9am-7pm.* $$

Hot Tip: Arrive in the late afternoon and there's plenty of time to take the belay safety class, climb until your arms are Jell-O, and loosen up in the sauna before a late dinner.

Sports Club/LA
747 Market St., SoMa, 415-633-3900 • Hot & Cool

The Draw: The immaculate, luxurious, extensive facilities will inspire you to achieve your personal best whether you play tennis, try a yoga class, hit the weights, or take the plunge in the city's most elegant lap pool.

The Scene: A good-looking clientele of moneyed, muscled professionals comes to work off the day's martinis and power lunches. You never know who you'll see, so leave the old sweatpants at home and opt for your most stylish workout gear. *Mon-Fri 5am-11pm, Sat-Sun 7am-8pm.* $$$$

Hot Tip: Bring your racquet and hit the courts, or abandon all pretense of a workout and retire to the spa to acquire that healthy glow the easy way. If you're not a member, stay at the Four Seasons to gain access.

EXPERIENCE SAN FRANCISCO

Dive into the San Francisco of your choice with one of our three themed itineraries: *Hot & Cool* (p.50), *Hip* (p.88), and *Classic* (p.122). Each is designed to heighten your fun-seeking experience by putting you in the right place at the right time—the best restaurants, nightlife, and attractions, and even the best days to go there. While the itineraries, each followed by detailed descriptions of our top choices, reflect our very top picks, the listings include a number of additional noteworthy options. So, whether you're looking to indulge in a decadent meal at one of the city's top restaurants overlooking the city lights or hit the dance floor late into the night, you'll find it all right here.

Hot & Cool San Francisco

You walk in and survey the surroundings. Nice. Let's get a drink. You find a place to relax and watch the action, which is looking sharp. You think, "This place is hot." Your drink arrives. The glass is perfectly frosted, the rim perfectly sugared, the Cosmo within a tiny artwork of liquid mastery. You take a sip. "Yes, very cool indeed." This is what we mean by hot and cool. From what to do to where to stay, eat, drink, and dance, this is your guide to the always-on spots.

Note: Venues in bold are described in detail in the listings that follow the itinerary. Those with an asterisk are recommended for both drinks and dinner.

Hot & Cool San Francisco: The Perfect Plan (3 Days and Nights)

Your Hotel: Hotel Vitale—A clever blend of fashion-forward boutique-hotel style and big-hotel assets, Vitale offers a chic restaurant downstairs and soaking tubs on the roof.

Thursday

The Perfect Plan Highlights

Prime Time: Thu-Sat

Thursday
Morning	Levi Plaza
	Jackson Square
Lunch	Globe, Myth
Afternoon	Union Square
Cocktails	Bar at XYZ
Evening	SFMoMA
Dinner	Ame, Slanted Door
Nighttime	Fluid Ultra Lounge
Late-Night	Loft 11

Friday
Morning	SBC Park Tour
Lunch	Tres Agaves, A16
Afternoon	Asian Art Museum
Cocktails	Jade Bar, Bacar
Dinner	supperclub San Francisco
Nighttime	Bambuddha Lounge
Late-Night	Suite one8one

Saturday
Morning	Tru Spa, Equinox Fitness, Ferry Plaza's Farmers Mkt.
Lunch	MarketBar, Pier 23 Cafe
Afternoon	Adventure Cat, Tiburon
Cocktails	Dolce, Cortez
Dinner	Frisson, Michael Mina
Nighttime	Redwood Rm., Mr. Smith's
Late-Night	Le Duplex, Ruby Skye

10am Built in what was an old warehouse district to provide a home for San Francisco's most famous home-grown business, Levi Strauss, the Levi Plaza office complex makes a wonderful contribution to the urban landscape. Drop by Piperade To-Go (Icehouse Alley between Union and Green and Sansome and Battery Streets) for coffee and a snack, then walk to the high-end antique shops and design stores of Jackson Square, a historical district that dates back to the Gold Rush era when it was the heart of the boom town. Today, its narrow streets and beautifully restored historical buildings (watch for period details) are filled with cafes, restaurants, antique shops, and furniture showrooms.

12:30pm Lunch Right in the neighborhood are two restaurants known for both power lunches of the artsy variety and great late-night dining: **Globe*** and **Myth***. If you are already heading toward Union Square, opt for **B44*** in nearby Belden Place. On sunny days, try to grab an outdoor table.

HOT & COOL

2:30pm If art sounds more inspiring than commerce, gallery-hop around Union Square, San Francisco's downtown. There are dozens of galleries within a few blocks. The best are Modernism at 685 Market Street and the collection of galleries housed at 49 Geary Street. (If it's the first Thursday of the month, save your gallery hopping for happy hour, when everyone stays open late and launches new shows.) Near Union Square is the **San Francisco Museum of Craft + Design**, just the slice of aesthetic refreshment a weary shopper needs.

4pm Many high-end stores face onto Union Square—Saks, Neiman Marcus, Macy's, and Gucci, among other heavy hitters. From Hermès, Chanel, and Prada to Mont Blanc, Gumps, and Banana Republic, almost every retail indulgence known to modern humanity is represented within a few blocks.

5:30pm Join the after-work crowd in the **Bar at XYZ** at the W Hotel, or try a Campari orange at **Chaya Brasserie*** facing the bay. Feeling social? Drop in at **111 Minna** for a hot party scene in a bare-bones art gallery space and mingle with a brainy, stylish crowd.

7pm Then, just down the street, enjoy art and the sounds of live music at the **San Francisco Museum of Modern Art (SFMoMA)**, which stays open late Thursday nights. Note: you could start with the museum and have your cocktails after.

9pm Dinner Choose among three dinner options, all of which exemplify the Asian influence on San Francisco's dining scene. Across the alley from SFMoMA, the St. Regis Hotel is home to **Ame*** (say "ah-may" to the doorman—he'll know you're no tourist), where you can dine at either the sashimi bar or in the modern chic dining room. **Slanted Door***, on the nearby Embarcadero, beckons with new Vietnamese cuisine served to a consistently full house in a stylish waterfront setting. Another slick option is the frequently packed Japanese restaurant and sake bar, **Ozumo***.

11pm Move over to **Fluid Ultra Lounge** for a slick, Miami-style scene in a small dance club, just a few blocks away. **Mezzanine** is the hot ticket for a night of heat and beats on the dance floor. A bit further away, the same goes for the slightly more polished **Loft 11**, where you can be assure of a scene that goes late, late into the night.

Friday

10am You don't have to be a die-hard baseball fan to get a kick out of taking the **SBC Park Tour**.

52

For those who want to experience another slice of San Francisco shopping, start your day earlier on Union Street in the Marina District. If it's bright out, choose a sidewalk table for an Italian breakfast at **Rose's Café**. From there, you're ideally situated for a window-shopping stroll east on Union Street. When the shops thin out, make your way down to Chestnut Street and more terrific shops, cafes, and restaurants.

12:30pm Lunch If you are leaving SBC Park, **Tres Agaves*** is nearby, a hot spot where people have been known to sample tequilas midday. Further down the road, join city bigwigs at **Town Hall** for a lunch of sophisticated comfort food. If instead you had a Marina morning, stroll to the Italian eatery **A16** on Chestnut, or head back up the hill to **Betelnut*** for pan-Asian cuisine.

2:30pm Cab to the Civic Center and the **Asian Art Museum** for a look at ancient Tibetan statuary, Japanese kimonos, jade figurines from China, and much more. You might combine this with exploring Hayes Valley (see Hip chapter, p.93).

6pm From the museum, walk over to Gough Street to **Jade Bar** for cocktails with the crowd getting off work. Sophisticates may opt instead for a pre-dinner wine-tasting at **Bacar***, South of Market, where jazz helps create a lively din. The patio at **Americano*** also hosts a solid after-work scene.

7:30pm Dinner For an experience like no other, unless you happened to go to earlier incarnations in Amsterdam or Rome, **supperclub San Francisco*** should be your first choice. There's only one seating for the three-hour-plus meal-cum-entertainment. Or dress your best and pay a visit to **Fifth Floor**, perhaps the most intimate and luxurious restaurant in town, in the South of Market Hotel Palomar. If you'd rather try a different neighborhood—or if you forgot to make reservations—try Cali-Med in an art- and film-themed setting at **Foreign Cinema** in the Mission, where a moderate wait in either of its two bars will generally produce a table.

11pm If it's Foreign Cinema for dinner, it must be **Laszlo**, the semi-attached DJ bar, for drinks afterwards. For a more eclectic scene, the **Bambuddha Lounge*** in the Phoenix Hotel will be buzzing from happy hour onward. Cab to **MatrixFillmore**, where the well-heeled crowd is sure to be spilling out the front door. And the later it gets, the hotter the scenes are at **DNA Lounge** and **Suite one8one**.

Saturday

9am Your aromatherapy massage, pedicure, and facial are waiting at **Tru Spa**. Close by, the new **Equinox Fitness Club** provides an extraordinary setting for a more active start to your morning. Golfers should cab to **Harding Park Golf Course**, the incredible 1920s public course recently given a PGA extreme makeover. You can also play nine holes at Harding's Fleming Nine.

11am Unless you've opted for golf, walk to the Ferry Building Marketplace on the Embarcadero to savor a Peet's coffee and a Frog Hollow pastry, the perfect snack as you stroll this gourmet heaven known as **Ferry Plaza Farmers Market**.

1pm Lunch The **MarketBar*** patio in front of the Farmers Market gives you a ringside seat for some of the best people-watching in town. Or, just down the Embarcadero is **Pier 23 Cafe***, where you can sit outside in back, watch the water, and hear a live band.

2:30pm Heed the bay's call of fresh breezes and salt spray on a 55-foot catamaran from **Adventure Cat**. Or resort to the iron sail and take a **Blue and Gold Ferry** from Fisherman's Wharf out to Tiburon where you can sit outside on the waterfront patio at Sam's and have an Anchor Steam. If possible, time your ferry trip back to the city for sunset.

6pm You look camera-ready; so should your cocktail lounge. Get the evening started at **Dolce**, North Beach's swankiest large-scale lounge, or in the modern bar at **Cortez*** downtown. Another good choice is **Suede**, depending on what's on their calendar that night.

8pm Dinner Few scenes or settings can rival Jetsons-esque and ultrasexy **Frisson***. For the culinary equivalent of ballet, head to the extravagant **Michael Mina** on Union Square. And for a Mission District experience that delivers delicious Asian fusion and an adjoining bar for après, head to **Circolo***.

11pm Launch your Saturday night with style at the **Redwood Room** in the Clift Hotel. Or try one of the newer hot spots, such as the tri-level extravaganza that is **Mr. Smith's**. If the night is bigger than all that, go all out at **Ruby Skye**, the reigning queen of San Francisco dance venues. If you've had dinner at Circolo and want to remain in the Mission, stop into **Levende Lounge*** to see and be seen. End at SoMa's **Le Duplex**, the French dance club with plenty of architectural and human eye candy, for a sweet finish to your weekend.

Hot & Cool San Francisco: The Key Neighborhoods

Downtown and the nearby **Financial District** (affectionately known as FiDi) are home to many of the most buzzing new hot spots in San Francisco. The streets are lined with the city's grand hotels, upscale shopping, slick restaurants, and posh nightclubs. By day, seek alfresco refreshment in Belden Place, a pedestrian alley packed with places to eat and drink with the hardworking natives. The suit crowd congregates for happy hour throughout the Financial District.

The Embarcadero, where Market Street bumps into the waterfront, is a sun-splashed, palm-lined esplanade with a view of the Bay Bridge, Treasure Island, and the East Bay hills. In addition to world-class restaurants and sparkling bars, it boasts the Ferry Building Marketplace, the gourmet center of San Francisco.

The Marina District offers upscale pleasures among an attractive, affluent local crowd along Chestnut, Union, and Fillmore Streets, and on weekends, at the Triangle, a cluster of bars at Fillmore and Greenwich Streets.

North Beach The eclectic scene runs the gamut from strip clubs to serious nightclubbing amidst the flashing neon lights of Broadway.

SoMa (South of Market) is where you'll find a trendy crowd ready to indulge in the luxury lounge scene. Many of the city's most happening nightclubs are clustered along the 11th Street corridor.

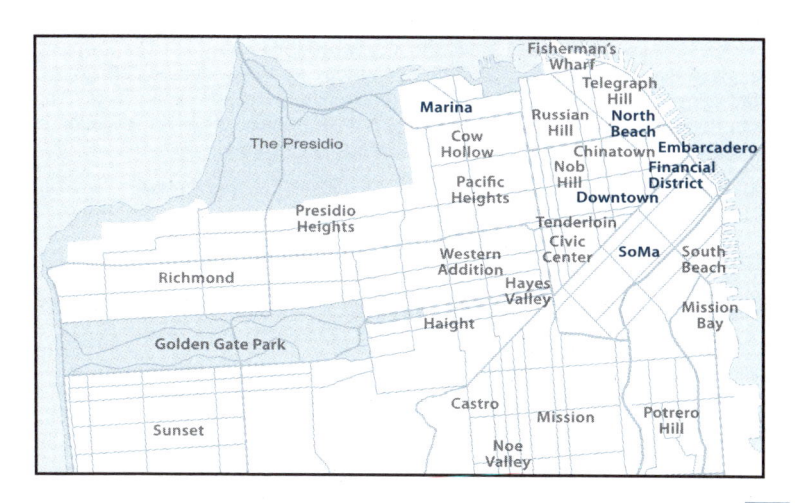

Hot & Cool San Francisco: The Shopping Blocks

Fillmore Street

Fillmore Street between Jackson and Bush Streets is a treasure trove of elegant independent boutiques carrying designer clothing, gorgeous footwear, beauty products, and more.

Cielo With a focus on European designers and cashmere, Cielo draws celebs and well-heeled locals. 2225 Fillmore St. (Sacramento St.), 415-776-0641

Flicka Scandinavian modernist fashion, accessories, and home furnishings. 1932 Fillmore St. (Bush St.), 415-292-2315

Gimme Shoes The destination for gorgeous designer shoes. (p.84) 2358 Fillmore St. (Washington St.), 415-441-3040

Kiehl's Long-standing destination for beauty lotions and potions with a knowledgeable staff. 2360 Fillmore St. (Washington St.), 415-359-9260

Margaret O'Leary High-end contemporary women's clothing. 2400 Fillmore St. (Washington St.), 415-929-0441

Nest Upscale and whimsical accessories and furnishings for the home. 2300 Fillmore St. (Clay St.), 415-292-6199

Toujours High-end silk and lace for the ladies in the house. 2484 Sacramento St. (Fillmore St.), 415-346-3988

Zinc Details A selection of modern home furnishings and playful décor from around the world. 1905 Fillmore St. (Bush St.), 415-776-2100

Union and Chestnut Streets

Few parts of town offer such great strolling opportunities as these two shopping streets in the Marina District. On Union, the shops are mostly between Gough and Steiner; on Chestnut, they're between Fillmore and Divisadero. While everything from fine housewares to designer eyewear is on offer here, the main attraction is unique, of-the-moment finery for hot bodies with high credit limits.

Abigail Morgan Upscale apparel from basics to lingerie to party dresses. 1640 Union St. (Franklin St.), 415-567-1779

Blue Jeans Bar Over 25 brands of jeans, from Rock & Republic to True Religion. 1827 Union St. (Octavia St.), 415-346-4280

Mingle Assorted handmade pieces by emerging local designers and artists. 1815 Union St. (Octavia St.), 415-674-8811

Rabat A chic selection of designers (Nicole Miller, French Connection, and the like) and fabulous shoes. 2080 Chestnut St. (Steiner St.), 415-929-8868

Riley James Upscale fashions for men and women. 3027 Fillmore St. (Union St.) 415-775-7956

Rin LA-style boutique with contemporary women's fashion and accessories. 2111 Union St. (Webster St.), 415-922-8040

Union Square

Downtown's Union Square—not to be confused with Union Street—is home to a mind-boggling number of shops—from national department stores to diminutive boutiques. Maiden Lane is one of the premier destinations for upscale goods. Here are a few of the highlights.

De Vera An unusual and intriguing assortment of home decor and accessories from across the globe. 29 Maiden Ln. (Kearny St.), 415-788-0828

Gimme Shoes From soaring heels to designer tennis shoes to sexy boots, this fashion-forward shop is mecca for anyone with a serious shoe fetish. (p.84) 50 Grant Ave. (Geary St.), 415-434-9242

Metier Sublime jewelry and beautiful clothing. 355 Sutter St. (Stockton St.), 415-989-5395

SoMa

Tucked into former warehouses amid the wide boulevards South of Market are some of the city's most innovative and exciting shops.

Jeremy's You want your Prada, Chanel, and Dolce, but you don't want to pay full price. This is your place. (p.84) 2 South Park (Second St.), 415-882-4929

Ligne Roset High-end French furniture maker specializing in modernism. 162 King St. (Third St.), 415-777-1030

Limn The ultimate emporium of modern European furniture and home and personal accessories. (p.85) 290 Townsend St. (Fourth St.), 415-977-1300

Ma Maison French home accessories, whimsical dishware, jewelry, and other distinctive gift items. 592 Third St. (Brannan St.), 415-777-5370

SFMoMA Museum Store An innovative selection of contemporary art books, jewelry, and signature gifts. (p.87) 151 Third St. (Mission St.), 415-357-4000

Vino Venue The wine shop that lets you try before you buy from a fancy vending machine. Busy like a bar after work. (p.87) 686 Mission St. (Third St.), 415-341-1930

Hot & Cool San Francisco: The Hotels

Clift Hotel • Downtown • Trendy (363 rms)
The Clift is Ian Schrager's contribution to San Francisco's downtown chic hotel collection. Schrager unveiled a Philippe Starck–driven remodel of this time-honored gathering spot in 2001, transforming it into the city's most trendy place to crash. As with most historic properties, the monochrome pale purple and cream-hued rooms can be small, but the high-end details are in place: Egyptian cotton sheets, duvet comforters, high-speed Internet access, in-room massage and spa services, and luxury fabrics throughout. The views get better the higher the floor you're on, naturally. Overall, the style factor is larger than life, from colored mirror accents to the gorgeous wood-paneled Redwood Room, still one of the sexiest bars in the city. Adjoining the bar is Asia de Cuba. Stay at the Clift and you'll never be more than an elevator ride away from a West Hollywood–style, beautiful people nightlife scene, but don't expect great water views or a spa. There's a fitness center that you will never see and that's about it. $$$ 495 Geary St. (Taylor St.), 415-775-4700 / 800-697-1791, clifthotel.com

Four Seasons San Francisco • SoMa • Modern (277 rms)
Boasting the city's largest guest rooms, the Four Seasons also offers direct access to the Sports Club/LA fitness center and spa, located within the hotel. Union Square is two blocks away. Moscone Center and SFMoMA are just a short walk. In short, you can set up shop in any of the rooms and do all your business, and pleasure, without setting foot in a cab. The décor in both the lobby and rooms, traditional with pan-Asian accents, transcends trendiness without being stodgy to arrive at a level of cool not achieved elsewhere. In the public areas, the art rivals that seen around the corner at SFMoMA. Rooms include luxury bedding, marble baths, deep tubs, products by L'Occitane, contemporary art, and floor-to-ceiling windows showing off the view. They take a discreet approach here. Walking by on the street, you hardly notice it. Only when you take the elevator up to the fifth floor (the hotel resides on floors five to 17) do you encounter its true opulence and luxury. For a refreshingly green view, ask for a room overlooking Yerba Buena Gardens. $$$$+ 757 Market St. (Third St.), 415-633-3000 / 800-819-5053, fourseasons.com/sanfrancisco

Harbor Court Hotel • Embarcadero • Modern (130 rms)
Kimpton Hotels bought the historic building that houses the Harbor Court in 1989. A few months later, the Loma Prieta earthquake brought about the demise of the elevated freeway that blocked its view of the bay. Down came the freeway, and presto, a luxury hotel with the city's best views of the water was born. Today the Harbor Court offers a triple threat that's hard to beat: great views, great location, and great amenities. This little stretch of Steuart Street includes a lavish YMCA with one of the city's largest indoor pools, to which hotel guests are invited, and several eateries and bars. One block away is the Ferry Building Marketplace, and a short walk in the other direction is the ballpark. As for décor, the Harbor Court is boutique chic, with rich fabrics, exotic lighting, and Japanese stylistic undertones. The rooms are on the small side, but elegantly

outfitted in autumn hues and dressed up with tailored canopy beds. Every evening there is complimentary wine service by the fireplace in the lobby, where you can mix with savvy couples on vacation and business travelers in the know. The hotel's in-house restaurant and sake bar, Ozumo, is a lively scene after work. Request a room with a view of Treasure Island. $$$ 165 Steuart St. (Howard St.), 415-882-1300 / 866-792-6283, harborcourthotel.com

Hotel Monaco • Downtown • Trendy (201 rms)

Where serious whimsy meets serious luxury, the Hotel Monaco is a decadent, silly place ideal for fun-loving sorts who don't mind smaller rooms and the lack of an all-out gym. All the rooms in the renovated 1910 Beaux Arts building have loads of character and include canopy beds draped in romantic fabrics and stripes. Stripes are the signature motif of the Monaco. Broad stripes adorn walls, bed skirts, and pillows, setting a theatrical but tasteful mood. Trompe l'oeil murals, such as the cloudscape in the lobby, add a touch of magic. Any other hotel might stop with decadent, highly original décor; a landmark restaurant such as the Grand Cafe; a terrific in-hotel spa; and a Theater District location convenient to downtown attractions. The Monaco goes far beyond with dozens of tiny flourishes, such as yoga accessories, Frette robes, Aveda bath goodies, and even a goldfish of your very own for the duration of your stay. Pop down to the living room in the morning for free coffee, and in the afternoon for fresh cookies. Return later for wine, cheese, a tarot reading, and a neck rub. Take the complimentary town car to one of the nearby shopping areas. Free your inner rock star in the Grace Slick Suite, packed with original artwork and memorabilia from Jefferson Starship and Jefferson Airplane. $$$ 501 Geary St. (Taylor St.), 415-292-0100 / 866-622-5284, monaco-sf.com

Hotel Palomar • SoMa • Modern (198 rms)

The Palomar is a Kimpton Hotel, which means penthouse-slick glamour is the name of the game. The Palomar has a distinctive, refined modernity. The rooms, lobby, and restaurant are all done in safari shades of tan, sand, and black, with touches of zebra print, emerald velvet, dark woods, and splashes of deep red or orange in art or accessories to liven things up. The in-house restaurant is the illustrious Fifth Floor, one of the best in town. The clubby dining room with its zebra-striped rugs, red leather and velvet banquettes, and Frette Italian table linens is downright racy. The small, sophisticated bar gives guests a place to mingle, but you won't find the crowds here. This is a boutique scene. The rooms are small, but offer upscale amenities like down comforters, Aveda bath products, and complimentary wireless access. It even has tall rooms for those who need it. Those with the most space are corner rooms overlooking Market Street. Ask about the Magritte suite with a ceiling of clouds and blue sky. $$$ 12 Fourth St. (Market St.), 415-348-1111 / 866-373-4941, hotelpalomar.com

Hotel Vitale • Embarcadero • Trendy (199 rms)

When the Hotel Vitale finally opened in 2005, seven long years and $53 million in the making, it was greeted, inexplicably, with a snarling chorus of catty remarks. Critics particularly annihilated the design of the building, which, one must admit, is less than inspiring from the street. However, once inside, the guest experience is undeniably exceptional. From the limestone floors and oaken walls of the lobby to the outdoor deep soaking tubs and secret gardens of the penthouse spa, Vitale brings together natural textures and tones with high luxury. It's located on the water and half of the rooms feature sweeping views of the bay and Bay Bridge (insist on one of them, the higher the better). As in the lobby, the style is Palm Springs retro meets uptown modernism. Throughout, the personal approach is closer to what you'd find in a boutique hotel than in a big operation. In addition to the up-to-the-minute design sensibilities, the main attractions are the location, spa, and lavish features such as flat-screen TVs, rainforest showerheads, and microfiber bathrobes. There's a fitness center, free yoga classes on the roof deck, and free passes to the Embarcadero YMCA. You can walk a block or less to any of a dozen excellent bars and restaurants, including Americano, the hotel's own stylish eatery (don't miss the ceiling art). $$$ Eight Mission St. (Steuart St.), 415-278-3700 / 888-890-8688, hotelvitale.com

Mandarin Oriental • Financial District • Modern (154 rms)
If you want spectacular bridge-to-bridge views all the way across the bay, a breathtaking level of opulence, and free passes to the nearby Equinox Fitness Club, this is your hotel. The Mandarin is close to Union Square and the Financial District, so it attracts the business crowd. It also boasts a few over-the-top suites for high romance. Besides Silks, their top-ranked restaurant, and the Mandarin Lounge, the cocktail bar sure to make you feel like Graham Greene, the major appeal here is the view. Guest rooms, billed as the highest in the city, are located between the 38th and 48th floors. They include the accoutrements you expect from a luxury hotel: fine linens, Italian marble baths, turn-down service, in-room massage, and furnishings with floral and Asian touches. Whatever your heart desires, it is only a phone call to the front desk away. Request a room with a tub-side view. $$$$+ 222 Sansome St. (California St.), 415-276-9888 / 866-526-6567, mandarinoriental.com/sanfrancisco

St. Regis Hotel • SoMa • Modern (260 rms)
Arriving at the end of 2005, the 40-story St. Regis Hotel—in a building the architects claim evokes Rodin's bold, overcoated sculpture of Balzac—is arguably the most luxurious hotel in San Francisco. From custom-designed Barcelona benches at the foot of every bed to lush leather wall coverings, huge plasma TVs, Pratesi linens, deep soaking tubs and separate showers, and 24-hour butler and room service, all the rooms offer serious decadence. The light-filled palette is done in many shades of cream, an effect both relaxing and uplifting. The top 18 floors are devoted to permanent residences, but most of the guest rooms feature fine views of the city, the bay, or Yerba Buena Gardens across the street (the St. Regis is next door to SFMoMA). Ask for one of the Grand Deluxe rooms, which are located on the higher floors and boast views of Yerba Buena gardens and the San Francisco hills. Downstairs is the impeccable restaurant Ame, serving fine New American food. In addition to an exclusive fitness center, there is the lavish 9,000-square-foot Remède Spa. Standard rooms average 450 square feet, while the suites range from 700 to over 3,200 square feet. The business resources are excellent, including Wi-Fi access, dedicated fax lines, and the ability to recharge a laptop or cell phone inside the in-room safe. Overall, the chic, ultramodern design is a resounding success that makes you want to stay an extra day, or week. $$$$+ 124 Third St. (Mission St.), 415 284-4000 / 888-625-5144, stregis.com/sanfrancisco

W San Francisco • SoMa • Trendy (423 rms)
The W has worked hard to please since its arrival just as the dot-com bubble burst. The lobby is surprisingly comfortable and inviting, considering the cutting-edge design sensibilities. Whether it's buzzing or empty (it is rarely empty), it makes an inviting place to order a drink and unwind. Grab a seat at the circular bar, or find a cozy spot in any of the sitting areas, where ultrachic versions of board games invite interaction with your neighbors. Behind the bar is the vibrant XYZ restaurant. Upstairs is the Bar at XYZ. W launched its first West Coast Bliss Spa in 2005. Signature products, movie-while-you-manicure stations, a brownie buffet, and 5,000 square feet devoted to pampering add up to a breathtaking place to get groomed. The guest rooms feel like your own modernist home, with shades of brown and blue, window seats, luxury linens, high-tech conveniences, Bliss bathroom products, and snacks. Most have city and Bay Bridge views, and the concierge has a stash of CDs and movies to plunder. Ask for one of the corner rooms, which are slightly larger. The service—swift and professional—is best exemplified in the "Whatever Whenever" button on the room telephones. There's also a pool, fitness center, and poolside yoga. The other guests? High-end business-pleasure travelers in favor of the national trend toward playful, modern, chic hotels. $$$$ 181 Third St. (Howard St.), 415-777-5300 / 888-625-5144, whotel.com/sanfrancisco

Hot & Cool San Francisco: The Restaurants

Ame • SoMa • New American (G)
Ame, next door to SFMoMA, is the first San Francisco endeavor of the creative duo behind the Napa Valley restaurant Terra, known for its innovative blend of Provençal, Tuscan, and Japanese culinary traditions. Ame continues the story with tuna done five ways, eel and foie gras with risotto, and other daring assemblages. The menu includes an impressive list of fine sakes, artisan cheeses, and more than 300 wines. The setting is understated but spectacular, on a level to match the impeccable modern style of the new St. Regis Hotel. The floors are done in mesquite wood, which contributes to the ambiance's dark, rich elegance, while a gorgeous sashimi bar creates a visual sensation. Throughout, the décor celebrates texture, with floor-to-ceiling bronze mesh panels, a wall of brush strokes, sheer curtains, and a dramatic fireplace. The bar serves a limited menu to an occasionally chic crowd, while the dining room caters to couples and sophisticated travelers. *Daily 11:30am-2pm and 6-10pm.* $$$ St. Regis Hotel, 689 Mission St. (Third St.), 415-284-4040, amerestaurant.com

Americano • Embarcadero • Italian
Americano features a beautifully subdued modern interior rich with dark woods, earthy textures, and plenty of green, in this case chairs in a vibrant shade of avocado. Americano has caught on swiftly. A poised and well-groomed crowd mostly on the easy side of forty fills up the arty space with pretty sights and sounds just about every night. The cocktail lounge is worth a visit even if you don't stay to eat—the food is excellent—for the ambiance, company, and bay view. Americano is located across from the Ferry Building Marketplace and draws heavily on its purveyors of fresh, organic produce and exceptional meats, dairy, and more. The cuisine is California-influenced Italian (think inventive pizzas) and changes seasonally. On warm days, consider lunch on the patio, and, whatever the weather, say yes to the ice cream sandwich for dessert. *Mon-Thu 6:30-10:30am, 11:30am-2:30pm, and 5:30-10pm, Fri 6:30-10:30am, 11:30am-2:30pm, and 5:30-11pm, Sat 7:30am-3pm and 5:30-11pm, Sun 7:30am-3pm and 5:30-10pm.* $$ Hotel Vitale, Eight Mission St. (Steuart St.), 415-278-3777, americanorestaurant.com

Asia de Cuba • Downtown • Fusion
Swanky, glamorous, Philippe Starck–ized Asia de Cuba opens onto the similarly decorated (and venerable) Redwood Room bar inside Ian Schrager's Clift Hotel. The restaurant is so dimly lit you'll need a flashlight to read the menu. The hit-and-miss food is a mélange of Asian and Cuban techniques and spices, characterized by rich, sweet sauces. The stratospheric prices have done little to dissuade visiting and local LA-style scenesters from making this a de facto headquarters. The frenzy has abated considerably, but on weekends the scene can still be quite a spectacle. *Sun-Wed 7am-2:30pm and 5:30-10:30pm, Thu-Sat 7am-2:30pm and 5:30pm-midnight.* $$$ Clift Hotel, 495 Geary St. (Taylor St.), 415-929-2300, clifthotel.com

A16 • Marina • Italian
Best Trendy Tables This newcomer to yuppie-laden Chestnut Street swiftly nailed down its turf and acquired a devoted following. The secret is the basic, hearty, and well-executed Southern Italian cuisine and an extraordinary list of Italian wines. The exterior and décor evoke the stylish, understated sophistication of New York's SoHo, and the clientele lives up to the challenge. This is the heart of the Marina, meaning young, affluent, well-heeled, and good-looking types looking to hook up, if the paperwork fits. As for the food, the wood-fired pizzas make a strong showing, as do the pastas and meats. *Sun-Tue 5-10pm, Wed-Thu 11:30am-2:30pm and 5-10pm, Fri 11:30am-2:30pm and 5-11pm, Sat 5-11pm.* $$ 2355 Chestnut St. (Divisadero St.), Marina, 415-771-2216, a16sf.com

Azie • SoMa • Asian
Azie is all 21st century, from its décor to its menu to its clientele. The ultra-modern décor gives you that downtown Tokyo feeling. Dark woods, a mirrored wall, and bold accents complete the bustling Pacific Rim ambiance. The spirit of innovation is obvious in the luminous, pagoda-style mezzanine rising from the middle of the dining room on four red columns. That pagoda, with its simultaneous exhibitionism and privacy, captures the mood well. There are even three booths with bronze curtains for total privacy. The menu changes frequently, but its always Asian fusion, from pomegranate-glazed pork riblets to triple-seared New York strip steak. Azie also makes a hot spot for a cocktail before or after dinner. *Mon-Thu 5:30-10pm, Fri 5:30-11pm, Sat 5-11pm, Sun 5-10pm.* $$ 826 Folsom St. (Fifth St.), 415-538-0918, azierestaurant.com

Bacar • SoMa • Mediterranean
Best Wine Lists A vast and lively tri-level shrine with an epic wine list and an impressive menu to accompany it. *See Hot & Cool Nightlife, p.72, for details.* $$$ 448 Brannan St. (Third St.), 415-904-4100, bacarsf.com

Bambuddha Lounge • Downtown • Asian
Dine poolside on south-Asian fusion and pretend you're in LA. *See Hot & Cool Nightlife, p.72, for details.* $ Phoenix Hotel, 601 Eddy St. (Larkin St.), 415-885-5088, bambuddhalounge.com

Betelnut • Marina • Asian
Best Chic Asian Restaurants Dark wood and plenty of cherry red accents—red stairs, red tabletops, a red bar along the open kitchen—lend Betelnut an exotic, Asia-of-the-imagination feel. It's as though you have found the back-alley spot where the Shanghai locals hang out, drink beer, and eat surprisingly great food. In fact, the owners refer to Betelnut as a beer house, and have strived to create an appropriately convivial atmosphere. Tables on the front patio let you people-watch and imbibe over lunch, while moody black leather banquettes in back give you a view of all who come and go. The bar in front can be a real scene on the weekends, when the crew of upscale local coeds comes out to play. *Sun-Thu 11:30am-11pm, Fri-Sat 11:30am-midnight.* $ 2030 Union St. (Buchanan St.), 415-929-8855, betelnutrestaurant.com

B44 • Financial District • Spanish
What do you do for lunch on a nice day downtown? Go straight to Belden Place, a block-long pedestrian alley packed with outdoor tables. Within a block you can journey from Paris to Barcelona to Tuscany, enjoying alfresco dining and cafe

society along the way. All of the restaurants are reasonably good, but the Catalan fare at B44 is a standout. White beans are delicious with homemade sausage and spicy aioli. Prawns, mussels, and baby squid populate the menu along with lamb and rabbit. A rare treat in San Francisco, B44 also offers a variety of succulent takes on paella. At lunch and happy hour, the crowd is very Financial District. Go at high noon to catch a spot of sun while it's directly overhead (later the skyscrapers cast dense shadows). At dinner, look for more visitors than locals. *Mon-Thu 11:30am-11pm, Fri 11:30am-10:30pm, Sat 5-10:30pm, Sun 4-9pm.* $$ 44 Belden Pl. (Bush St.), 415-986-6287

Bocadillos • Financial District • Basque/Tapas

These days, you hear "bocadillos" popping up in conversations all over town. What is it? Spanish for finger food or appetizer. As a restaurant, it means a place that is stylish yet inviting and happy to see you any time of day. Stop by in the morning for a frittata with the troops on their way to work. Drop in at lunch for a tuna melt and a fresh fruit sorbet. Or come for dinner and choose from a menu with such sections as "marinated" or "roasted." For a splash of Spanish-style socializing, swing by for a glass of wine. In the evening, the crowd tends to the young and affluent. Otherwise, it's worker bees fueling up and killing time (many of the same people, but in a different mood). *Mon-Fri 7am-11pm, Sat 5-11pm.* $ 710 Montgomery St. (Washington St.), 415-982-2622, bocasf.com

Butterfly • Embarcadero • Asian

Butterfly is a large, modern-looking restaurant on the waterfront. The vast dining room has high ceilings, a bar with a mesmerizing blue backdrop, and an incredible view of the bay. It serves tasty California-Asian fusion cuisine. At times, a DJ spins and the young trendy types gather. Other times, there is live jazz. Generally the crowd is a mix of scene-y types and suits who have migrated across the road from the Financial District. Sometimes, the sea of tables is sparsely populated. At brunch, there is seldom a wait, always a view, and plenty of good things to eat. An after-dinner drink may be sleepy or packed depending on the night. To play it safe, order several appetizers instead of the mains. *Mon-Fri 11:30am-3pm and 5-10pm, Fri 11:30am-3pm and 5-11pm, Sat 11am-3pm and 5-11pm, Sun 11am-3pm and 5-10pm.* $$ Pier 33 (Bay St.), 415-291-9482, butterflysf.com

Café Maritime • Marina • Seafood

Reviewers raved about Café Maritime from the instant it opened in 2004. The reason was its simplicity. San Francisco had a shortage of good seafood restaurants. One could hit places for high-brow, big-ticket dining, but for a more relaxed setting, there were precious few solid options. Then came cheery, welcoming, summery, tranquil Maritime. With its lack of 'tude, crisp décor, and homey menu of seafood dishes and comfort foods, it was destined to be a new favorite, especially among the sporty Marina crowd. The location, on a busy thoroughfare, leaves much to be desired, but they've done a good job shutting out traffic noise. The kitchen is open until 1am, in case you need some oysters to finish off the evening. *Daily 5:30pm-1am.* $ 2417 Lombard St. (Scott St.), 415-885-2530, cafemaritimesf.com

Chaya Brasserie • Embarcadero • Fusion
East meets west at this waterfront restaurant serving nouvelle French-Japanese cuisine. *See Hot & Cool Nightlife, p.73, for details.* $$ 132 Embarcadero (Mission St.), 415-777-8688, thechaya.com

Circolo • Potrero Hill • Asian
Best Restaurants with Bars Circolo will be the first to welcome the next big uptick in the economy. Unabashedly ambitious, it serves an innovative menu of Nuevo Latino–Southeast Asian fusion cuisine in a dark, industrial-chic setting. That might have been enough for others, but Circolo went the extra mile, opening a slick lounge next door in 2005. It's called the Wa Ultra Lounge. By "ultra lounge", it means the usual, albeit welcome, combination of futuristic lighting, minimalist décor, and trendy cube furniture. Circolo makes a fine place to stop for a drink, dinner, and, on the right night, a bit of rhythmic booty jiggling, ultra-wa style. *Sun-Thu 5-10pm, Fri-Sat 5pm-2:30am.* $$ 500 Florida St. (Mariposa St.), 415-553-8560, circolosf.com

Coco500 • SoMa • Californian
There's plenty to love about Coco500, perhaps because the purveyors seem to have made a genuine effort to understand what people want in a restaurant and deliver it with style. One small example is the "noncommittal" portion of the dessert menu, where you can order one little brownie or a single ounce of chocolate. The fare focuses on sustainably produced artisan ingredients, from the seafood and local produce to the fine wines. The chic but comfortable ambiance caters to a stylish crowd, some having a drink, some nibbling appetizers, many seated for a full meal. *Mon-Thu 11:30am-10pm, Fri 11:30am-11pm, Sat 5:30-11pm.* $$ 500 Brannan St. (Fourth St.), 415-543-2222, coco500.com

Cortez • Downtown • Mediterranean
Trendy small plates in a contemporary setting and cosmopolitan crowd. *See Hot & Cool Nightlife, p.74, for details.* $$ Hotel Adagio, 550 Geary St. (Taylor St.), 415-292-6360, cortezrestaurant.com

Farallon • Downtown • Seafood (G)
Best Seafood Restaurants The undersea theme is executed with such panache and imagination, you may feel like Captain Nemo on an oceanic culinary adventure. Blown-glass chandeliers with hanging tendrils evoke breezy jellyfish, while columns encrusted with crustaceans give you that Little Mermaid feeling. If it sounds silly, it's not. It is magical, dreamy, and elegant, like the haute seafood dishes on the menu. Look for lobster, scallops with black caviar, and any fish with beurre rouge. Farallon is entertainment dining at its finest, though it's not the best bet for a romantic dinner, as the dining room can be noisy. The crowd consists largely of out-of-town visitors, ladies and gentlemen of a certain age, and those dressed up for a special evening. *Mon 5:30-10pm, Tue-Thu 11:30am-10pm, Fri-Sat 11:30am-11pm, Sun 5-10pm.* $$$ 450 Post St. (Powell St.), 415-956-6969, farallonrestaurant.com

Fifth Floor • SoMa • French (G)
Best Fine Dining It's not much from the street, but Fifth Floor makes up for what it lacks in curb appeal with a decadent experience few restaurants can match. The décor is safari chic meets silken boudoir, and tables are situated for maximum privacy. The silence is heavy like a snowstorm and for the same reason:

Other diners' conversations are buffered to a soft hum by so much cushion and crepe. This is the place to woo the demure and refined or to indulge as though it were the last night for luxury. The food is high French executed with precision. The common denominator among those dining is the willingness to spend a great deal of money for an impeccable meal, but the vibe is grownup sexy and intimate, so couples of a certain age predominate. *Mon-Fri 7-10am and 5:30-10pm, Sat 8-11am and 5:30-11pm, Sun 8-11am.* $$$ YB◨ Hotel Palomar, 12 Fourth St. (Market St.), 415-348-1111, hotelpalomar.com/palsf_dining.html

First Crush • Downtown • New American
Wine bar focusing on California wines and flavors. *See Hot & Cool Nightlife, p.75, for details.* $$ F◨ 101 Cyril Magnin St. (Ellis St.), 415-982-7874, firstcrush.com

Foreign Cinema • Mission • Mediterranean
Best Always-Hot Restaurants Offering a rare mix of high elegance and trendy style, industrial-chic Foreign Cinema has been a favorite of the well-heeled artsy crowd for years. This is the sort of grand-scale place you would normally find downtown, where it would be filled with expense-account types. Thanks to its location in the scruffy Mission, it attracts a younger, more stylish crowd that can nonetheless afford to dine well. With high ceilings, a crackling fireplace, and your favorite art house film showing on the patio wall, Foreign Cinema offers all you could want and more. As for the food, it just gets better. Don't miss Laszlo Bar, where you'll find a cool mojito every night and a hot crowd most weekends. *Mon-Thu 6-10pm, Fri 6-11:30pm, Sat 11am-11:30pm, Sun 11am-10pm.* $$ YB◨ 2534 Mission St. (21st St.), 415-648-7600, foreigncinema.com

Frisson • Financial District • New American
Best Restaurants with Bars Several catty reviewers sniped at Frisson when it opened, perhaps out of jealousy, for it is beautiful, sexy, and smart. However, Frisson does several things exceedingly well. The DJ lounge–inspired scene is seriously fresh, as in fresh enough to keep up with hot new places in Paris and New York. The bar exudes sexy like no place else in town, and several architectural elements (a co-ed fountain for washing up, a downstairs hideaway, an outdoor smoking alley) are apt to provoke conversations with strangers. Dress your Euro-chic best, cop a James Bond attitude, and order your favorite aromatherapy-style basil-infused cocktail from the list of beverages. If the thump of the DJ beat and the sight of young scenesters sets you off, spend your time elsewhere. *Tue-Fri 5pm-2am, Sat 6pm-2am, Sun 11am-5pm.* $$ YB◨ 244 Jackson St. (Sansome St.), 415-956-3004, frissonsf.com

Globe • Financial District • Californian
Best Late-Night Eats For those nights when you get a late start, Globe can be a lifesaver. At Globe, you can sit down to a perfectly roasted chicken, the irresistible pizza du jour, fancy mac and cheese, or a big T-bone steak at midnight. Even if it isn't late, Globe makes a fine choice for dinner. The exposed brick walls of the historic building set off the artwork nicely and lend satisfying texture to the otherwise simple-chic, Lower East Side–style décor. A stylish local crowd makes the scene, which is peppered with foodies getting off work as the night wears on. The compact room can get noisy, but the close quarters also make it festive when crowded. *Mon-Fri 11:30am-3pm and 6pm-1am, Sat 6pm-1am, Sun 6-11:30pm.* $$ F◨ 290 Pacific Ave. (Battery St.), 415-391-4132

HOT & COOL • RESTAURANTS

La Suite • Embarcadero • French Brasserie
La Suite is a French brasserie magically transported to San Francisco, complete with red and gold trim. The bar is backed by windows facing the street and bay. As you move deeper into the restaurant, the dining areas feel progressively more intimate. The space is tamed by a longing for traditional, perhaps even staid, Parisian ways, but it makes up for it in Continental sophistication and poise, complete with banquettes, chandeliers, dark woods, and honey-colored walls. This is the grownup date zone, with high romance in the air. The food successfully mimics that served in better Parisian restaurants. The filet mignon is superb, the grilled fish excellent, the salads perfectly assembled, and the sauces whipped up with expertise. *Sun-Thu 11:30am-3pm and 5:30-11pm, Fri-Sat 11:30am-3pm and 5:30pm-midnight.* $$ 100 Brannan St. (Embarcadero), 415-593-5900, lasuitesf.com

Levende Lounge • Mission • Fusion
Best Restaurants with Bars Trendy small plates in a lounge setting. *See Hot & Cool Nightlife, p.76, for details.* $$ 1710 Mission St. (Duboce Ave.), 415-864-5585, levendesf.com

MarketBar • Embarcadero • Californian
Rare indeed are nights when it is warm enough to dine alfresco in San Francisco, but when they do arrive, MarketBar achieves its full glory. Outdoor tables facing the Embarcadero offer excellent people-watching, especially at lunch, on sun-drenched weekends, and during happy hour, when the Ferry Building Marketplace attracts big crowds. While the food is good-quality California-style fare, it's the wine list, handsome bar, homey vintage feel, and prime location that make it all worthwhile. On Saturdays, when the Farmers Market is in full swing, the atmosphere is positively gay with people high on fresh organic fruits and vegetables. *Sun-Fri 11:30am-10pm, Sat 11:30am-11pm.* $ One Ferry Building (Market St.), 415-434-1100, marketbar.com

Michael Mina • Downtown • New American (G)
Best Fine Dining The result of the serious 2004 makeover to this landmark space is cool sophistication, creamy white pillars, and visual and culinary perfectionism, the ideal setting for a truly glamorous evening. Chef and namesake Michael Mina is an exacting, theatrical sort. His touch is evident on everything from the linen of the napkins to the shade of dusty blue on the chairs, and certainly every plate of food. His specialty is the riff on an ingredient. For example, he'll do a Kobe rib roast and let you try it au poivre, with horseradish mash, and with caramelized onion. Go nuts and get the lobster pot pie, or try the caviar cart. While you're at it, peruse the list of more than 1,500 wines with prices up to $14,000. *Mon-Sat 5:30-10pm, Sun 5:30-9:30pm.* $$$ Westin St. Francis, 335 Powell St. (Geary St.), 415-397-9222, michaelmina.net

Myth • Financial District • New American
Myth has an artfully secluded bar area, a row of private booths, waves of shimmery fabric, and walnut lattice on portions of the ceiling. The private booths, like your own three-sided wooden cabin straight out of Kyoto, are utterly unique. As for the food, it is an unusual mix of froufrou art food and dig-in hearty classics. You can start with a pear salad with Danish blue cheese and candied cashews, add a half-order of citrus-glazed salmon medallions with lobster

lemongrass sauce, then finish with a New York steak with cipollini onions. The crowd is an upscale blend in its thirties and forties, but the youngsters are catching on, thanks, perhaps, to the dance music and slick lounge area. It all feels very New York, very savvy, very, dare we say, boom-ish. *Tue-Thu 5:30-10pm, Fri-Sat 5:30-11pm.* $$ 470 Pacific Ave. (Montgomery St.), 415-677-8986, mythsf.com

Nectar • Marina • Wine Bar
Global small plates menu complements the wines at this comfortable wine bar. *See Hot & Cool Nightlife, p.78, for details.* $ 3330 Steiner St. (Chestnut St.), 415-345-1377, nectarwinelounge.com

One Market • Embarcadero • Californian
Best Power Lunch Spots There aren't many better-looking dining rooms in town than this vivacious space. Its huge windows and high ceilings give it the grand feel of an event hall, but the white table cloths and candlelight cozy it up. The clock tower of the Ferry Building just outside lends an archetypal backdrop to the dining experience. The sturdy fare that has made One Market famous is reliable and well-executed. The menu changes often to remain seasonal, but meat and fish dishes are the specialty; the roast pork shoulder atop a bed of farro is out of this world. For a dining experience you won't forget, come in a group and request the chef's table inside the kitchen. *Mon-Fri 11:30am-2pm and 5:30-9pm, Sat 5:30-9pm.* $$ One Market St. (Embarcadero), 415-777-5577, onemarket.com

Oola • SoMa • American
Best Late-Night Eats Not far from the club corridor around 11th and Folsom Streets, Oola has courted the late-night club set with some success (the kitchen stays open until 1am). The setting works in elements of polished concrete, exposed brick, and steel for a loft-style industrial modernism. On the menu, you'll find hearty dishes with exotic touches, such as a tomato tart with goat cheese and onion jam and baby back ribs with cilantro, ginger, and soy glaze. Come late night for elegant sustenance with a fun crowd. Ideally, drop in for dinner around 10pm. *Sun 6-11pm, Mon 6pm-midnight, Tue-Sat 6pm-1am.* $$ 860 Folsom St. (Fourth St.), 415-995-2061, oola-sf.com

Ozumo • SoMa • Japanese
Best Sushi Restaurants You want great sushi; a view of the water, and a cosmopolitan look and feel, and you don't want to have to leave the Financial District. Ozumo has it all. In addition to a scenic sushi bar with a view of the bay, it also has a candlelit sake lounge and something called the Robata Grill, where it serves grilled fish, Kobe beef, lobster, chicken, lamb, duck—you name it. The sake lounge features an intriguing list of sakes to sample, served chilled, like the scene, with its minimalist bench seating in monk robe–orange fabric. At lunch, it's the expense account crew, and happy hour brings out the Financial District crowd for cocktails and a lively scene. *Mon-Wed 11:30am-2pm and 5:30-10pm, Thu-Fri 11:30am-2pm and 5:30-10:30pm, Sat 5:30-10:30pm, Sun 5:30-10pm, lounge until closing.* $$ Harbor Court Hotel, 161 Steuart St. (Mission St.), 415-882-1333, ozumo.com

Pier 23 Cafe • Embarcadero • Traditional American
Three main points of appeal keep people coming to Pier 23: the sun-baked patio on the water, the live music, and the down-home, no-frills seafood. You've got your sun, your view of the water, your fish and chips, and your salsa, rock, jazz, or reggae band. What else could a person possibly need? Sunday brunch and Saturday afternoon are almost always a party. The crowd is a mix of regular folks kicking back with sunglasses on and beer in hand. The mood is rambunctious and friendly. This is not the place to pose and be seen. *Mon-Fri 11:30am-10pm, Sat 10am-10pm, Sun 10am-9pm.* $ ⊥F≡ Pier 23 (Lombard St.), 415-362-5125, pier23cafe.com

Piperade • North Beach • Basque
Piperade serves authentic food from the Basque country in a cozy cave-like setting. Wood beams in the ceiling, chipper lamps, bold art, a brightly lit bar, and wood floors warm the place up. The feel is European, like a secret find in a Spanish village. Basque classics change each day and include sautéed calamari in ink sauce (Tuesday) and braised rabbit with prunes (Thursday). To start, try the warm piquillo peppers with goat cheese, raisins, and muscatel vinaigrette. The evening brings a mixed crowd, from bridge-and-tunnel married folk to young couples and executives doing dinner. *Mon-Fri 11:30am-3pm and 5:30-10:30pm, Sat 5:30-10:30pm.* $$ ⊟ 1015 Battery St. (Green St.), 415-391-2555, piperade.com

Quince • Pacific Heights • Californian (G)
Tasteful in every detail, Quince quickly became a favorite among locals from the surrounding upscale neighborhoods. The décor in the small, square Shaker-plain dining room is light and open. Inside, aside from a few Victorian flourishes, only the photographs of quince hung on the cream-colored walls attract attention. Chef Michael Tusk worked at Chez Panisse, where the ingredient is king, and the influence is evident. The cooking style is devoted to selecting ingredients so flawless they command notice, then preparing them in order to let their character shine. The menu of rustic Italian cuisine with Spanish and French influences changes daily based on what is available. Expect dishes like asparagus ravioli with white asparagus sauce, duck roasted with cherries and grappa, and lavender cake with Meyer lemon cream. The fresh pastas are a rare treat. Call several weeks in advance to make a reservation. *Tue-Sun 5:30-10pm.* $$ ≡ 1701 Octavia St. (Bush St.), 415-775-8500, quincerestaurant.com

Roe • SoMa • Asian
Plan to order plenty of food at Roe, as the portions are small. What they lack in size they make up for in flavor. Imagine your favorite Thai place with an expanded list of ingredients, a penchant for sushi, and a mission to reach artistic heights. That's the menu at Roe, and it is done exceedingly well. The curried shrimp with garlic noodles is a must-have. The dining room is sultry and comfortable, with a wall of plush, undivided seating, the better to know your neighbors. The whole room has an inclusive feel, as though you were having dinner at a party. Gold lamé, velvet, and chain-mail accents lend the room a decadent, Shanghai boudoir feel. Upstairs is a dance club called Privé. After a hot beginning, the vibe has slumped a bit, but weekends are holding steady. The crowd depends on the DJ or event. Dinner is the sure thing. If upstairs is happening, consider it gravy. *Tue-Thu 5-10pm, Fri 5pm-11pm, Sat 6-11pm. Upstairs Fri-Sat until 4am.* $$ ⊥≡ 651 Howard St. (Third St.), 415-227-0288, roerestaurant.com

Rose's Café • Marina • Comfort Food

Location is part of the fun with Rose's. Situated on a sunny corner at the base of Pacific Heights, it has a privileged feel. Rose's evokes the happy ease of certain bistros in France and trattorias in Italy, with its cafe tables and red velvet booths in a bright, fresh setting. Though the food is well prepared, it's foot traffic, people-watching, the outdoor seating, and meals of convenience that keep Rose's on the map. In the morning, it's all about stroller-pushing moms out to catch some rays with their caffeine fix. At lunch, the shoppers arrive. And in the evening, affluent couples drop in for a casual meal. The burger and pizzas are solid choices. The weekend brunch is popular as well, where you'll find the same crowd digging into waffles and eggs. *Daily 7am-10pm.* $ 2298 Union St. (Steiner St.), 415-775-2200

Shanghai 1930 • Embarcadero • Chinese

Sophisticated food and ambiance, reminiscent of another era, is accentuated with live jazz. *See Hot & Cool Nightlife, p.80, for details.* $$ 133 Steuart St. (Mission St.), 415-896-5600, shanghai1930.com

Slanted Door • Embarcadero • Vietnamese

Best Chic Asian Restaurants This is one of the city's premier hot spots, especially in its new location at the water's edge, so if you want to dine here, reserve as soon as you can. Friday and Saturday nights see a seemingly endless stream of stylish locals gathered at the bar and clustered around tables crammed with a tantalizing medley of small plates late into the evening. It's been packed solid every day from the very beginning. The reason is mostly the food, which is good enough to become an addiction, though the friendly scene has something to do with it as well. Don't miss the spring rolls and the lemongrass tofu with fresh shiitake mushrooms, onions, and chili sauce. *Sun-Thu 11:30am-2:30pm and 5:30-10pm, Fri-Sat 11:30am-2:30pm and 5:30-10:30pm.* $$ One Ferry Building, (Market St.), 415-861-8032, slanteddoor.com

supperclub San Francisco • SoMa • French/Italian

Best Trendy Tables Born in Amsterdam and raised in Rome, the sublimely over-the-top supperclub landed in San Francisco in fall 2005 and the place went wild. The scene is a rare, highly entertaining blend of techno-chic décor and Burning Man theatrics, attracting a crowd of daring young hotties in fashion-forward attire. In case you're not familiar with the concept, here goes: There is only one seating each night. Everyone is seated on plush white beds in La Salle Neige (The Snow Room). The menu is a surprise, but is generally French-Italian and always five courses artfully presented. Vegan and vegetarian options are available. The décor is fantasyland white on white. Drag queens, acrobats, and other exotics—some resemble human anime characters—perform as well as serve, and a DJ works the evening. Around dessert, the place turns into a dance club. For weekend reservations, call as far in advance as possible, and check to see if there is a theme the night you're there. You wouldn't want to miss a chance to eat dinner in your favorite white bikini (or bikini briefs). The best way to do supperclub is in a small group. The bar boasts quite a hot scene on weekends. *Bar Tue-Sun 6:30pm-2am. Dinner at 7:30pm.* $$ 657 Harrison St. (Third St.), 415-348-0900, supperclub.com

Town Hall • SoMa • Traditional American
Best Power Lunch Spots The vintage brick building that houses Town Hall is handsome and well-proportioned, and the hearty cuisine is eminently edible. This isn't small plates or art food or fusion anything, it's straight-ahead good food you will want to come back for again and again. The service is solid. The bar is inviting but not the main attraction. The tables are big, comfortable, and spaced wide enough apart to maintain privacy. The menu changes frequently, but it runs to classic dishes like butter lettuce with candied walnuts and blue cheese dressing, veal meatballs with potato purée and green peppercorn sauce, and bacon-wrapped quail. *Mon-Thu 11:30am-2:30pm and 5:30-10pm, Fri 11:30am-2:30pm and 5:30-11pm, Sat 5:30-11pm, Sun 5:30-10pm.* $$
342 Howard St. (Fremont St.), 415-908-3900, townhallsf.com

Tres Agaves • SoMa • Mexican
Best Latin Restaurants An all too rare thing even in San Francisco, Tres Agaves is a stylish and sophisticated Mexican restaurant with a buzzing bar scene. In a cavernous industrial-chic space with exposed brick and pipes punctuated by bright spots of Mexican art, creative professionals gather after work for tantalizing upscale fare. The carnitas and spit-roasted chicken are among the most popular items on the menu. But the real star is the extensive menu of tequila cocktails. Although the vibe is fairly casual, reservations are recommended even on weeknights. *Mon-Thu 11am-1am, Fri-Sat 11am-2am, Sun 10am-3pm.* $
130 Townsend St. (Second St.), 415-227-0500, tresagaves.com

Zuppa • SoMa • Italian
The space is very deep-boom 1999, with cement walls, loft-style steel accents, and a long communal table. Incarnated as Zuppa, the warmth of Southern Italy has flooded in, complete with a sunny yellow wall, wooden accents, and colorful modern art. The servers wear tuxedos and smiles, a nice combination, especially when they set down a generous portion of savory fare. What a pleasant change from all those small plates! The wood-burning oven turns out herbed focaccia and pizzas with thin, delicious crusts. The rest of the menu covers cured meats, pastas, salads, seafood, steaks, and Italian wines. The bone-in ribeye and the spaghetti with prawns are sure to please. Avoid the bar—it's too cramped—and ask for a table upstairs if you want to eye-spy the cooks in action. *Mon-Fri 11:30am-2:30pm and 5:30-11pm, Sat-Sun 5:30-11pm.* $
564 Fourth St. (Brannan St.), 415-777-5900, zuppa-sf.com

Hot & Cool San Francisco: The Nightlife

Americano • Embarcadero • Italian
The bar and patio are both buzzing after work with young professionals. *See Hot & Cool Restaurants, p.62, for details.* F≡ Eight Mission St. (Steuart St.), 415-278-3777, americanorestaurant.com

Azie • SoMa • Restaurant Bar
Polished, exotic, and sophisticated downtown-Tokyo-style hot spot for a cocktail. *See Hot & Cool Restaurants, p.63, for details.* F≡ 826 Folsom St. (Fifth St.), 415-538-0918, azierestaurant.com

Azul Bar and Lounge • Downtown • Jazz Club/DJ Bar
Azul feels like a secret, mostly due to its location. You wouldn't expect a loungy, chic DJ club tucked into a tiny alley right in the middle of retail Mecca off Union Square. Azul is, naturally, done up in shades of metallic blue. During the week it attracts the young and presentable retail talent indigenous to its hood, as well as the happy-hour crowd from the nearby Financial District, for laid-back sipping and mingling action, often set to Latin jazz. Regular dance parties pepper its calendar, and on weekends it can get moving. *Mon-Tue 2pm-midnight, Wed-Sat 2pm-2am.* ≡ One Tillman Pl. (Grant Ave.), 415-362-9750, azul-sf.com

Bacar • SoMa • Lounge
Building a big, ambitious, tri-level shrine to fine wine and food seemed like a great idea at the peak of the dot-com boom. Trouble is, by the time Bacar opened, most of its hometown was unemployed. But the next wave has finally come. With an enormous bottle selection—some 1,400 international selections with 65 offered by the glass—the emphasis remains on wine. The wine bottles are even part of the sleek décor, looming in a glass-enclosed wall. The food tends to reliable American and Mediterranean dishes, such as wood-fired pizza and grilled lamb chops. These days, the loungy basement level is the best of the three floors, catering to SoMa trendsetters looking for a pre- or post-dinner cocktail. Seating down there is limited and fills up quickly, so be ready to stand. The bar upstairs is next to the band, so you won't be able to talk unless you get a table. *Sun 5:30-10pm, Mon-Thu 5:30-11pm, Fri 11:30am-midnight, Sat 5:30-midnight.* F≡ 448 Brannan St. (Third St.), 415-904-4100, bacarsf.com

Bambuddha Lounge • Downtown • Hotel Bar/Lounge
Best Trendy Hangouts The Phoenix Hotel maintains a solid rock-star reputation, frequently boasting large and very beautiful crowds to prove it. This is the Sky Bar of San Francisco. Despite plenty of private parties mid-week, on weekends you can expect a flow of well-coiffed LA-style cuties looking for same. Grab your drink and set up shop under one of the palapas by the pool, where you'll have the space to dance if the DJ gets to you, or pass the big gold Buddha and secure a wee table inside, where you can order up a little caramelized onion naan and five-spice duck. When the chemistry clicks, Bambuddha can be a great scene. *Tue-Thu 5:30-10:30pm, Fri-Sat 5pm-2am.* C F≡ Phoenix Hotel, 601 Eddy St. (Larkin St.), 415-885-5088, bambuddhalounge.com

Bar at XYZ • SoMa • Hotel Bar/Lounge
The lobby bar at the W, a good place to meet up with friends or make new ones, is inviting and well-appointed with post-Starckien décor in serious autumn shades, but the XYZ lounge upstairs takes things up a notch. Obviously they were going for a sexy, urbane, deep-nightlife glam look, and they nailed it. Part the curtain of metal beads and the small space feels intelligently intimate, like a private party in a futuristic living room, complete with a noteworthy nude on the back wall. On one side of the room, the bar glows, changing color every few seconds. On the other, a civilized crowd vies for the limited couch and cube seating, with areas divided by white curtains that can be pulled around for privacy. Because it is so often crowded, XYZ is particularly nice on a weeknight, presuming you bring your own company. *Tue-Sat 7pm-2am.* W San Francisco, 181 Third St. (Howard St.), 415-817-7836, xyz-sf.com

Betelnut • Marina • Restaurant Bar
Perennially popular bar and restaurant with streetside tables and sleek Asian décor. *See Hot & Cool Restaurants p.63, for details.* 2030 Union St. (Buchanan St.), 415-929-8855, betelnutrestaurant.com

B44 • Financial District • Restaurant Bar
Snag an outdoor table at happy hour and watch the world go by. *See Hot & Cool Restaurants, p.63, for details.* 44 Belden Pl. (Bush St.), 415-986-6287

Bocadillos • Financial District • Restaurant Bar
A fine choice for a glass of wine and a chat with the FiDi types who work nearby. *See Hot & Cool Restaurants, p.64, for details.* 710 Montgomery St. (Washington St.), 415-982-2622, bocasf.com

CAV • Hayes Valley • Wine Bar
Best Wine Bars Don't let the wall of wine intimidate you. CAV is friendly enough to welcome even the wine illiterate into its dimly lit, urban-chic midst. Have a seat and sample any of scores of wines from around the globe by the glass, flight, or taste. Where else can you hop from an Andalusian sherry to a Chilean Sauvignon Gris to a St. Emilion Bordeaux and wind up—hopefully after dinner—with a glass of 1963 Grahams vintage port? The menu offers distinctive wine-friendly snacks, including truffle tastings, crudo, sardines, charcuterie, various small plates, and a delightful assortment of artisan cheeses. Flights change weekly, each exploring a region or style of interest. *Mon-Thu 5:30-11pm, Fri-Sat 5:30pm-midnight.* 1666 Market St. (Franklin St.), 415-437-1770, cavwinebar.com

Chaya Brasserie • Embarcadero • Restaurant Bar
With its back to the Financial District and its nose pointed at the Bay, Chaya has a marvelous location that echoes its mood: With work behind you, the night is yours. The happy-hour scene generally lives up to its name and is a great place to turn up in business attire, soak up the view, and make new acquaintances. As the name implies, the food is nouvelle French-Japanese. You can have a mango Chayapolitan, salmon tartare potato blinis, seaweed salad with ginger soy vinaigrette, and hit the sushi bar, all without leaving one room. *Mon-Fri 11:30am-2:30pm and 5:30-10pm, Sat 5:30-10:30pm, Sun 5-9:30pm.* 132 Embarcadero (Mission St.), 415-777-8688, thechaya.com

Circolo • Potrero Hill • Restaurant Lounge
Young urbanites gather to dance and drink at this trendy, minimalist lounge. *See Hot & Cool Restaurants, p.65, for details.* B 500 Florida St. (Mariposa St.), 415-553-8560, circolosf.com

Cortez • Downtown • Hotel Bar/Lounge
For a bar-restaurant so high on style, including ultramodern Calder-esque lamps, the Cortez opened to surprisingly little fanfare. But the truly cool spots usually do. It's a surprising find, set off the lobby of the Hotel Adagio. Once inside, you'll quickly focus on the boldly eclectic surroundings and lengthy menu of tantalizing small plates. The influences range from the Far East to the American West, and diners are instructed to order several items to share. A meal might consist of a foie gras terrine, chopped ahi tuna, butternut squash ravioli, and the "Croque Madame." It's easy to pile up a hefty tab, especially since it takes the "small" in small plates pretty seriously. But the fact that you're among a good-looking, cosmopolitan crowd will take away some of the sting. If that doesn't work, try a few of the Cortez specialty cocktails in the intimate bar area. *Daily 5:30-10:30pm for dinner, 5pm-1am for drinks.* F Hotel Adagio, 550 Geary St. (Taylor St.), 415-292-6360, cortezrestaurant.com

DNA Lounge • Mission • Lounge/Nightclub
Best Late-Night Hangouts DNA Lounge is not only one of the best places in the city to dance all night to the latest music, it is a little piece of San Francisco modern dot-com history, thanks to its owner, Jamie Zawinski. Zawinski was one of the first faces at Netscape, helping to bring the Internet revolution to the people back around 1994-95. He rode it out all the way through open-source Mozilla, but finally gave up when that faltered and turned to serious night play with the DNA Lounge. As you might expect, the place is genuinely cutting-edge cool, not trumped-up mainstream. The décor is sparse, the sound system is Goliath, the crowd varies depending on the show but is always ready to dance, and the shows include everything from strange new bands to world-famous DJs. No surprise, you can take a break and surf the Internet. *Hours vary depending on event.* C 375 11th St. (Harrison St.), 415-626-1409, dnalounge.com

Dolce • North Beach • Lounge
Best Sexy Lounges Of the several clubs on this block, Dolce can be distinguished from the others by the fact that it is the most beautiful, with ultramodern, sleek décor done in tasteful chocolate, cream, and honey hues. The backlit bar illuminates a long panel of roses for a delicate touch. It features well-known local DJs spinning house and hip-hop and has a large dance floor that can be standing room only on weekends, with most of the seating areas reserved by "VIPs." On Wednesdays and Thursdays, Dolce can be a charming place to stop in for some sexy, mellow beats and more open space. You might even get a seat on one of the beds. (It hosts private parties that can be invitation only, so check the website before you head out.) *Wed-Sat 9pm-2am.* C 440 Broadway (Kearny St.), 415-989-3434, dolcesf.com

DragonBar • North Beach • Nightclub
One man's hipster is another man's dork. Nowhere is this truth more evident than at DragonBar, where locals go on Wednesdays and Thursdays, because it's less crowded with early-twenties bridge-and-tunnel losers, and where B&T folk

flock by the hundreds on Friday and Saturday nights because that's when all the cool early-twenty-somethings are there. Vive la difference. Sultry DragonBar has great black and red décor, with loads of pan-Asian motifs, such as geisha pictures, bamboo elements, and paper lanterns. Beyond the setting, the big attraction is the expansive dance floor and the many energetic people on it. For the ladies, look your best to pass the red rope test, get in free, and make the ongoing guest list. Gentlemen, the above mentioned policy wisely ensures that the ladies keep coming back. *Tue-Thu 9pm-2am, Thu-Sun 8pm-2am.* C≡ 473 Broadway (Kearny St.), 415-834-9383, maximumproductions.com

First Crush • Downtown • Wine Bar

Best Wine Bars First Crush boasts a vast wine list that encompasses virtually every aspect of California wine imaginable, but the food is equally impressive, with a wide selection of New American–style small and large plates to accompany your wine choice. The location is convenient for after shopping or before theater, which means the clientele includes a fair number of tourists, which only adds to the festive atmosphere. For anyone interested in sampling California wines—from the classics to the smaller, lesser-known labels—First Crush is a must. They even list how many cases are made of each wine, which adds more to the picture than one might imagine. *Sun-Wed 5-11pm, Thu-Sat 5pm-midnight.* F≡ 101 Cyril Magnin St. (Ellis St.), 415-982-7874, firstcrush.com

Fluid Ultra Lounge • SoMa • Lounge/Nightclub

Best Scene Bars Done up in white and designed right down to its toes, Fluid Ultra Lounge starts with a futuristic island bar glowing from within and backed by a wall of white couches. Some lounges are about reclining and drinking, and some are about dancing. Fluid moves. As you pass the bathrooms, you enter a den of funk, where a roster of mostly A-list DJs spins to an enthusiastic crowd packed tightly on the small dance floor. A nook off to the side of the dance floor offers a place for VIPs to whisper and snuggle. Numerous regular parties keep the action fresh, including something called the Bedroom, which encourages scanty dress and naughty behavior. Dress uptown fashion-forward to make sure you get in and fit in. *Wed-Fri 5pm-2am, Sat 10pm-after hours.* C≡ 662 Mission St. (New Montgomery St.), 415-615-6888, fluidsf.com

Frisson • Financial District • Restaurant Lounge

Sexy DJ lounge that draws a fashionable crowd. *See Hot & Cool Restaurants, p.66, for details.* B≡ 244 Jackson St. (Sansome St.), 415-956-3004, frissonsf.com

Jade Bar • Hayes Valley • Bar

Best Neighborhood Bars Although it's stranded by itself on the three-lane thoroughfare of Gough Street, Jade Bar attracts a solid crowd nightly. One reason is its proximity to Hayes Valley. Another is its proximity to Civic Center's big venues. Once you're there, you can enjoy the glass floor-to-ceiling waterfall, the main floor's tiny and often extremely crowded bar, the windowless lounge-cum-cave downstairs, and the very enticing carpeted and cushioned lounge upstairs. But wait, there's more. If you get started reasonably early, you can also order up Thai fusion snacks from around the corner. The crowd tends to young, single professionals looking to let their hair down after work or, on weekends, chat up a new titillating companion. *Mon-Sat 5pm-2am, Sun 8pm-2am.* B≡ 650 Gough St. (McAllister St.), 415-869-1900, jadebar.com

La Suite • Embarcadero • Restaurant Bar
French brasserie with an inviting bar. *See Hot & Cool Restaurants, p.67, for details.* F 100 Brannan St. (Embarcadero), 415-593-5900, lasuitesf.com

Laszlo • Mission • Bar/Nightclub
Next to parent restaurant Foreign Cinema, this industrial-style bar is well suited to the location, set as it is among the post-industrial structures of the Mission District. Although it's within the same building as the restaurant, it manages to have an identity all its own. A long bar flanking one side makes it easy to get a cocktail even on busy nights. Upstairs is a balcony overlook and mezzanine. DJs provide the nightly beat—chilled-out breaks and down tempo along with visuals projected on the far wall on occasion. Early in the evenings, it will still be empty and quiet enough to talk over a cocktail and even order in appetizers from Foreign Cinema. Later, a cover, a line, loud music, and droves of Mission nightlifers transform the scene. Laszlo is pre-lounge, so don't expect an Italian sofa to drape yourself across or much room to dance. This is a drink and schmooze and groove-in-one-place kind of space. *Tue-Sun 6pm-2am.* C B 2534 Mission St. (21st St.), 415-648-7600, foreigncinema.com/laszlo

Le Duplex • SoMa • Lounge/Nightclub
Best Late-Night Hangouts It's not just the definite article, Le Duplex really does have a European feel, complete with a fairly consistent supply of actual French people. The setting is sophisticated. A gentleman might even wear a blazer without irony and still be let in. The not-too-big main level has a long mahogany bar, modern accents, and an attractive crowd, which can swell to capacity on nights when things get moving (Friday night is a good bet). They do the VIP bottle service thing upstairs, a great way to go if you've brought your posse and want a place to regroup off the dance floor. *Tue-Wed 7pm-2am, Thu-Sat 5pm-2am.* C 1525 Mission St. (11th St.), 415-355-1525, duplexsf.com

Levende Lounge • Mission • Lounge
Levende has swiftly become a mainstay in San Francisco nightlife, not to mention host to a popular after-after-after-party for Sunday brunch. DJs set the mood through dinner, and as the night deepens the place transforms into a popular club. There has been some grumbling about the prices. The issue may be the turf war between Levende's two personalities. One side wants to be an upscale restaurant serving critic-worthy small-plate world-fusion cuisine. The other spins house music and wants to attract a crowd of beautiful young things. No matter. Levende is cool enough to be reeling in a stylish crowd at the dinner hour and well after. *Tue-Fri 5-11pm, Sat 6-11pm, Sun 11am-4pm and 6-11pm. Bar Tue-Sat until 2am.* C F 1710 Mission St. (Duboce Ave.), 415-864-5585, levendesf.com

Loft 11 • SoMa • Lounge/Nightclub
Best Club Scenes Busty girls, muscled dudes, faux tans, expensive drinks, and a seriously slick setting combine to make Loft 11 a fine destination for those who can make the doorman's cut. It's a dramatic, expensive place fueled by money, fashion, and straightforward sex appeal. The music may not be the most cutting edge, but it will definitely get you moving. While it serves Asian fusion cuisine, you're better off eating elsewhere because the big draw here is the scene, which doesn't get going until well after the dinner hour. However, having dinner does spare you the red rope treatment. Thursday nights yield the best crowd, with

HOT & COOL • NIGHTLIFE

weekends taking a bridge-and-tunnel beating, which nonetheless fills the place to the second floor with ladies and gentlemen in their Saturday night finery. *Thu-Sat 6:30pm-2am.* C≣ 316 11th St. (Folsom St.), 415-701-8111, loft11sf.com

MarketBar • Embarcadero • Restaurant Bar
Popular outdoor terrace at weekend farmers market and weekday happy hour. *See Hot & Cool Restaurants, p.67, for details.* F≣ One Ferry Building (Market St.), 415-434-1100, marketbar.com

MatrixFillmore • Marina • Bar
Best Scene Bars Contemporary and even slightly edgy in décor, MatrixFillmore is just the right size. It's big enough to offer an appetizing variety of prospects to cruise and to lose track of whomever you came in with for a few minutes, and yet small enough to be comfortable, inviting, and not intimidating. The crew of smokers out front give a hint of what's inside, which is almost always thirty-something business dudes posing, with moderate success, as upscale hipsters, and the girl version of same. All in all, it's a fine spot for a drink under the elevated fireplace, as well as an excellent place to chat up the talent, and to succumb to being chatted up. *Daily 5:30pm-2am.* ≣ 3138 Fillmore St. (Greenwich St.), 415-563-4180, matrixfillmore.com

Mezzanine • SoMa • Nightclub
Best Club Scenes As with many clubs, the quality of the Mezzanine experience depends largely on a given night's DJ or event. Check the calendar on the website, or keep an open mind and try your luck. Of the elements that remain constant, the most important is the expansive, industrial, warehouse-conversion space. Cement and steel make a muted, serious, authentically modern backdrop for ultramodern art shows. The vast dance floor takes a solid crowd of hundreds of revelers to fill up; when it does—when a great DJ brings the party people out of their nooks and crannies—it rocks until 5am (no alcohol after 2am). Upstairs are a couple of chill areas, tastefully done in a minimalist loft-chic style. C≣ 444 Jessie St. (Fifth St.), 415-625-8880, mezzaninesf.com

Mr. Smith's • SoMa • Bar
Best Trendy Hangouts Even though it's just a couple of blocks from Union Square, this little stretch of Seventh Street is good and dodgy. All the better to make you feel very insider-ish when you stop before the nothing-special doorway, only to enter a plush, tri-level nightlife paradise. The main floor has soaring ceilings, exposed brick walls, a vast central bar of polished dark wood, modern chandeliers, retro-Victorian speakeasy-style wallpaper and accents, and plenty of room to mingle. Upstairs is the VIP zone with bottle service, views of the action, and opulent lounge seating. And when it's time to get down and dirty? The low-frill basement level offers all-out dance music and a bar, plus enough space to shake your funk out. Though the décor, amenities, and arrangement are ideal for a never-ending party, the real magic touch is the management, who draw a good, lively, attractive crowd of single twenty- and thirty-somethings, especially on weekends. *Wed-Fri 6pm-2am, Sat 8pm-2am.* ≣ 34 Seventh St. (Mission St.), 415-355-9991, maximumproductions.com

Myth • Financial District • Restaurant Bar
The slick restaurant-lounge with dance music draws a festive young crowd. *See Hot & Cool Restaurants, p.67, for details.* F☰ 470 Pacific Ave. (Montgomery St.), 415-677-8986, mythsf.com

Nectar • Marina • Wine Bar
Best Wine Bars Nectar is strategically designed to be the perfect place for a glass of wine after work, as well as a nightcap. Solo sippers find a comfortable spot at the bar, while couples and groups can nestle into Zinfandel-purple suede banquettes in the lounge area. The small, skinny space is a tasteful blend of contemporary modernism—stark white, powder-coated steel tables and espresso-hued wood floors—and softer elements, such as the furry ottomans. Nectar serves 40 wines by the glass, and changes that list frequently, so even locals can broaden their repertoire. The bottle list includes a staggering 800 carefully selected listings. It's fun to read the over-the-top menu, which pokes fun at wine snobs even as it suggests someone behind the scenes really knows their grape juice. The inventive small-plates menu changes weekly and includes such offerings as asparagus tempura and scallops with tikka masala and strawberry polenta. *Mon-Thu 5:30-10:30pm, Fri-Sat 5:30pm-midnight, Sun 2-9pm.* F☰ 3330 Steiner St. (Chestnut St.), 415-345-1377, nectarwinelounge.com

111 Minna Gallery • SoMa • Bar/Art Gallery
Best Trendy Hangouts Set in a large gallery space in an alley just south of Market, the attraction began here with Qool, a Wednesday evening happy-hour party. From its modest beginnings, word spread quickly and soon the crowd of casually dressed downtown dot-com kids gave way to an influx of people from all over the city and beyond. Soon 111 Minna expanded and began offering more evening events to accommodate them. Now, the schedule features happy hour, often accompanied by live music and a regular array of top DJs hosted by some of the city's best-known party throwers. It's generally very stylish, especially given its art gallery location. The mood can be snooty, but it is mostly friendly and welcoming. *Mon-Thu 11am-10pm, Fri 11am-2am, Sat 8pm-2am.* C☰ 111 Minna St. (Second St.), 415-974-1719, 111minnagallery.com

Oola • SoMa • Restaurant Bar
Industrial-chic space that draws the late dinner, post-dinner, and pre-club crowds. *See Hot & Cool Restaurants p.68, for details.* ☰ 860 Folsom St. (Fourth St.), 415-995-2061, oola-sf.com

Otis • Downtown • Lounge
Otis is 1,300 square feet of semiprivate, high-style, white-and-gold glam with a '70s smack. A new concept in San Francisco, Otis arrived in mid-2005 announcing it would be open exclusively to members and their select guests from 9pm to 2am each night, with membership by invitation only to ensure that only the right sort of people grace the white leather furniture during party hours. The public is welcome to drop by for a cocktail and a snack from 2 in the afternoon until 9pm. After that, the certifiably hippest strata of the city's socialites, artists, DJs, party girls, and suits take over. Elitist? Definitely. Snobby? Absolutely. Ridiculously cooler than thou? Yep. But you wouldn't want to party with just anyone, would you? Stop by for a couple of Uncle Otis concoctions made of dark Caribbean rum and exotic juices in the early afternoon. Who

knows, if you strut your stuff just right, maybe a member will invite you to stay. *Daily 2pm-2am; members and invited guests only after 9pm.* 25 Maiden Ln. (Kearny St.), no public phone, otissf.com

Ozumo • SoMa • Restaurant Bar
A lively happy hour takes place at the stylish bar of this Japanese restaurant. *See Hot & Cool Restaurants, p.68, for details.* F Harbor Court Hotel, 161 Steuart St. (Mission St.), 415-882-1333, ozumo.com

Pier 23 Cafe • Embarcadero • Restaurant Bar
The best place in town for casual fish and chips by the water. *See Hot & Cool Restaurants p.69, for details.* F Pier 23 (Lombard St.), 415-362-5125, pier23cafe.com

Redwood Room • Downtown • Hotel Bar
Best Scene Bars The Redwood Room has been around since 1934 and had matured into a somewhat portly but endearing old fellow when Ian Schrager and Philippe Starck got hold of it a few years ago. Many feared their remake would obliterate a much-loved bit of local history, but Starck's typically high-concept modernism plays beautifully here. The new Redwood Room is a real eye-popper, with moving "paintings" on the redwood walls and a towering bar all aglow from within. The servers are hot numbers in skimpy cocktail dresses, catering to the needs of the would-be in crowd. Doormen keep the riffraff out while socialites, business types, and party girls sip sweet, powerful drinks. Even the real trendsetters can't resist its allure, especially late at night. *Sun-Thu 5pm-2am, Fri-Sat 4pm-2am.* Clift Hotel, 495 Geary St. (Taylor St.), 415-929-2372, clifthotel.com

Roe • SoMa • Restaurant Lounge
Sexy, sophisticated dance club (also called Privé) with a leopard-print bar. *See Hot & Cool Restaurants, p.69, for details.* C 651 Howard St. (Third St.), 415-227-0288, roerestaurant.com

Ruby Skye • Downtown • Nightclub
Best Club Scenes Every night is a party at Ruby Skye, where grand pomp and high style reign. Especially when the big-name DJs show up, you'll find a dance floor full of twenty and thirty-something revelers eager to show off their latest skimpy outfit (the Bebe look) and hottest moves. Ruby Skye is San Francisco's most opulent dance club, the sort of place where sophisticated light shows, a mega sound system, trapeze artists, and go-go dancers on platforms are all part of the standard fare. The theme parties, such as the Caribbean White party in June, when everyone dresses in their brightest whites, can be very fun. Show up around 11pm. *Thu 9pm-2am, Fri 9pm-3am, Sat 8pm-4am.* C 420 Mason St. (Geary St.), 415-693-0777, rubyskye.com

Sake Lab • North Beach • Bar
The Jetsons used to be way in the future, but it seems lately that we have caught up with them at last. Witness the arrival of the Sake Lab, a disarmingly space-age restaurant and bar done in silver and neon blue that makes you want to wear experimental fabrics, sit in a chair shaped like a snow cone, and drink a bright green cocktail. Instead, you will drink sake, since there are more than 40 different varieties on offer, as well as creative sake-enriched cocktails. This is all very refreshing in North Beach, home to old-school bars and restaurants that

seem to blend together. The Sake Lab gets high marks for daring and originality, as well as for good music played at reasonable volume and sushi that's a cut above the ordinary, plus some delicious grilled robata skewers. *Sun-Thu 6-10pm, Fri-Sat 6pm-1:30am.* ≡ 498 Broadway (Kearny St.), 415-837-0228, sakelab.com

Shanghai 1930 • Embarcadero • Restaurant Bar

Remember when cigar bars were all the rage? Shanghai 1930 was new then. Today it is no longer on the cutting edge, but it is still an elegant spot for an evening drink or sophisticated Chinese dinner. Descend the stairs and you enter a secret world underground, where decadence flourishes. It succeeds in creating a fantasy of another time and another place, the "Paris of the Orient" at its height of indulgence. Live jazz plays Tuesday through Saturday, the cocktails flow, and in the private lounge, the high rollers fire up their contraband Cubans. The crowd, as you might guess, is of mixed ages and ethnicities who want an ambiance of intelligence, polish, and savoir faire. *Mon-Thu 11:30am-2pm and 5:30-10pm, Fri-Sat 11:30am-2pm and 5:30-11pm.* F≡ 133 Steuart St. (Mission St.), 415-896-5600, shanghai1930.com

Slanted Door • Embarcadero • Restaurant Bar

Perennial hot spot on the waterfront with a buzzing bar scene after work. *See Hot & Cool Restaurants, p.70, for details.* F≡ One Ferry Building (Market St.), 415-861-8032, slanteddoor.com

Suede • Fisherman's Wharf • Lounge

Best Sexy Lounges One of the more handsome additions to arrive on the lounge scene, Suede caters to young professionals who expect their dance and romance spots to be at least as well-furnished and lavish as their homes. True to its name, Suede has plenty of European-designed furniture in earth-toned suede. Tea lights and fabric-draped ceilings soften the mood, while sleek, modernist lines set an appropriate stage for the patrons' latest fashions. Suede is big into VIP bottle service and special events, so it's hard to say what you'll find on any particular night. The general cast, however, is a monied set of pretty faces staking out their VIP sofa turf and showing off their well-coiffed stuff on the dance floor. For those looking for bigger crowds, louder music, and a more rave-like scene, 383 Bay, a much bigger club downstairs, should serve nicely. It's just a few blocks from Chestnut Street's many restaurants. *Fri-Sat 9pm-2am, plus special events.* C≡ 383 Bay St. (Mason St.), 415-399-9555, suedesf.com

Suite one8one • Downtown • Lounge

Best Sexy Lounges Go-go dancers working the pole? Check. House DJs spinning hip-hop? Check. Bouncers with headsets and loads of 'tude, a mix of ladies showing some skin, dance floors on multiple levels? Check, check, and check. If you want to get in without a painful wait, arrive before 10pm dressed LA/Miami club style. Better yet, reserve a table in the VIP zone, a swanky retreat from the crush of dancers, where your own server will mix you a drink while you recline on the Euro-chic plush furniture. It's only a matter of money. *Thu-Sat 9pm-4am.* C≡ 181 Eddy St. (Taylor St.), 415-345-9900, suite181.com

HOT & COOL • NIGHTLIFE

supperclub San Francisco • SoMa • Restaurant Bar
This trendy newcomer draws a hot, Eurochic crowd for decadent nights. *See Hot & Cool Restaurants, p.70, for details.* C≣ 657 Harrison St. (Third St.), 415-348-0900, supperclub.com

Tres Agaves • SoMa • Restaurant Bar
Stylish Mexican hot spot known for its impressive tequila drinks menu. *See Hot & Cool Restaurants, p.71, for details.* F≡ 130 Townsend St. (Second St.), 415-227-0500, tresagaves.com

Voda • Financial District • Bar
Voda is a high-concept, Miami-style, understated neon–enhanced lounge where the seating looks like beds and colorful cubes abound. With over 100 different vodkas to choose from, it definitely has something for the serious martini drinker. Voda (the word is Russian for water) is part of the Belden Place melee, where throngs vie for an outdoor table at happy hour, and the outdoor seating is the big draw at Voda, too. Claim one of the orange banquettes and ogle the passersby coming and going from the many other restaurants and bars. As the evening turns to night, the DJs take over, the after-work crew thins, and the club-loving set—those that feel at home in a futuristic setting—arrives. *Mon-Fri 4:30pm-2am, Sat 7pm-2am.* ≡ 56 Belden Pl. (Pine St.), 415-677-9242, vodasf.com

Zebra Lounge • North Beach • Lounge/Nightclub
It's early days yet for the Zebra Lounge, but its prospects look good. A large dance floor, safari-inspired décor, a key location on the Broadway nightclub corridor, and parties with some of the city's best DJs add up to good times ahead. Zebra is all about big weekend nights out dancing the night away with a couple hundred new acquaintances. Judging by the crowd, those acquaintances are bound to be singles in their twenties and early thirties, many from the areas surrounding San Francisco, all dressed in their best Saturday-night finery. Zebra claims to have the "best sound and lighting system in the city." Put on your dancing shoes and give it a spin after 10pm. *Fri-Sat 10pm-2am.* C≣ 447 Broadway (Kearny St.), 415-788-0188, zebrasf.net

Hot & Cool San Francisco: The Attractions

Adventure Cat • Embarcadero • Sailing
While summer is the big time to sail, the bay can serve up a gorgeous day on the water any time of year. Adventure Cat has a 55-foot catamaran (with a 70-foot mast!) that it takes out for 90-minute cruises three times a day—1pm, 3pm, and sunset—between March and October, and less frequently in the winter. The mood is festive, with everyone—there may be twenty people on board—oohing and ahhing over the views and the exhilarating salty spray. Because catamarans have two hulls, the ride is smoother and less scary than in regular sailboats. Sit back, hit the cash bar, grab a snack, and enjoy silently skimming along at a pleasantly swift speed. Adventure Cat also does a fully catered, all-day picnic excursion to Angel Island, plus other special outings, such as whale and bird watching off the Farallon Islands, a Fourth of July night sail, and an October cruise to watch the Blue Angels air show. *90-minute cruises.* $$$ J Dock, Pier 39, 415-777-1630, adventurecat.com

Asian Art Museum • Hayes Valley • Art Museum
Now settled into its remarkable digs near Civic Center and City Hall, the Asian Art Museum has emerged as one of the city's preeminent arts and culture institutions. Built in the former home of the Main Library, a 1917 Beaux Arts gem, the museum is a dazzling combination of modern elegance and historic architecture. It is one of the largest museums in the West devoted exclusively to Asian art, with some 15,000 pieces spanning 6,000 years of Asian history. Since the grand reopening, the Asian has become, somewhat unexpectedly, a trendy hangout, with a calendar of arts-themed events aimed at the beautiful people. The Art After Hours evenings offer a heady mix of art, cocktails, DJ music, and mingling. Unfortunately, they only happen four Wednesdays each year. *Tue-Sun 10am-5pm, Thu until 9pm.* $ 200 Larkin St. (Grove St.), 415-581-3500, asianart.org

Blue and Gold Ferry • Fisherman's Wharf • Tour
The Blue and Gold Ferry service makes regular runs across the bay, leaving daily from Fisherman's Wharf (and on weekdays during commute hours from the ferry building). An exhilarating and scenic 45-minute ride will drop you in Tiburon, a quaint village that's home to the seriously affluent. The center of the action is Sam's Anchor Café, a casual bar and restaurant with a patio famous locally for its sunshine and party people. A bright Saturday on the patio at Sam's, surrounded by smiling, slightly rowdy fellow patrons, beer in hand, fish and chips on the way, water glistening, sailboats gliding by—such is the sum of earthly pleasure. $ Pier 41 (Powell St.), 415-705-5555, blueandgoldfleet.com

Club Sportiva • SoMa • Car Rental
Join Club Sportiva and a stable of the finest rides in the city is at your disposal. You can also rent by the day. Dream of cruising the Golden Gate in your Ferrari 308 GTSi Quattrovalve? For a pretty penny, you can. Or consider a day behind the wheel of a Morgan Plus 8 roadster. Now that should turn some heads. Or you can pretend to be Dustin Hoffman in *The Graduate* and drive across the Bay

Bridge in your Alfa Romeo. (It's British racing green, but Club Sportiva has a red Triumph TR6 that could work even better.) It also has a Lotus, several Porsches (including a 356 Cabriolet from 1961—sort of makes your palms sweat just thinking about it, doesn't it?), a Bentley, an E-type Jag, and other heart-thumpers. $$$$ 840 Harrison St. (Fourth St.), 415-978-9900, clubsportiva.com

The Embarcadero Promenade • Embarcadero • Waterfront Walk
Looking at the Embarcadero today, it's hard to believe that it was until recently a wasteland covered by a noisy freeway. In 1989, the earthquake happened, the freeway came down, the palm trees went up, the 60-foot Claes Oldenburg bow and arrow sculpture struck home, and a new center of urban bliss was born. If you bike, rollerblade, or jog, take to the path that runs along the water from SBC Park, past the Ferry Building Marketplace, all the way to Pier 39. On Saturday mornings, the Ferry Plaza Farmers Market *(see below)* is a wonderful way to eat, relax, and catch some sun. Though the view faces mostly east, and is thus especially nice in the morning, you can still catch the glow of the sunset as you round the horn after the Ferry Building. King Street to Fisherman's Wharf

Equinox Fitness Club • Financial District • Health Club
Call it sweat equity. The New York–based and decidedly New York–style Equinox Fitness Club opened its doors in 2005 in the historic and lovely Pacific Stock Exchange building. The setting, with its Grecian columns and to-the-sky ceiling, should inspire some heroic feats. In contrast to the regal structure, the design style throughout the 33,000-square-foot space is modern, bright, and airy, with all the latest equipment and classes in every discipline the 21st-century urbanite could want. It even offers something called the Commotion Class, a circuit of medicine balls, jump ropes, body balls, and resistance training with partners, encouraging you to get to know your fellow athletes. When it's time to get wet, descend to the old vault area, where you'll find a lap pool and plush locker rooms. There's a full-service spa, juice bar, thumping workout beats, and a shop. If you're not a member of an Equinox Club elsewhere, stay at the Mandarin Oriental to receive a free day pass. *Mon-Thu 5am-10pm, Fri 5am-9pm, Sat 8am-6pm.* $$$$ 301 Pine St. (Sansome St.), 415-593-4000, equinoxfitness.com

Ferry Plaza Farmers Market • Embarcadero • Shopping
San Francisco's much-loved parking lot farmers market got a serious upgrade a few years ago, when it moved into the Ferry Building Marketplace. It's still held in a parking lot in back, but now it is attached to a wonderland of fine restaurants and high-end gourmet specialty shops that stay open all week. You want fresh local oysters and a stylish place to swallow them? Done. You want Acme bread, local caviar, fresh flowers, ripe fruits, Peet's coffee, world-class wines, an artisan cheese shop, Miette pastries, organic meats, a fishmonger, and a food-obsessed bookstore? Done. It is hard to imagine any locally produced or harvested delicacy not beautifully represented here. Add incredible views and space to walk, relax, and stretch out on the grass nearby, and the Farmers Market is no longer just a place to fill a basket with groceries. It's a highly enjoyable destination for visitors and locals alike—and has also become a highly social, see-and-be-seen affair on Saturday mornings for beautiful people sipping lattes and exchanging gossip over ripe peaches. *Market open Sat 8am-2pm, Tue and Sun 10am-2pm, Thu 4-8pm. Shop and restaurant hours vary.* One Ferry Building (Market St.), 415-291-3276, ferrybuildingmarketplace.com

The Gardener• Embarcadero • Shop
The simple name belies the sophistication of the merchandise found here. Sure, the shop is small, but when you're this good at selecting irresistible loot, you don't need a lot of space. Look for an original and earthy collection of treasures that might include a perfect handbag, an elegant wooden spoon, a sumptuous body lotion, a dramatic vase, or any number of other non-essentials you can't live without. *Mon-Fri 10am-6pm, Sat 8am-6pm, Sun 10am-5pm.* One Ferry Building (Market St.), 415-981-8181, thegardener.com

Gimme Shoes • Downtown • Shop
San Franciscans rely on Gimme Shoes to supply a steady stream of highly original designer footwear. These are shoes that say to themselves (to say so out loud would be immodest), "I am without contest the most distinctive and marvelous pair of shoes in this room, and perhaps even in the whole city." The selection leans toward understated quality and originality more than bobbles and bells. Expect leather like butter, handcrafted excellence, superior styling, the slightly idiosyncratic but crucial detail. They also carry a small but equally distinctive selection of handbags and jewelry. *Mon-Sat 11am-7pm, Sun noon-6pm.* 50 Grant Ave. (Geary St.), 415-434-9242; 2358 Fillmore St. (Washington St.), 415-441-3040, gimmeshoes.com

Harding Park Golf Course • Sunset • Golf Course
Harding Park has been making San Francisco golfers go all mushy since 1925. Tucked into the southwestern edge of the city, washed by sea breezes, it is surrounded by scenic Lake Merced, which lovingly bends an arm around it. Its challenging yet accessible course is lined all the way with majestic cypress trees. In 2002, the PGA got hold of it and launched major renovations. A year later, the course reopened to relieved acclaim. The *San Francisco Chronicle* gushed, "People who play it want to remember it forever," calling it "one of the finest municipal golf courses in the West, and perhaps in all of America." In 2005, it hosted the American Express Championship, officially putting the course back on the world-class map. These days, Harding has it all: awesome views, a spectacular course, a spiffy new clubhouse, and the beloved Fleming Nine nestled in the middle of the 18-hole main course. $$$$ 99 Harding Rd. (Skyline Blvd.), 415-664-4690, harding-park.com

International Orange Day Spa • Pacific Heights • Spa
Best Spas Certainly one of the most handsome spas in town, International Orange is yoga-centric, exudes sophistication, emphasizes wellness, and feels European in style, with plenty of white. In addition to your massage, facial, or other treatment, you can indulge in a yoga class in a minimalist-chic space. The location makes it convenient for the Pacific Heights crew, meaning well-groomed young ladies and the occasional well-groomed young gentleman. After your treatment you can lounge outdoors on the patio or indoors on pillows, where you won't be shooed out even if you linger awhile. *Mon-Fri 11am-9pm, Sat-Sun 9am-7pm.* $$$ 2044 Fillmore St. (California St.), 888-894-8811, internationalorange.com

Jeremy's • SoMa • Shop
Imagine a random assortment of designer fashions plucked from the racks of, say, Barney's New York, tossed around until a few pieces are slightly damaged, then hung up in a spare but handsome retail space at massive discounts. That's

Jeremy's. You want a Nanette Lepore dress for $180? Last season's Prada driving moccasins for $160? A TSE cashmere sweater with a minuscule hole in the armpit for $90? A Burberry shearling coat trench for $1,200? It's all here, or at least something close. Both men and women will love to rummage the racks at Jeremy's. *Mon-Sat 11am-6pm.* 2 South Park (Second St.), 415-882-4929

Kamalaspa • Downtown • Spa
New to the spa scene in 2005, Kamalaspa subscribes to the 6,000-year-old Ayurvedic tradition of India. Before your massage, you will need to identify your dosha in order for your Ayurvedic diagnosis to be made and the oils and other products customized appropriately. Don't worry, it sounds more complicated than it is. All you really need to do is relax and admire the views of Union Square. Kamalaspa is opulent, inspired by the decadent Raj era. Think velvet tapestries, ornately carved dark woods, low light, and spice hues. The roster of services is equally inspired, with the usual spa and salon fare, plus options for men such as the Maharaja Royal Shave. The foyer has a soothing tank full of colorful fish, while the treatment area entrance includes a night sky overhead populated with Ayurvedic constellations. *Mon-Sat 10am-7pm, Sun 11am-5pm.* $$$$ 240 Stockton St., 7th Fl. (Maiden Ln.), 415-217-7700, kamalaspa.com

Limn • SoMa • Shop
If they called it an art gallery, you'd happily pay admission. Limn takes modern design and décor to the next level, elevating the experience to a sensory delight on a par with what one expects from grand public institutions. Lately they opened an official art gallery adjoining the furniture and accessories floors. It's a nice addition, but rarely competes with the glam factor of the spectacular showrooms. Visit to dream, to fill your home with Italian sofas and German kitchen cabinets, and to buy that iconic Pablo Pardo lamp you've always wanted. *Mon-Fri 9:30am-6pm, Sat-Sun 11am-6pm.* 290 Townsend St. (Fourth St.), 415-977-1300, limn.com

Remède Spa • SoMa • Spa
Remède at the St. Regis Hotel is the best thing you can do for your appearance, not to mention your state of mind. Step into the lavish surroundings and champagne and truffles arrive (chocolate, not fungus); separate men's and women's lounges beckon. Then the customized, personalized pampering begins. Some spas have a way of inducing anxiety rather than erasing it by tacking on extra fees with every "suggested" ointment. Not so chez Remède. One fee includes a professional's expert assessment of your needs as the treatment progresses. The approach is strictly high-end, state-of-the-art skin care, using ultra-potent, restorative French Laboratoire Remède products exclusively. Treatments include customized deep-cleansing facials, indulgent body treatments, relaxing massages, precision waxing and nail treatments, body bronzing, and more. Billed as offering "the most indulgent skin care and body treatments available in San Francisco," Remède is an oasis of luxury. $$$$ *Daily 9am-9pm.* St. Regis Hotel, 125 Third St. (Mission St.), 415-284-4000, remede.com

San Francisco Helicopter Tours • Tour
Get your bearings fast with a whirly-bird's-eye view of the city. For the last 25 years, San Francisco Helicopter Tours has been lifting off from SFO and Sausalito and buzzing the hot spots in four- and six-seater helicopters. The

views are genuinely breathtaking as you nuzzle up to the Golden Gate Bridge, the Bay Bridge, Alcatraz Island, the San Francisco skyline, and Fisherman's Wharf, then up the coastline to the lush slopes and jagged cliffs of the Marin Headlands, and drop down over the bayside village of Sausalito. *Call ahead to make a reservation; shuttle service picks you up from downtown. 15-minute tour.* $$$$ 800-400-2404, sfhelicoptertours.com

San Francisco Museum of Craft + Design • Downtown • Art Museum
Diminutive but ambitious, the Museum of Craft + Design is just two blocks off Union Square and makes for a brief, uplifting stop if you are in the neighborhood. The museum opened in 2004 and is attempting to amass a permanent collection. Meanwhile, traveling and home-curated shows are on display. What is the difference between art, craft, and design? A hint lies in utility. The objects on view here epitomize good design (that's the design part), meaning a perfect marriage of beauty and utility, and are often rendered by hand (that's the craft). Is it art? You decide. *Tue-Sat 10am-5pm, Thu 10am-7pm, Sun noon-5pm.* $– 550 Sutter St. (Mason St.), 415-773-0303, sfmcd.org

S Factor • Marina • Health Club
Ladies, free your inner stripper at S Factor, the newest and sexiest workout in town. Pole dancing? Oh yes. Have you ever seen an erotic dancer with flabby abs? Of course not. All those calorie-burning, muscle-toning gyrations and sultry moves keep a girl looking tight. Augmented with Pilates and yoga moves, the S Factor workout is all about exploring sensuality, gaining confidence, and improving strength and flexibility. Participants, the same youthful and reasonably fit green-minded crowd that keeps dozens of yoga studios around town in business, are guaranteed to walk out feeling hot. *Call for schedule.* $$ 2159 Filbert St. (Fillmore St.), 415-440-6420, sfactor.com

SBC Park Tour • SoMa • Tour
One of the prettiest ballparks in the country, SBC Park sits on the edge of the bay with views to the east of the Oakland hills. On most game days, you can stroll down and buy a ticket, find a seat, sip a glass of Cab over fancy take-out or garlic fries, and soak up some of the best of American culture. On days when there isn't a home game, it offers a behind-the-scenes, player's-eye tour, arguably even more fun than watching a game. Tours go into the Giants' dugout and the visiting team's clubhouse, and even onto the hallowed field itself. Even if you're not a huge baseball fan, the tour is a hoot. *Ballpark tours daily 10:30am and 12:30pm, except home day games.* $$ 24 Willie Mays Plaza (King St.), 415-972-2400, sbcpark.com

SFMoMA • SoMa • Art Museum
Unveiled in 1995, the new SFMoMA helped a budding art movement in the SoMa neighborhood blossom and flourish. The landmark structure houses the nation's second-largest collection of modern art. Enter and you are greeted by the gleeful hues of a permanent Sol LeWitt installation. An atrium construction fills the lofty space with light, while a somber staircase invites you to ascend the four levels. The permanent collection includes more than 15,000 works, from paintings by Magritte, Man Ray, and Matisse to sculpture by Calder and Modigliani. Special exhibitions showcase the best of modern art, photography, and design. On Thursdays the museum stays open late and often has live music.

The first Thursday of the month is more festive still, when art buffs migrate from gallery to gallery for the monthly art walk. The cafe is quite good for light meals and snacks. *Fri-Tue 10am-6pm, Thu 10am-9pm in the summer, from 11am in winter.* $ 151 Third St. (Howard St.), 415-357-4000, sfmoma.org

SFMoMA Museum Store • SoMa • Shop
If you're looking for a tasteful gift for the folks back home, a special someone, or even a baby shower present, SFMoMA has your answer. They offer a unique and stylish collection of jewelry, most of it handmade, some of it very reasonably priced. Other highlights include the baby and kids sections, where the selection is full of colorful and useful toys and gifts you won't find everywhere, and the home and office accessories, featuring modernist takes on everything from salad bowls to paperclip holders. The collection of art and photography books is also hard to beat. *Daily 10am-6:30pm, Thu until 9:30pm.* 151 Third St. (Mission St.), 415-357-4000, sfmoma.org

Sports Club/LA • SoMa • Health Club
Best Workouts As gyms go, this one is 100,000 square feet of eye candy. Beautiful people, beautiful equipment, beautiful building, designer lighting and details, floor-to-ceiling downtown views, and a peach of a lap pool add up to some serious motivation. After your yoga, tennis, or weight training, you can spruce up at the well-appointed spa and salon, then sip a fruit smoothie and get to know your exercise neighbors at the Sidewalk Café. Unless you are a member or go with someone who is, the only way to get in is to stay at the Four Seasons, where guests have free access to the club. *Mon-Fri 5am-11pm, Sat-Sun 7am-8pm.* $$$$ 747 Market St. (Grant Ave.), 415-633-3900, thesportsclubla.com

Tru Spa • Financial District • Spa
Best Spas Chic, sexy, and convenient, Tru Spa is a relatively new arrival on the spa scene. It is sleek in décor and progressive in its approach. Step inside for some pampering and you enter a world of heightened sensations. The women's lounge area is eye-poppingly pretty in blue and white. Drop in after a day of shopping or sightseeing for a cutting-edge facial, aromatherapy massage, or mani-pedi. Choose between Energizing, Relaxing, or Detoxifying therapies. Each is paired with a tailored, heat-sensitive aromatherapy balm and a unique program of coordinated light. It even has something called the Tropical Rainforest Room that transforms into a steamy paradise after your treatment to open your pores. *Mon-Tue, Thu-Fri 9am-9pm, Wed noon-9pm, Sat 9am-6pm, Sun 9:30am-6pm.* $$$$ 750 Kearny St. (Washington St.), 415-399-9700, truspa.com

Vino Venue • SoMa • Shop
The "try before you buy" model revolutionized the music business. Now the same approach is being applied to wine. Vino Venue is not a bar, it's a wine store where you can sample the wines before you buy—for a price and from an automated tasting station. As a shopping experience, it's all very entertaining. Buy a debit card, insert it in your station of choice, choose a wine, and voilà, you are served a one-ounce pour. The selection spans a range of price points and includes more than 100 wines, many locally made by small, family-run businesses. After work, the scene can get lively. *Mon-Thu noon-9pm, Fri-Sat noon-10pm, Sun 2-6pm.* 686 Mission St. (Third St.), 415-341-1930, vinovenue.net

Hip San Francisco

The restaurant doesn't have to be expensive. The bar doesn't have to be an ultra lounge. The hotel doesn't have to have five stars. But they'd better have that certain confidence that is the provenance of those who reside naturally on the cutting edge. Hip is youthful but savvy, fashionable but independent. In San Francisco, hip is SoMa dance clubs and Mission District dive bars. Not that hip means slumming. Far from it. Hip venues are just a little riskier and a little more raw, and in San Francisco, there are plenty of them.

Note: Venues in bold are described in detail in the listings that follow the itinerary. Those with an asterisk are recommended for both drinks and dinner.

Hip San Francisco:
The Perfect Plan (3 Days and Nights)

Your Hotel: Hotel Rex—It's centrally located, comfortable, pleasantly quirky, a great home base, and a fine venue for meeting new people, especially at the lobby bar.

The Perfect Plan Highlights

Prime Time: Fri-Sun

Friday
Breakfast	Boogaloo's
Morning	The Mission
Lunch	Luna Park, Slow Club
Afternoon	Twin Peaks Castro
Cocktails	Bissap Baobab
Dinner	Limón, Range
Nighttime	Beauty Bar, Whisper
Late-Night	Club Six

Saturday
Breakfast	Café Andrée, Canteen
Morning	West Coast Live
Lunch	Citizen Cake
Afternoon	Hayes Valley Kabuki Springs and Spa
Cocktails	Oxygen Bar, Lime
Dinner	Andalu, Delfina
Nighttime	Pink, Mighty
Late-Night	The EndUp

Sunday
Morning	Glide Memorial
Brunch	Universal Cafe
Afternoon	Haight, Golden Gate Park
Cocktails	Dogpatch Saloon, Mecca
Dinner	RNM Restaurant, Tallula
Nighttime	Café du Nord, Swig
Late-Night	El Rio

Friday

9am Breakfast Trek out to the Mission District, the soul of the city, for pancakes and a messy scramble at **Boogaloo's**.

10:30am Explore the historic cathedral and fascinating backyard graveyard of **Mission Dolores**. Then stroll the eclectic array of shops along Valencia Street. From 16th Street, work your way up the numbered streets to 19th and beyond, exploring the local take on furnishings, fashion, and literature. The vibe is shopper-friendly, especially if you like your shopping bags full of unique items not found in chain stores. The Mission's large Latin population lends a dose of color, spice, and diversity seen in everything from the local art to the plethora of taquerias. Those feeling curious can explore the gritty five-and-dimes along Mission Street.

12:30pm Lunch On Valencia Street you can pop into **Luna Park** for a hearty lunch of upscale comfort food. Or visit the **Slow Club** for an unbeatable gourmet burger among a bustling Media Gulch lunch crowd.

2pm Hop in your car, turn your sights due west and aim for the radio tower atop **Twin Peaks**. You'll get a sweeping bird's-eye view of the entire Bay Area that is hard to match without getting in a helicopter.

3pm On your way back down the hill, cruise the shops and rainbow scene in the **Castro District**. The shops carry everything from decorative household items and froufrou body lotions to potted plants, antiques, and music. Or stroll 24th Street in Noe Valley for boutique fashion. Le Zinc French Bistro is the place to caffeinate. Feeling more adventurous? Zip down to **Mission Cliffs**, one of the largest and friendliest climbing gyms in the country.

6pm As evening falls, join the locals for a cocktail at African-influenced **Bissap Baobab*** in the heart of the Mission District or **Emmy's Spaghetti Shack***, far enough down Mission Street to shake off any threat of tourists. The sunny **Medjool*** is a pleasant spot to nibble on a few tapas along with your cocktails before moving on to dinner.

8pm Dinner Try delicious Peruvian fare in a bright and festive setting at **Limón**. Just down the street at **Range** you'll find a quieter atmosphere for enjoying outstanding comfort food. Alternatively, sample the delicious and inventive North African–inspired dishes at **Baraka** (be sure not to miss the white sangria) perched on a corner atop Potrero Hill.

10pm For a martini and manicure (no kidding), squeeze into the **Beauty Bar**. When your nails are dry, try the sexy lounge and dance space at **Whisper**, a short cab ride away and good until the early hours. The very edgy DJ bar called **Sublounge** requires a car and a very open attitude—think Burning Man. To wrap up your evening, make a visit to the steamy, sweaty, thumping basement at **Club Six** for some seriously late-night fun.

Saturday

9am Grab breakfast at your hotel—especially if that means Café Andrée at the Hotel Rex or Canteen at the Commodore Hotel. Then wake up your mind at the live recording of the weekly radio show **West Coast Live**. Another option is a drive across town to scenic **Baker Beach**, where you can admire the Golden Gate Bridge from the ocean side, not to mention the heavy dose of exposed skin passing you by.

HIP • ITINERARY

12:30pm Lunch Make a trip to Hayes Valley for lunch at **Citizen Cake**. While the food is excellent, eat dessert first. You won't want to miss it. Also in the neighborhood is **Suppenküche**, where the young and hip take their wiener schnitzel and beer.

2pm Hayes Valley is home to some of the city's best and most eclectic high-end retail, including stores devoted to lingerie, fine designer clothes, distinctive home accoutrements, upscale gadgetry, Italian shoes, and more. In the afternoon, browse the design and fashion boutiques, then top things off with a coffee at one of the cafes nearby.

4pm Does your body need a break? Rejuvenate at the **Kabuki Springs and Spa**. On Saturdays, gentlemen can enjoy the communal baths, and everyone is welcome at the spa. Or head back to SoMa and check in with the leading edge of the art world at the **Yerba Buena Center for the Arts**.

7pm For a breath of fresh air—literally—start your night at the **Oxygen Bar**. But if you need something with a little more punch than oxygen, join the scene at **Lime*** in the Castro. Another fine option is a glass of wine at the diminutive and charming **Hôtel Biron** in Hayes Valley.

9pm Dinner Try small, sensational plates at **Andalu*** in the Mission District. Italian comfort food, consistently top of its class, can be had at the now famous **Delfina** up the street. For DJ-lounge ambiance, few outclass SoMa's **Sushi Groove South**.

11pm Fueled up and ready to party, work your way across the city, touching down at such venues as the tiny, very hip DJ bar called **Pink**; an exposed-brick warehouse space, **Mighty**, where serious dancing happens when the event is right; or **The Velvet Lounge** in North Beach, where the patrons come in from far-flung Bay Area villages. Wherever you end up, be sure to wind up at **The EndUp** for one of the best after-hours parties in town. Don't worry about arriving late—the party goes on until Monday morning.

Sunday

9am Feed your soul at **Glide Memorial United Methodist Church**'s famously uplifting services at 9am or 11am. Cecil Williams, a San Francisco institution, preaches social justice with a toe-tapping cadence. If church doesn't appeal, check out activities from one of the other *Perfect Plans*—perhaps a quick visit to the de Young Museum (see p.154) or the Asian Art Museum (see p.82).

11am Brunch It is simply impossible to do better than **Universal Cafe**, the perfect combination of delicious food and modern industrial ambiance. On sunny days, pray for one of the coveted outdoor tables—you just may get lucky. Brunch is also a great time to visit the famed **Zuni Café**.

1pm Have your cab drop you off at Haight Street (at the corner of Ashbury, of course). You're in the heart of the **Haight**. Remnants of the '60s remain, but for the most part fashion has moved on to the cutting edge. Stop in at one of the shops—especially Villain's Vault—you're guaranteed to find things here you won't find on Union Square.

2pm Go west, young man, to **Golden Gate Park**. On Sundays, the main road through the park is closed to traffic, giving those on rollerblades and bikes free reign. Near the park, there are several places to rent gear by the hour.

4pm If you like jazz, drop by the scruffy **Dogpatch Saloon** from 4 to 8pm for a weekly impromptu jam session of the highest quality. If the sun is out, check out the buzzing outdoor patio at **Pilsner Inn**. If a slicker scene appeals, try the bustling Sunday happy hour from 5 to 7pm at **Mecca***. (Note that it serves a Southern-inspired prix fixe dinner on Sundays.)

7pm Dinner Skate late and still in the Haight? You're in luck. It's an easy walk to **RNM Restaurant**, where you can settle in to enjoy their very original take on tapas in a very un-Haight-like high-design setting. Elegant **Eos*** in nearby Cole Valley offers its own heavy dose of sophistication, in the form of outstanding food, wine and décor. To sample something a bit more exotic, try the nouveau Indian small plates at lovely **Tallula** in the Castro, a short cab ride away.

9:30pm Hopefully you had dinner early, because so much great live music and dancing awaits on Sunday nights. In the Mission, there's Salsa Sundays at **El Rio** starting at 8 and at the **Elbo Room** at 9pm. In the Castro, you can hear bands at Prohibition-style **Café du Nord** starting around 8pm, or work your Sunday Top 40 groove thing at **SF Badlands**. Near the downtown hotels is multilevel **Swig**, where an electric blues jam (a tradition in the space that predates the current remodel) starts at 9pm. Cancel your Monday morning meetings and let the good times roll.

Hip San Francisco: The Key Neighborhoods

Castro District, located along Upper Market and south along Castro Street, is the rainbow-power center of the city and a prime stomping ground both day and night for arty, fashion-conscious locals.

The Haight, ever hip and scruffy, is the original hippie heaven and conveniently adjacent to Golden Gate Park. Shopping opps, cheap eateries, and several hipster bars line the Upper Haight from Masonic to Stanyan.

Hayes Valley is adjacent to Lower Haight Street where cutting-edge shops deliver assorted fashionable must-haves for all aspects of life and great restaurants beckon from every corner.

The Mission District is San Francisco's ground zero for hipsters. They flock to its Victorians and gritty streets. On Mission Street, crowds of recent arrivals shop for produce by day, while at night, the young and hip crowd into scores of bars and restaurants.

Potrero Hill and 18th Street, to the east of the Mission District, has been a bastion of iconoclasts and leather-clad hipsters for years. Now it is home of trendier, more affluent sorts and the neighborhood restaurants that cater to them.

SoMa draws hipsters of all stripes to its nightlife scene. It's known for its edgy and eclectic bars and dance clubs—sometimes located on pretty sketchy blocks. Plan accordingly.

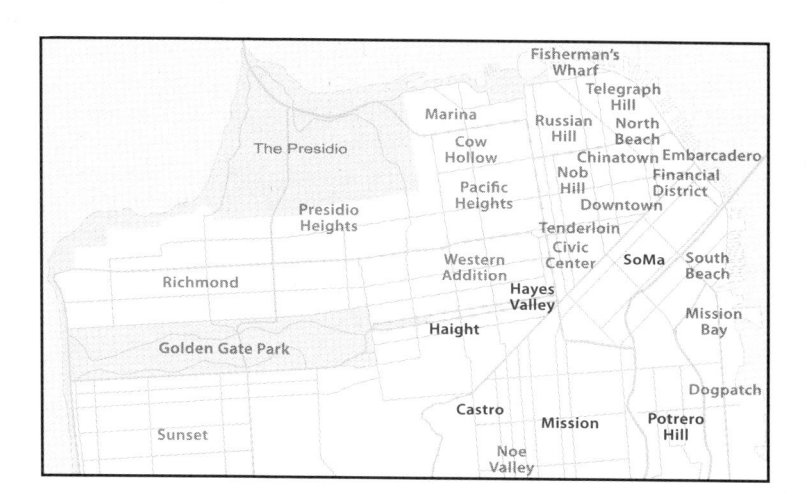

Hip San Francisco:
The Shopping Blocks

Hayes Street

A colorful array of boutiques and art galleries has sprung up along this once-grungy corridor between Franklin and Laguna Streets.

Alabaster An all-white selection of exotic beautiful gifts for the home. 597 Hayes St. (Laguna St.), 415-558-0482

Friend High-end modern accessories and furnishings from across the globe. 401 Hayes St. (Gough St.), 415-552-1717

Minnie Wilde Well-designed hipsterwear for urbanites. (p.119) 519 Laguna St. (Hayes St.), 415-863-9453

Propeller High-end home accessories and furnishings by local artists and designers. 555 Hayes St. (Laguna St.), 415-701-7767

Zonal An eclectic mix of rustic home furnishings and vintage accessories for the home. 568 Hayes St. (Laguna St.), 415-255-9307

Valencia Street

The stretch between 16th and 24th Streets provides an eye-popping variety of places to shop. The retail fare focuses on home furnishings and accessories, both modern and vintage; hipster attire; artsy boutiques; and used books.

Good Vibrations The nationally renowned women-positive sex toy shop. (p.118) 603 Valencia St. (17th St.), 415-522-5460

Laku Locally designed neo-bohemian clothing and accessories in rich textures and colors. 1069 Valencia St. (22nd St.), 415-695-1462

Minnie Wilde Well-designed hipsterwear for urbanites. (p.119) 3266 21st St. (Valencia St.), 415-642-9453

Paxton Gate A boutique where taxidermy mice and flesh eating plants mingle. (p.120) 824 Valencia St. (19th St.), 415-824-1872

Rayon Vert A small and eclectic assortment of whimsical gifts and a staff with impeccable taste in flowers. 3187 16th St. (Guerrero St.), 415-861-3516

Sunhee Moon A wonderful collection of unique fashion-forward clothing designed locally. 3167 16th St. (Guerrero St.), 415-355-1801

X-21 Modern Eclectic, unusual, and vintage items all crowded into one huge space. 890 Valencia St. (20th St.), 415-647-4211

Hip San Francisco: The Hotels

Commodore Hotel • Downtown • Trendy (113 rms)
In mid-2004, the Commodore reopened its cafe as Canteen, a tiny, retro-trendy gem of a place with gray walls and a clover-green counter serving "daring home cooking." On the other side of the hotel entrance is the Red Room, an equally tiny club done entirely in ruby red, which is long past being a new scene but is still a fun place to get a drink among the young and adventurous. The rooms are small and lack views, but they're comfortable, with full baths, amusing Neo-Deco décor, and nautical touches reminiscent of a 1920s cruise ship. Ask for one of the rooms in back, as they tend to be quieter than those facing the street. The sort of people who stay at the Commodore like character, a bargain, and a youthful environment. The typically eclectic group might include a French couple, a young music entrepreneur, a party girl and her friends, an up-and-coming photographer, and a few free spirits. The neighborhood can feel a bit far from the center of things until you realize you're just a couple of blocks from Union Square and North Beach, and very close to hot spots like the Redwood Room, Cortez, and Ruby Skye. Rooms feature walk-in closets. $ 825 Sutter St. (Leavenworth St.), 415-923-6800 / 800-338-6848, thecommodorehotel.com

Hotel des Arts • Downtown • Trendy (51 rms)
One suspects, and earnestly hopes, that this is the way of the future for urban hotels. Hotel des Arts is clean, crisp, situated in an ideal location, ridiculously inexpensive, hip, and favorably predisposed to green policies and practices. The real appeal here, however, is the dramatic art. All of the suites and some of the other rooms have been given over to emerging artists to paint and re-create, floor to ceiling, guided entirely by their muse, whimsy, and vision. The results are, well, jaw-droppingly fabulous. The rooms are each so different that there is no best room per se—just check the options on the website before making a reservation. Certainly that would be enough to recommend this ultramodern hotel in the sly Victorian-era building, but there is much more. The lovely French brasserie Le Central is right downstairs. Chinatown, Union Square, and the Financial District are all within a couple of blocks. It serves a complimentary continental breakfast, offers free wireless Internet, and features all the usual basics, from hair dryers to TVs and irons. In the European tradition, the basic rooms have shared baths, all of which have original Victorian claw-foot tubs. All the rooms have sinks, and many have small refrigerators and microwaves. The lively, diverse clientele ranges from hipster students to savvy business visitors and young European families on holiday. $ 447 Bush St. (Grant Ave.), 415-956-3232 / 866-285-4104, sfhoteldesarts.com

Hotel Diva • Downtown • Modern (115 rms)
The Diva's day has come again. All that edgy Italian furniture from the late '80s feels completely au courant again. Sculptural, brushed-steel headboards, dark purple carpets, futuristic lighting, and dramatic, lounge-style curtains will make you feel all Studio 54–ish. Not to imply it is at all tired or shabby. An investment in great European design rarely goes sour, and thanks to a recent round of

renovations, any tatters have been mended for a smooth, glossy finish across the board. The fact that you can rent an iPod from the concierge says it all. This is home base for hipster fun, from the hard-candy colors of the glass and stainless steel entryway to the free Internet lounges on four floors. If you plan to party all night at the city's premier club, Ruby Skye, the Diva is extremely convenient. For that reason, in addition to the clubby décor, the dance crew likes the Diva. You'll also find a mix of other travelers, from honeymooners to business executives breaking their routine, as well as those in the theater industry. The units include luxury linens, free wireless Internet access, CD players, and all the standard amenities. For a larger bathroom, ask for an 08 or 09 room. Night owls will appreciate the free 24-hour business center for those 3am faxes. If you plan to use your car frequently, choose another hotel, as the valet wait can be infuriating, and if you want a view, look elsewhere. Diva guests are eligible for certain discounts and specials at Tru Spa. $ 440 Geary St. (Mason St.), 415-885-0200 / 800-553-1900, hoteldiva.com

Hotel Rex • Downtown • Timeless (94 rms)

San Francisco has a thriving literary community, including scores of renowned local writers, loads of great bookstores, tons of cafes, several remarkable literary festivals, and now the Hotel Rex. The Rex has been working hard to establish itself as the Algonquin of the West, hosting a variety of book-related events in the 1920s-literary-salon style and infusing the guest experience with a thinking person's pleasures. Hotel Rex is run by the Joie de Vivre company. The name of its game is originality, with plenty of amusing little extras. Here the charming lobby is furnished like Henry James's study, with a globe, leather chairs, reading lamps, antiquarian books, and tasteful portraits of famous writers. The small adjoining bar is the sort of dark-wood and golden-bottle kind of place that makes you want to stop off for a nightcap and a bit of rousing conversation before bed. The rooms, recently renovated, are pure pleasure for those who like a bit of home in their hotel. This is not ultramodern sleek décor. The rooms are aimed more at comfort, wit, and creativity, with sunny paint jobs and comfortable chairs, bold stripes and patterns, unique works of art, a travel book or two, and a number of thoughtful touches, such as pillow-top mattresses and two-line cordless phones with voice mail. Ask for one of the quieter rooms located in the back of the hotel—the best are the King Executives on higher floors. The hotel hosts a wine hour in the evenings, giving guests a chance to socialize. Rex is close to Union Square and the theater district, and not far from the Financial District. Real writers stay here. Those who've been spotted include novelist Po Bronson, mystery writer Domenic Stansberry, and memoirist Tony Cohan. Travelers who enjoy a literary but never stodgy atmosphere will love the Rex. $$ 562 Sutter St. (Mason St.), 415-433-4434 / 800-433-4434, thehotelrex.com

Hotel Triton • Downtown • Trendy (140 rms)

More stylized than stylish, this fun, trendy boutique hotel is a regular haunt for film and music types, as well as hip gays and lesbians and folks who just want to have fun. A few of the small but eye-poppingly furnished rooms have been designed by or in honor of showbiz luminaries, including Jerry Garcia, Carlos Santana, Andy Dick, Woody Harrelson ("Woody's Oasis"), the Red Hot Chili Peppers, and the set designer from *Rent*. The Triton has taken the lead in the city in making its hotel eco-friendly, with impressive efforts to reduce waste, recycle resources, and keep chemical use to a minimum. The entire hotel is cleaned with green products. One whole floor of rooms—the seventh—takes environmental concerns even more seriously, with energy-saving lightbulbs and water saving devices, water and air filtration systems, and organically grown cotton linens and towels. The opportunities to mingle abound: morning coffee in the lobby; a complimentary wine party every evening with a visiting DJ on Friday nights, plus surprise debuts by local musicians, bartenders, and artists, tarot card readings, and chair massage; and the 3 o'clock cookie service. Other freebies include a daily *New York Times*, a 24-hour yoga channel and free yoga kit upon request, a basic workout facility, and morning town car services for the downtown area. If you're traveling solo and seeking some peace, book a tiny Zen Den, complete with incense, a bamboo plant, mechanized wind chimes, the Book of Buddha, and your own image of Goddess Tara to watch over you. $$ 342 Grant Ave. (Bush St.), 415-394-0500 / 800-800-1299, hoteltriton.com

The Phoenix Hotel • Downtown • Trendy (41 rms)

Party like a rock star, and maybe even with a rock star, at the hotel that started the whole hip hotel trend in San Francisco. Accommodations are little more than motor-lodge–style rooms with nicer beds, dressed up with cool paint jobs, tropical bungalow styling, imported island furnishings, and even contemporary pieces by local artists, not to mention in-room bamboo xylophones. Music celebs like REM, Ben Harper, and Sonic Youth name the Phoenix a favorite crash pad. Three rooms and three suites (which include adjacent "tour manager" suites) are situated around a tropical-theme courtyard complete with palapas and a heated outdoor swimming pool with a mural painted on the bottom. The newly incarnated Bambuddha Lounge on the street level provides built-in nightlife. A cost-effective oasis in this somewhat sketchy part of town, the Phoenix is not for everyone. Some people are drawn to its funky charm, friendly staff who know where and when to have fun around town, free parking, free poolside continental breakfast, and the often-rocking bar scene. Others, who should not stay here, find fault with the lack of plush amenities, the trashy 'hood (which is actually fairly central), and the late-night party noise (not a problem if you join the party). Cranky or not, guests enjoy free entrance to the communal baths at the Kabuki Springs and Spa. $ 601 Eddy St. (Larkin St.), 415-776-1380 / 800-248-9466, thephoenixhotel.com

Hip San Francisco: The Restaurants

Andalu • Mission • Fusion/Tapas
Best Latin Restaurants A plush and festive oasis in the still-gritty Mission, Andalu serves up an international take on the small plates craze. Call it tapas if you like, but Spain is only one of the cuisines influencing the kitchen here. Andalu is big on flavor and whimsy. The room is stylish, from the blue ceiling layered with clouds to the huge glassy bar in back to the avant-dressed clientele. Order the delicious but agonizingly tiny ahi tartar tacos with chili and lime (better make that two). The polenta fries are sure to vanish in seconds, and the mini paellas are always a hit. The well-crafted wine list includes sangria, 60 wines by the glass, and tempting flights. Have a drink before or after dinner to chat with natty locals. *Sun-Tue 5:30-10pm, Wed-Thu 5:30-11pm, Fri-Sat 5:30-11:30pm.* $$ 3198 16th St. (Guerrero St.), 415-621-2211, andalusf.com

Bagdad Café • Castro • Diner
Best Late-Night Eats Sure, the spiced fries are good and the burgers are certain to satisfy, but the real reason to visit Bagdad Café, situated on one of the busiest corners of the hip and busy Castro District, is for the people-watching. Grab a table near the big windows—it's hard not to—and enjoy the parade of fit and fashionable residents. The other big appeal is its 24-hour service, a rarity in San Francisco, especially for decent food and a fun atmosphere. By day, men should walk up Market St. toward Castro after their meal in order to visit Rolo, a clothing store worth the effort. *24 hours.* $– 2295 Market St. (16th St.), 415-621-4434

Bar Tartine • Mission • French
The folks behind the fanatically popular Tartine bakery opened a dinner and wine spot in late 2005, complete with antler chandelier. With its easy poise and flawless good taste, Bar Tartine makes a refreshing change to the surrounding dive bars. Stop in for a hearty country-French supper or a glass of good wine and conversation at the marbletop bar. Quiet enough to promote conversation and quirky enough to be inviting, it's a good place to eat or have a drink solo (with a reasonable chance of chatting up your neighbor), as well as a romantic spot to bring a date. *Mon-Wed 5:30-10pm, Thu-Sat 5:30-11pm.* $ 561 Valencia St. (16th St.), 415-487-1600, tartinebakery.com/bar_tartine.htm

Baraka • Potrero Hill • North African
Perched on a windy corner, Baraka occupies a space so small it had to open an equally diminutive lounge around the corner where it sends people waiting for a table. That only adds to the charm of this intimate, romantic spot. The interior has a Moroccan feel, meaning pinhole tin lamps, velvet upholstery in shades of red, and dark, richly draped fabrics. As for the food, it is slightly exotic by California standards, offering Latin and North African flavors that still feel new to our corner of the world. Meatballs with yogurt, stuffed dates with chorizo and Serrano ham, seafood paella—the flavors are arrestingly powerful. A crowd of in-the-know locals packs in here every night. *Daily 5:30-11pm.* $ 288 Connecticut St. (18th St.), 415-255-0387, barakasf.net

HIP • RESTAURANTS

Bissap Baobab • Mission • Senegalese
Drop in at this sexy, unpretentious West African outpost and you may find a sweet bossa nova quintet serenading you as you sip a rum cocktail flavored with hibiscus juice, ginger, or tamarind. You will definitely find your plate heaped with a hearty feast. Dinner is simple and spicy, relying heavily on fried plantains, spicy marinated chicken, stews flavored with cumin and chilies, and couscous. Other satisfying home-style Senegalese dishes include accra, vegetarian beignets made with black-eyed peas and spicy tomato sauce. The scene is refreshingly international and multiethnic, with both an African and Brazilian presence. The servers, like much of the clientele, are young, accented, multiethnic hotties from far-off ports. On weekends, it's crowded and noisy, but that's part of the fun. Dance off that imported African beer around the corner at Little Baobab (3388 19th St.), where DJs spin Afro-Cuban and reggae beats to a hip Mission crowd. *Bissap Baobab: Tue-Sun 6-10:30pm. Little Baobab: Mon-Sat 6pm-2am.* $ 2323 Mission St. (19th St.), 415-826-9287, bissapbaobab.com

Blowfish Sushi • Mission • Japanese
In the early days of the digital era, Blowfish felt like something out of *Blade Runner,* with racy anime features running on TVs above the sushi bar, sexy electronica turned up loud, and tattooed, counterculture divas with weird hair and radical fashions serving overengineered Japanese cuisine. All that is still true, it's just that the times have caught up to the place, so it all feels slightly less avant-garde. The crowd remains urban-edgy, though some of them have grown up and cashed in on their techie-savant skills. Now they bring their Treo and their biz dev guy for deal talk and sushi. Asian fusion dishes are also available. Music is baked into the experience; a pulsing beat keeps things lively even on a Tuesday night. Singles can happily eat and drink at the small bar. *Mon-Thu 11:30am-2:30pm and 5:30-11pm, Fri-Sat 5:30pm-midnight, Sun 5:30-10pm.* $$ 2170 Bryant St. (20th St.), 415-285-3848, blowfishsushi.com

Blue Plate • Mission • Californian
This scruffy, far-off stretch of Mission Street hides several funky gems. The best of them is Blue Plate, a narrow strip of a restaurant with a secluded garden space out back, a crew of intriguing servers, and a consistent knack with highbrow comfort food. Enter and you instantly feel you are on the inside track, eating where the locals-in-the-know eat. The front room is lighter and noisier; tables in the back dining room are more moody and romantic. A favorite is the grilled hearts of romaine salad with bacon, cherry tomato, and avocado. While it does an especially good job with its classic meatloaf and mashed potatoes, the daily collection of dishes rarely stumbles. After dinner, walk a block to El Rio for live music. *Mon-Thu 6-10pm, Fri-Sat 6-10:30pm.* $$ 3218 Mission St. (Valencia St.), 415-282-6777, blueplatesf.com

Boogaloo's • Mission • Diner
After a night out carousing, folks turn up at Boogaloo's starting around 10am. The line, like the breakfast, lasts all day, as young bohemians in their slacker gear gather to hang out and nurse hangovers with bad coffee and inexpensive, generously portioned pancakes, omelets, and scrambles. The weekend crowd matches the servers tattoo for tattoo and piercing for piercing. Weekdays, it's urban mommies with their babies and freelancers with their laptops and newspapers. The food is pretty basic, but the blueberry pancakes are a consis-

tent crowd-pleaser. If you want to observe (and eavesdrop on) the indigenous Mission tribe in its gritty natural habitat, this is the place. *Daily 8am-3pm.* $– ⌷ 3296 22nd St. (Valencia St.), 415-824-4088

Caffe Centro • SoMa • Cafe

South Park reminds one of a quaint, residential cul-de-sac in London, as it was designed to. In the early days of the multimedia explosion, South Park was ground zero and its unofficial midday headquarters and refueling station was Caffe Centro. How many hundreds or even thousands of dot-com deals were done at those green metal tables! Today, it still does a brisk and lively lunch and coffee business serving the hip SoMa media types and brainy entrepreneurs who survived the bust. The sidewalk tables face the park's trees, lawn, and swings, and are invariably sun-dappled. The lunch fare is informal, with the sandwiches, bread salad, and niçoise salad with balsamic vinaigrette the reliable winners for a quick meal. *Mon-Fri 7am-5pm, Sat 8am-4pm.* $– ⌷ 102 South Park (Second St.), 415-882-1500, caffecentro.com

Catch • Castro • Seafood

While the scene in this Castro restaurant is gay friendly, it is also entirely friendly to the non-gay crowd. The vibe is mellow-festive and everyone should feel welcome. Those dining are mostly affluent locals in their thirties and forties looking for great seafood in a beautiful setting without pomp. This handsome spot with exposed brick walls, natural light, and tasteful furnishings serves excellent food and a mean mojito. Take a seat on the sheltered patio or in front of the illuminated array of bottles behind the bar and listen to the chilled-out lounge sounds. The menu is packed with favorites like pan-seared halibut and pepper-seared ahi tuna. The bar, a lively chatting zone before and after dinner, makes a decent nightcap, especially if you are interested in hooking up with a well-groomed local boy. *Mon-Tue 11:30am-3pm and 5:30-9:30pm, Wed-Thu 11:30am-3pm and 5:30-10pm, Fri 11:30am-3pm and 5:30-11pm, Sat 11am-3:30pm and 5:30-11pm, Sun 11am-3:30pm and 5:30-9:30pm.* $ ⌷ 2362 Market St. (Castro St.), 415-431-5000, catchsf.com

Chez Papa Bistrot • Potrero Hill • French Bistro

Where do they find such sizzling-hot French guys to wait tables? Heavens! Gentlemen, don't be alarmed, there are plenty of French women on hand to cut the vibe, but a sexy vibe it remains, one way or another. The tiny dining room and sidewalk tables cram everyone elbow to elbow, which is not necessarily a bad thing. It makes both lunch and dinner a noisy, exciting affair, like a Euro-chic party about to take off. The French bistro cuisine is top notch, serving favorites like New York steak frites, ahi tuna au poivre, and chocolate hazelnut pot de crème. The quiet neighborhood overlooking the high-rises of downtown will make you want to sit back and have another Lillet before ordering. *Mon-Thu 11:30am-3pm and 5:30-10pm, Fri-Sat 11:30am-3pm and 5:30-11pm, Sun 5:30-10pm.* $$ ⌷ 1401 18th St. (Missouri St.), 415-255-0387, chezpapasf.com

Chez Spencer • Mission • French

Chez Spencer seems to sink away into the brickwork. Look closely and you notice the sheltered front patio and the buzz of the pleasantly crowded little bar inside. Tucked into this industrial space is one of the best and most enjoyable French restaurants in town, which attracts a steady crowd of youngish hipsters (in the well-groomed sense) from all over the city. What looks tiny from the outside opens up to double-high ceilings and hunting-lodge rafters that make you want to order the pan-seared antelope, which is excellent. In the middle of the scene is the wood-burning oven, churning out perfect pizzas. In back, another kitchen cranks out the rest of the French country fare. *Mon-Sat 5:30-10:30pm.* $$ ≡ 82 14th St. (Folsom St.), 415-864-2191

Citizen Cake • Hayes Valley • Californian

Hyperbole does not exist strong enough to describe how delicious the cookies and other desserts at Citizen Cake are, but it's not only about sweet stuff. Dinners routinely convert newcomers to the Citizen Cake faith. On weekends, brunch is packed with the young, arty, and disturbingly good-looking denizens of the surrounding neighborhoods. Pass by the window-filled corner and it's hard to resist going in, even if you're not hungry, because after all there's always room for a cookie, a scoop of handmade ice cream, a glass of wine at the bar... The place makes it very easy to feel welcome and at ease, all without compromising on urban style and sophistication. Ideally situated for a meal before or after the symphony, opera, or ballet, it's also a destination restaurant of solid merit. *Tue-Fri 8am-10pm, Sat 10am-10pm, Sun 10am-5pm (9pm when there are symphony, opera, or ballet performances).* $$ ⓘ≡ 399 Grove St. (Gough St.), 415-861-2228, citizencake.com

Delfina • Mission • Italian

Cute waitresses with abundant tattoos and piercings still serve your food at Delfina, where it is still possible to feel like a hipster, and still worth a visit, since the food is so good. However, the glossies have discovered the place, sending droves of upper-middle-class stylish retirees and their platinum Amex cards rushing for the phone to make reservations months in advance. That is the price a restaurant pays for being consistently on, and Delfina has been that for several years now. The Italian menu changes daily and offers organic greens, handmade pastas, roasted chicken, flatiron steak, and other favorites. Desserts and the accompanying dessert wines are notably well chosen. It's a tight fit in the dining room, so leave the train and bustle at home. In warm months, the patio in back is the way to go. *Sun-Thu 5:30-10pm, Fri-Sat 5:30-11pm.* $$ ≡ 3621 18th St. (Guerrero St.), 415-552-4055, delfinasf.com

Emmy's Spaghetti Shack • Mission • Comfort Food

A good place to grab a casual late-night supper among local hipsters. *See Hip Nightlife, p.110, for details.* $ F≡ 18 Virginia St. (Mission St.), 415-206-2086

Eos • Haight • Fusion

Eos was one of the first restaurants locally to do sophisticated Asian fusion cuisine, and one of the first to open an ambitious (though minuscule) wine bar. Part of the secret to its ongoing success has been an inclination to continue to evolve. The menu has shifted from large plates and elaborate desserts to small plates. The décor has kept pace with the times as well, currently done in shades of pale green with bamboo accents and a jet-black bar. The minimalist aesthetic with emphasis on tasteful modern art remains. Unbeatable dishes include the ahi tuna and mango rolls, and lemongrass prawn cakes. If dinner is not on the agenda, wedge yourself into a seat, if you can get one, at the postage-stamp of a wine bar next door and sample from the hefty wine list. The crowd mirrors the inhabitants of the neighborhood, 99 percent of whom are under forty and dressed urban à la mode. *Sun-Thu 5:30-10pm, Fri-Sat 5:30-11pm.* $ ⓘⒷ≡ 901 Cole St. (Carl St.), 415-566-3063, eossf.com

Home • Castro • Traditional American

It's all about the fireplace patio at Home. And brunch, when you can build your own Bloody Mary. And dinner, when the comfort food runneth over and the succulent pot roast arrives just the way you always wished mom would make it. And the macaroni and cheese, which can cure anything from the blues to the mean reds. It's also about the people-watching, some of the best in the city, with walls of windows facing the pedestrians of the Castro District, most of whom are some combination of fashionable, eccentric, and good-looking. The atmosphere is relaxed and cozy, but still modern and festive. Stop by for a glass of wine in the evening, when the bar is bustling with the young and fashionable. *Mon-Thu 5-10pm, Fri 5-11pm, Sat 10am-2pm and 5-11pm, Sun 10am-2pm and 5-10pm.* $ ⓘⒻ≡ 2100 Market St. (Church St.), 415-503-0333, home-sf.com

Iluna Basque • North Beach • Tapas

Iluna Basque offers a tempting range of hearty small plates, from crab meat and thyme croquettes to chicken stew with onions and bell peppers. The dining room is small but sexy, with red walls, dark wood tables, and brushed steel accents. Windows look out on Washington Square. Its long communal table, perfect for solo diners, creates a convivial atmosphere conducive to good conversation and meeting new people. It stays open late on the weekends, catering to the crowds coming and going from the many night spots nearby. Popular with the young—but not impossibly young—set, Iluna Basque feels too racy for business dinners. Save it for something juicier. *Sun-Thu 5:30-11pm, Fri-Sat 5:30-midnight.* $ ⓘ≡ 701 Union St. (Powell St.), 415-402-0011, ilunabasque.com

Lime • Castro • American/Tapas

Swinging '60s décor, buzzing Castro scene, and global comfort food in a fun neighborhood. *See Hip Nightlife, p.112, for details.* $ ⓘⒻ≡ 2247 Market St. (Noe St.), 415-621-5256, lime-sf.com

Limón • Mission • Peruvian

Best Latin Restaurants Savory, hearty Peruvian food in its most basic form is already quite delicious. When it gets polished up and refined with international influences, it's an instant winner. Limón occupies a sleek, modern, vibrant space, laid out like a loft, with a split-level dining room. In front, the ceiling rises two stories, giving the fresh lime-colored walls and bold art a chance to shine. The best tables are downstairs in front, where the lighting and the view of the ultra-hipsters inside and out is best. The trademark flavors are spicy cayenne and tangy lime, which turn up in hearty meat and seafood dishes. Paper-thin slivers of onion add extra flavor to the already flavor-packed spicy Chicharron de Pollo. *Mon-Thu 11:30am-3pm and 5–10:30pm, Fri 11:30am-3pm and 5-11pm, Sat noon-11pm, Sun noon-10pm.* $$ ≡ 524 Valencia St. (16th St.), 415-252-0918, limon-sf.com

Luna Park • Mission • Traditional American

A Mission favorite, Luna Park feels like a dark, seedy bar but dishes out American fare with abundant skill. The reasonable prices keep the crowd young and hip, while the superior mojitos help diners maintain a healthy outlook. Many of the menu items, like the ambiance and service, reflect a love of comfort. The food is all about hearty satisfaction via the tried-and-true route, such as Cobb salad, lemon risotto with grilled shrimp, and roast chicken. Indulge, converse, laugh, then walk to any of a dozen nearby bars. Beware the long wait for a table. *Mon-Thu 11:30am-2:30pm and 5:30-10:30pm, Fri 11:30am-2:30pm and 5:30-11:30pm, Sat 11:30am-3pm and 5:30-11:30pm, Sun 11:30am-3pm and 5:30-10pm.* $ 694 Valencia St. (18th St.), 415-553-8584, lunaparksf.com

Mecca • Castro • Californian
Local hipsters congregate here for the excellent cuisine and lively bar scene. See Hip Nightlife, p.113, for details. $$ 2029 Market St. (Dolores St.), 415-621-7000, sfmecca.com

Medjool • Mission • Mediterranean/North African
Medjool is a relative newcomer with style and bravado. The dining room has proportions like a gymnasium, yet it exudes warmth like a Tunisian oasis. The walls and furniture are done in Van Gogh yellow, zesty tangerine, and cornflower blue, echoing the vibrant cuisine on offer, which covers southern France, Italy, Spain, Morocco, Tunisia, and parts of the Middle East. From chicken with almond-pomegranate sauce to lamb and fig tagine, a lively array of dishes are served as small plates. Medjool is committed to creating an environment where the young and hip will flock. Don't miss the rooftop brunch. *Restaurant Mon-Thu 5-10pm, Fri-Sat 5-11pm. Bar 5:30pm-2am.* $$ Elements Hotel, 2522 Mission St. (21st St.), 415-550-9055, medjoolsf.com

The Public • SoMa • New American
The SoMa nightlife district along the 11th Street corridor has been experiencing a renaissance of late. A key element of the new, fresh vibe is the Public, an adept blend of nightclub energy with fine dining sophistication. Housed in a historic brick building with loft ceilings, exposed beams, and large arching windows, this relative newcomer feels like it's been around for years—in a good way. The foyer gives onto a comfortable bar area where friends and friends-to-be can gather and chill while they wait for a table. DJs and an occasional trio provide musical ambiance. In the kitchen, American-Italian comfort food is the theme. Highlights include the Tuscan vegetable soup with a poached egg and duck sugo with fresh pappardelle. *Tue-Sat 6-9:30pm. Drinks Tue-Thu 6pm-midnight, Fri-Sat 6pm-2am.* $$ 1489 Folsom St. (11th St.), 415-552-3065, thepublicsf.com

Range • Mission • New American
Range is a sunny, inviting, sophisticated venue in a great location with a hip mood that appeals both day and night. Light walls, diner stools around the bar, wood accents, and plenty of original artwork and photography set a comfortable, uplifting ambiance conducive to conversation. The food focuses on seasonal ingredients and dishes such as slow-cooked halibut, coffee-rubbed pork shoulder, and marinated fennel with peaches and chèvre. In addition to wine, Range pours a lovely white sangria and an extensive list of vodkas and tequilas. *Sun, Mon, Wed-Thu 5:30-10pm, Fri-Sat 5:30-11pm.* $ 842 Valencia St. (20th St.), 415-282-8283, rangesf.com

RNM Restaurant • Haight • New American/Tapas

Best Trendy Tables RNM feels like New York, a compliment suggesting it conveys an attitude of easy, even worldly sophistication. A welcome bit of polished, modern style in the otherwise nitty-gritty Lower Haight, RNM specializes in small-plate servings. Grab a table in the upper-level dining area and you'll be well perched to observe the action in the main dining room. Menu highlights include porcini-crusted day boat scallops and a succulent rack of Australian lamb on mint and Parmesan-scented farro. If you need further proof that the place feels like New York, check out the tribute to the White Castle burger, classed up for the refined West Coast audience. The crowd is hip and sexy, drawing from a large pool of slick hipsters indigenous to the area. Go on a Thursday night and hit Milk, a few blocks west, for a hip-hop session afterward. *Tue-Thu 5:30-10pm, Fri-Sat 5:30-11pm.* $$ 598 Haight St. (Steiner St.), 415-551-7900, rnmrestaurant.com

Slow Club • Mission • Californian

The Slow Club was slow before slow food was cool, as they say. It is an institution in what has been, until very lately, a no-man's-land neighborhood. Today it serves excellent California-style cuisine to a loyal crowd of hip Media Gulch locals. The space is small and dark with low ceilings and minimal, industrial accoutrements—concrete floors, steel railings, porthole windows, plain wooden tables and chairs, open kitchen, tiny rectangle of a bar in back. The star is the flawless food. The pastas are fresh, lively, and succulent, the meats done to perfection. With aioli and balsamic onions, this is the best burger in town. While the atmosphere is friendly, don't expect to make new acquaintances. The bar is too small to encourage much mingling, and locals focus on eating and talking to their friends. *Open for coffee and pastries weekdays 7-11am; Mon-Thu 11:30am-2:30pm and 6:30-10pm, Fri 11:30am-2:30pm and 6:30-11pm, Sat 10am-2:30pm and 6-11pm, Sun 10am-2:30pm.* $ 2501 Mariposa St. (Hampshire St.), 415-241-9390, slowclub.com

Sneaky Tiki • SoMa • Polynesian

Sneaky Tiki is a decidedly modern and yet entirely retro take on the beloved tiki theme. We're not talking kitsch, or not entirely. This is wee but high-end tiki complete with spherical fish tanks, *Star Trek*-ish uniforms, draped semi-private booths (adjustable stereo! personal call buttons!); a cocktail lounge serving fruity drinks; DJs spinning (loud) house music; valet parking; and, yes, pan-Asian fare prepared with style. The menu focuses on grilled meats and fish with various dipping sauces. Try the beef jerky with coriander and peppercorn and the whole bass steamed in a banana leaf with chili and kaffir lime, then satisfy your island sweet tooth with the Bikini Platter assortment of tropical desserts. *Mon-Fri 11am-4pm and 5-10pm, Sat-Sun 5-10pm.* $ 1582 Folsom St. (12th St.), 415-701-8454, sneakytiki-sf.com

Soluna Cafe & Lounge • Hayes Valley • American

This place somehow manages to do it all. Velvet booths, velvet pillows, and velvety drapes help create a relaxed and cozy but still chic living room feel at Soluna. The menu is similar; full of well-wrought favorites, including a number of tasty salads, that are quite content not to push any boundaries. With a handsome view of City Hall, they get a bustling, business-oriented lunch crowd, then cross over to a quieter scene in the evenings, which, surprise! turns clubby around 10pm. The DJs start spinning, the hotties in their heels and halters arrive, and the place gets bumpin' with the local crew of partiers. *Mon-Fri 11:30am-2:30pm, Tue-Sat 5-9:30pm and happy hour Tue-Sat 4-6pm.* $$ 272 McAllister St. (Larkin St.), 415-621-2200, solunasf.com

Suppenküche • Hayes Valley • German
Perched at the western end of the Hayes Valley strip, Suppenküche is a robustly lively German outpost staffed by Bavarian hotties of both sexes who will make you scrub your brain for a good come-on line. The seating—mostly benches—and the décor—simple blond woods and whites with the occasional lederhosen display—evokes an Alpine wirtshaus or local pub. It's nearly always crowded for dinner, with the young and stylish crammed shoulder to shoulder around the central bar, lifting, what else, great, tall glasses of golden beer. The food is what you might expect: sausages, lentil soup, potato pancakes, wiener schnitzel (breaded pork loin), and pork chops, all skillfully prepared. The bar can be a great place to meet new people, some of whom you might end up sharing a bench with for dinner. *Mon-Sat 5-10pm, Sun 10am-2:30pm and 5-10pm.* $ 525 Laguna St. (Hayes St.), 415-252-9289, suppenkuche.com

Sushi Groove South • SoMa • Sushi
Best Sushi Restaurants Oh, it's hip all right. Very hip. So hip, in fact, that those uncertain of their hipster status may balk and run at the big, unmarked iron door guarding the entrance. Fear not, it's a surprisingly friendly place (not that you shouldn't step out looking your fashion-forward best) and the hostess will make you feel right at home. The sushi? Excellent. Modern. Slightly creative, tending to California-influenced rolls. Other dishes, such as the lettuce cups filled with barbecue beef, will delight those not in the mood for fish. Ambiance? Edgy, bordering on night-clubby. The crowd? Hot, young, sexy, and often dressed to make the most of all three. Several good lounges are within walking distance for those with an escort (the neighborhood is a bit gritty). As for the beat, with DJs spinning nightly, there definitely is one. *Mon-Tue 6-10pm, Wed-Thu 6-10:30pm, Fri-Sat 6-11:30pm.* $$ 1516 Folsom St. (11th St.), 415-503-1950

Tablespoon • Various • New American
Not unlike its moniker, Tablespoon is long and skinny, with tables suited to couples, not groups, and a strip of bar seating running along one side. Upscale comfort food is their shtick—think macaroni and cheese, Caesar salad, pork tenderloin, and succulent braised lamb shanks. Flattering amber lighting, handsome minimal décor, friendly service, and plenty of smart-talking, designer-clothes-wearing local talent complete the favorable feel of the place that has a loyal following. Tablespoon isn't a destination restaurant, but if you are in the neighborhood, you will feel like you've discovered a hidden treasure. *Mon-Sat 6pm-midnight, Sun 5-10pm.* $$ 2209 Polk St. (Vallejo St.), 415-268-0140, tablespoonsf.com

Tallula • Castro • Indian/Fusion/Tapas
Alternately described as bohemian, ethnic, and artistic, Tallula is a fantasy come to life. What if you knew a sexy Indian artist who trained in the kitchens of Paris and had connections in the California organic farming community, and she invited you to a fabulous dinner party at her intimate loft apartment? What if, indeed. That's Tallula, our lady of the crimson rose, blushing peach, and sunset

gold walls. Tallula of the open beams, stained glass, and gauzy curtains. Tallula of the lemon and cilantro potato pancakes with tamarind and date chutney. Unique, inviting, and entirely stylish, this is life beyond curry. Bring a companion and partake of a sake concoction at the small lounge downstairs among the colorful Castro crowd (meaning energetic, coiffed, and varied), then climb the curving, beat-up, narrow staircase to your table in one of four dining rooms. San Francisco is only now getting its Indian groove thoroughly on. Tallula, with its warmth and idiosyncratic style, is leading the way. *Daily 5pm to close.* $$ 4230 18th St. (Diamond St.), 415-437-6722, tallulasf.com

Tartine • Mission • Bakery/Cafe
Never try to deny Tartine devotees of their fix. They will be ruthless in the pursuit of their sugary cinnamon-orange morning bun, Scharffen Berger pain au chocolat, or lemon meringue cake. Better to give in and join the line out the door, as this is perhaps the best bakery in town. The crowd of diehard, dyed-in-the-wool San Franciscans of all ages that hangs out here will delight most any visitor. Doesn't anyone around here have a job? No. They are all freelance creatives, artists, dot-com millionaires in disguise, professional foodies, or Noe Valley mommies. Studded lesbians, bike messengers, woolly intellectuals, keen-eyed novelists, they're all here, worshipping the almighty latte. For a light lunch, have a pressed mozzarella and tapenade sandwich and a glass of wine. *Mon 8am-7pm, Tue-Wed 7:30am-7pm, Thu-Fri 7:30am-8pm, Sat 8am-8pm, Sun 9am-8pm.* $ 600 Guerrero St. (18th St.), 415-487-2600, tartinebakery.com

Universal Cafe • Mission • Californian
Best Brunches Universal has found a nice groove over the years. The tiny space, outfitted with industrial-grade metal and wood gear, is used with remarkable efficiency. A bentwood bench runs the length of one wall, with tables spaced along it. A tiny marble bar looks over the open kitchen. On sunny days and warm nights, outdoor tables fill up out front. It is a friendly, handsome scene populated with friendly, handsome people. Weekend brunch is pure pleasure, with dishes that go above and beyond the ordinary. At dinner, it often includes a grilled steak, well-composed salads, salmon, risotto, and pasta. The romance factor is high at Universal, where the crowd is couples or pairs of couples. Brunch lures in gaggles of friends lounging after a long week or night out and young urbanites showing off a hip city spot to their parents. *Tue-Thu 5:30-9:30pm, Fri 11:30am-2:30pm and 5:30-10:30pm, Sat 9am-2:30pm and 5:30-10:30pm, Sun 9am-2:30pm and 5:30-9:30pm.* $ 2814 19th St. (Bryant St.), 415-821-4608, universalcafe.net

Walzwerk • Mission • German
The East Germans have arrived! This funky cache of über-hipdom kicks out hearty East German fare with no-frills panache. Walzwerk accurately re-creates a saucy little dive typical of an East German village, complete with saucy waitresses, saucy cooks, saucy visitors crowding the tables and carrying on in a host of Euro languages, and saucy dishes that will leave you well fueled and ready to hit the town. The décor evokes a clean and creative but impoverished aesthetic common to shared student apartments in, say, Leipzig, circa 1994, meaning sixties-era album covers used as art, a big HiFi poster, nostalgic framed portraits of Lenin, and retread chrome chairs. Beyond the fun ambiance and hip crowd, the food makes a nice change. The breast of chicken stuffed with apples and bacon with

sun-dried cherry sauce is a big favorite. A dozen German beers round out the good times. You are mere blocks away from the Mission hot spots and not far from the 11th Street nightlife corridor. *Daily 5:30-10pm.* $ 381 S. Van Ness Ave. (15th St.), 415-551-7181, walzwerk.com

Woodward's Garden • Mission • Californian
Woodward's Garden is a quiet, unassuming, artful little place. Though there are all of eleven tables, you will probably land one without too much of a wait. Due to its diminutive stature, location, or possibly its slightly eccentric style, Woodward's Garden has remained a secret known only to foodie locals. Stop in for the grilled persimmon and baby arugula salad, the pork chop with apple-shallot sauce, or the caramelized pear stuffed with chèvre with prosciutto and frisée and you will understand what they're raving about. For dessert, be sure to order the vanilla crème brûlée with chocolate mousse and walnut biscotti. *Tue-Sat 6-11pm. Cafe Sat-Sun 8am-8:30pm.* $$ 1700 Mission St. (Duboce Ave.), 415-621-7122, woodwardsgarden.com

Zuni Café • Hayes Valley • Mediterranean
Best Always-Hot Restaurants Chef Judy Rodgers has made Zuni Café a landmark in the city, serving rustic Mediterranean cuisine of the highest mark for over twenty years in the same location. The restaurant itself, with its copper bar extending from the tiny cocktail tables up front to the art-filled dining room in back, feels like a rambling house. Along with the Caesar salad, the dish everyone loves is the roasted chicken for two with Tuscan bread salad with pine nuts and currants. Beyond the stylish yet comfortable setting, savory dishes expertly prepared, and festive mood, one of the nicest things about Zuni is the service. Servers are friendly, professional, and know what they are talking about. The Zuni style crosses all borders between people. From young hipsters to gay businessmen to suburban couples, everyone feels at home. Brunch is excellent, and the cocktail scene is lively. *Tue-Sat 11:30am-midnight, Sun 11am-11pm.* $$ 1658 Market St. (Franklin St.), 415-552-2522

Hip San Francisco: The Nightlife

Andalu • Mission • Restaurant Bar
A handsome crowd gathers at the sparkling bar for wine, sangria, and cocktails. See Hip Restaurants, p.98, for details. F= 3198 16th St. (Guerrero St.), 415-621-2211, andalusf.com

Anú • SoMa • Bar/Nightclub
This postage stamp of a bar in a persistently seedy stretch of town can be surprisingly hip. DJs spin every night, mixing solid house, techno, and hip-hop. Once in a while, a local or even an international celebrity DJ drops in, word gets out, and the line spills out the door. The crowd is eclectic, but uniformly young and hip; the sort of folks who know what "solid house" means. The skid-row environs make the relatively non-dive interior a surprise. The fact that the small plates are edible is even more of a shocker. And most surprising of all? The bartenders do their own fruit-infused vodkas, then shake them into delicious cocktails. The dance floor is minuscule—not necessarily a bad thing, at least not until it goes from crowded in a naughty way to crowded in an uncomfortable way on the weekend and Wednesday nights. Watch your step on arrival and departure in this sketchy 'hood. *Mon 9pm-2am, Tue-Fri 5pm-2am, Sat 7pm-2am.* C B = 43 Sixth St. (Market St.), 415-543-3505, anu-bar.com

Bar Tartine • Mission• Wine Bar
An ideal spot to perch at the bar with a fine glass of red wine before heading out on the town. See Hip Restaurants, p.98, for details. F= 561 Valencia St. (16th St.), 415-487-1600, tartinebakery.com/bar_tartine.htm

Beauty Bar • Mission • Theme Bar
Quirky doesn't go far enough to describe tiny, pink, eccentric Beauty Bar, a Mission District favorite with a drag queen tinge. Often it's too crowded to dance or even wedge your way inside, which makes for a festive, if claustrophobic, scene. If you like the chaotic energy of a crowded night spot, you're in business. The place takes the kitschy '60s-era beauty salon motif pretty seriously, with hairdryer chairs and free Urban Decay manicures when you buy a cocktail Wednesday-Friday from 6 to 10pm. While there are better places to talk and dance, there are few better for meeting fellow hipsters over a stiff drink and hard-to-resist music. On weekends, wiggle room is at a premium as dressed-up twenty- and thirty-year-olds take the place by storm. During the week, it's more low-key. *Mon-Fri 5pm-2am, Sat-Sun 7pm-2am.* = 2299 Mission St. (19th St.), 415-285-0323, beautybar.com

Bissap Baobab • Mission • Restaurant Bar
When was the last time you had a Senegalese cocktail serenaded by live music. See Hip Restaurants, p.99, for details. B= 2323 Mission St. (19th St.), 415-826-9287, bissapbaobab.com

Blue Cube • Downtown • Nightclub
Have you been to Burning Man? Do you own more than one article of Diesel clothing? Have you danced until at least 4 in the morning within the last six months? If you did not answer yes to at least one of these questions, you probably won't feel at home at Blue Cube. But if you're ready to go deep underground or mingle in and fake it, grab your faux-fur vest and your platform go-go boots and head to Blue Cube to hook up with your raver brethren. The venue is a bi-level behemoth of a place in an ultramodernized brick-and-steel warehouse, fitted out with a state-of-the-art sound system and very edgy art shows. *Open for events. Check the website.* C B ≡ 34 Mason St. (Market St.), 415-392-4833, bluecubesf.com

Café du Nord • Castro • Performance
It's easy to believe Café du Nord was a notorious Prohibition speakeasy nearly a century ago. The interior boasts genuine Victorian accents and flavor, from the exposed brick to decorative paneling and wainscoting to a 40-foot hand-carved mahogany bar. Descend the stairs and you enter a dark, red-walled subterranean world where the bartenders know what they are doing and the tiny stage in back hosts great live acts seven nights a week. They book plenty of swing and bebop, and all kinds of great bands show up here. Try to catch Lavay Smith and Her Red Hot Skillet Lickers, a homegrown diva with a voice to melt your kneecaps. *Open daily one hour before showtime until 2am.* C F ≡ 2170 Market St. (15th St.), 415-861-5016, cafedunord.com

Catch • Castro • Restaurant Bar
The bar at this seafood spot draws a chatty Castro crowd before and after dinner. *See Hip Restaurants, p.100, for details.* F ≡ 2362 Market St. (Castro St.), 415-431-5000, catchsf.com

Club Six • SoMa • DJ Bar/Nightclub
The neighborhood may be a bit ragged, but Club Six is on top of its gritty, slightly punk-flavored game. Grab a drink upstairs in the loft-style lounge, relax on any of the many sofas, contemplate the art of the moment, and listen to a live band of just about any persuasion imaginable. When you're ready, plunge into the basement, where the ceiling is low, the air is hot, the music is loud, and everyone is dancing. Tuesdays host a mixed bag, including live jazz and spoken word; Thursdays is the regular reggae dance party called Give Thankz; weekends bring all kinds of talent, from famous DJs to electronica to experimental videos. The crowd is young and hip. Club Six was transformed into the S&M-flavored Cat Scratch Club for the filming of *Rent*. Still not convinced? Mos Def is said to have done his after-show here. Now that's hip. *Tue and Thu 9pm-2am, Fri-Sun 9pm-4am.* C ≡ 60 Sixth St. (Mission St.), 415-863-1221, clubsix1.com

Dogpatch Saloon • Potrero Hill • Dive Bar/Jazz Club
Want to feel like the ultimate jazz insider? Drop by the Dogpatch Saloon on Sunday at 4pm to witness an impromptu jazz jam with local musicians. The place is a tiny dive on the wrong side of Potrero Hill—all the more surprising when you settle into a booth and start soaking in the musical genius. A fiver opens the door to cocktails, four hours of live jazz, and free snacks and chili. You can get your fill and still have time for a Sunday night dinner somewhere glam. If you are in the mood for live jazz other nights of the week, it is worth

calling, as they often have something of interest on stage. *Mon-Wed 4pm-close, Thu-Sun noon to close (usually around midnight). Live jazz Sun 4-8pm.* C B = 2496 Third St. (22nd St.), 415-643-8592

El Rio • Mission • Dive Bar/Performance
Best Neighborhood Bars Scruffy but lovable, El Rio offers a consistently good time for young hipsters looking to get their groove going on the cheap. Several rooms, a patio decorated with Christmas lights, and a mixture of DJs and live music keep things lively all week. TeMA, the regular Friday night world beat dance party, is a sure hit that pulls in big crowds of twenty-somethings. It's also fun to stop by for Sunday Salsa, starting at 3pm with a free barbecue while it lasts out on the patio. There's always something going on, from mini film festivals with movies shown outdoors (dress warmly) to live flamenco music and dance, free local oysters at 5pm on most Fridays, and late afternoon DJs spinning reggae and hip-hop—plus Caribbean snacks—on second Saturdays. *Mar-Nov Mon-Thu 5pm-2am, Fri-Sun 3pm-2am. Dec-Feb hours vary. Call ahead or check website.* C B = 3158 Mission St. (César Chavez St.), 415-282-3325, elriosf.com

Elbo Room • Mission • Dive Bar/Performance
Scruffy, dim, and not terribly clean, the Elbo Room might be the sort of place to avoid, if it weren't for the terrific repertoire of daily live music. Downstairs is a bar, nothing fancy, but popular. Upstairs is live music just about every night of the week. The music varies from acid jazz to electronica to indie rock to Afrofunk to Latin rock—anything likely to appeal to the musically omnivorous post-collegiate city kids that throng the place. Thirty-somethings and even open-minded forty-somethings can throw on their favorite pair of Diesel jeans, the latest retro Pumas, and a smartass T-shirt to taste what the younger generation is listening to these days. *Daily 5pm-2am.* C = 647 Valencia St. (17th St.), 415-552-7788, elbo.com

Element Lounge • Nob Hill • Lounge
A stylish lounge and dance spot done in naturalistic, Zen-inspired, elemental materials—steel, slabs of stone, wood, and the glow of candles—Element Lounge attracts a well-dressed party crowd that's ready to dance. Even the exposed brick walls take on a natural feel. The music is hip-hop and house dance music, sure to keep the crowd moving. Best of all is the Akasha Room, separated from the dance floor by windowed steel partitions, with a stone center that seems to glow, attracting people to the surrounding couches like moths to a flame. Element can be hit or miss as far as the crowd goes. Keep an open mind and drop by on a Saturday night. *Tue-Thu 9pm-2am, Fri-Sat 9pm-3am.* C = 1028 Geary St. (Polk St.), 415-440-1125, elementlounge.com

Emmy's Spaghetti Shack • Mission • Restaurant Bar
Emmy's evokes scrappy East Village hip and caters to a crowd of down-home Mission hipsters in their twenties and thirties. It is small and funky, with an artsy vibe, vintage aprons strung across the room, and Thursday-Saturday a DJ cooking up some magic from the middle of the tiny dining room. There's a four-seater bar that makes a great spot for a single to roost over a glass of wine and a late supper. The food is good, reasonably priced, and served after most places are closed. Some locals virtually live on the spaghetti with meatballs. *Fri-Sat 5:30pm-midnight, Sun-Thu 5:30-11pm.* F = 18 Virginia St. (Mission St.), 415-206-2086

HIP • NIGHTLIFE

The EndUp • SoMa • Nightclub
Best Late-Night Hangouts A nightlife institution, the EndUp is exactly what it sounds like: the place to end up after all the other clubs and parties shut down. The facilities are comfortable but not fancy. There's a heated patio that gets bumping, a small dance floor, a fireplace. The crowd includes everything from gay to scruffy Burning Man hip to dance floor divas in their slinky Prada whatever. Saturday night keeps right on going through Sunday and into Monday, and has for thirty years. Fridays from 10pm to 6am are Fag Fridays immediately followed by the mother of all after-after-after parties from 6am-1pm. The best, however, is Sunday night's long-running Devotion party, starting at 8pm and going strong until 4am Monday. Job? What job? *Thu 10:30pm-4:30am, Fri 10pm-6am, Sat 6am-1pm and 10pm-6am, Sun 6am-4am.* C= 401 Sixth St. (Harrison St.), 415-646-0999, theendup.com

Eos • Haight • Wine Bar
A tiny wine bar that draws a casually sophisticated local crowd. *See Hip Restaurants, p.101, for details.* B= 901 Cole St. (Carl St.), 415-566-3063, eossf.com

EZ5 • Financial District • Bar/Nightclub
EZ5 is best around happy hour, when a weird mix of Chinese hipsters, business geeks, and loungy types mingle side by side. The décor is part nightclub, part boudoir, and part retro Chinese love den, with a dash of 12-year-old-girl bedroom thrown in for good measure. The walls are orange. The bar is reflex blue. The cushions are pink, red, and orange. And it's all topped with a disco ball. DJs mix whatever they please starting at 6pm nightly. *Mon-Fri 4pm-2am, Sat 6pm-2am.* = 682 Commercial St. (Kearny St.), 415-362-9321, ez5bar.com

Home • Castro • Restaurant Bar
The bar that runs the length of this popular Castro restaurant is always packed *See Hip Restaurants, p.102, for details.* F= 2100 Market St. (Church St.), 415-503-0333, home-sf.com

Hôtel Biron • Hayes Valley • Wine Bar
Burrow into this tiny but tasteful hole in the exposed brick wall, and you will discover a Parisian-style wonderland of art, wine, light snacks and good music. The wine list bears the signs of having been very carefully selected by someone who knows his reds. Hôtel Biron is an ideal stop for a glass of wine and some intelligent conversation before dinner—you can actually hear what the other person is saying. But unless you want to chat up the bartender, bring your own companion, as the scene is generally fairly subdued—better for friends and couples than mingling. *Daily 5pm-2am.* B= 45 Rose St. (Gough St.), 415-703-0403, hotelbiron.com

Lexington Club • Mission • Bar
Best Gay Bars and Clubs A sea of gritty young sexy girls in their gritty, twenty-something tattoos and tank tops awaits at the Lexington Club most nights. Technically, guys are allowed in, but you'd best behave, as this is a formidable crew. One wrong move, and you'll get the mass stink eye of your life. A new female arrival is sure to get the once over at the bar, especially if she is looking sharp in her boy-cut hair or hipster dreadlocks. The setting is bo-ho fantasy, with beautiful vintage woodwork, church pews for benches, blood red walls, and art

shows of good quality, plus a pool table and jukebox. Get a can of cheap beer and do your best to chat up the smart, educated, sexy young things. Be sure to check out the artfully embellished bathrooms. *Mon-Thu 5pm-2am, Fri-Sat 3pm-2am.* 3464 19th St. (Lexington St.), 415-863-2052, lexingtonclub.com

Lime • Castro • Bar

The swinging '60s décor at brand-new Lime will make you wish you had a pair of white vinyl gogo boots to go with your best polyester miniskirt. Futuristic white plastic designer chairs contrast with the dark walls and floor for a visual ka-pow, and the front windows are tinted pink, like much of the interior, which says something about the Lime outlook. The cocktail scene both before and after dinner is a winner, with a full stock of great-looking fashionistas and Castro-zone hipsters to ogle and schmooze. If you dine, you will enjoy a global menu of comfort foods, such as the trio of miniburgers and the tandoori chicken with yogurt sauce. Yeah, baby! *Mon-Thu 5pm-midnight, Fri-Sat 5pm-1am, Sun 10:30am-3pm and 5pm-midnight.* 2247 Market St. (Noe St.), 415-621-5256, lime-sf.com

Little Baobab • Mission • Nightclub

DJs spin Afro-Cuban and reggae beats to a hip Mission crowd. *See Bissap Baobab in Hip Restaurants, p.99, for details.* 3388 19th St. (Mission St.), 415-826-9287, bissapbaobab.com

Luna Lounge • SoMa • Lounge/Nightclub

Part bar, part lounge, part dance club, Luna succeeds best at the last, notably when a specially promoted party (such as the on-again, off-again Sensual) brings in the peeps. The setting is pleasing enough, with spacy lunar-landscape blue lighting in the bar area, peekaboo windows onto the main dance floor, and a ventilated smoking lounge. There's a futuristic white room for overflow dancing and a second DJ. The crowd is young and ready to party hard on weekends. Things don't usually get going until 11pm, and often run after hours. Dress your best and prepare to do battle with the doorman. *Wed-Sat 10pm-close.* 1192 Folsom St. (Eighth St.), 415-626-6043, lunaloungesf.org

Madrone Lounge • Haight • Bar/Art Gallery

Madrone is the low-key hangout of choice on Tuesday nights, when it hosts the no-cover Spread Love party from 6pm to midnight, spinning Latin beats, roots, reggae, and other soulful sounds. The emphasis is on world cultures and art, with mismatched furniture, handmade flourishes, and different art shows going up every few weeks. Wednesdays there's live music, Thursdays funk, and Fridays more world beat. Drop in early for happy hour and appetizers, when a crowd—young, casual, and diverse—shows up even mid-week. Choose from the wide range of home-infused vodkas and fruit juices. *Sun-Mon 6pm-midnight, Tue-Sat 6pm-2am.* 500 Divisadero St. (Fell St.), 415-241-0202, madronelounge.com

Martuni's • Mission • Piano Bar

Dinner is over but you don't want to go home. You want to hear show tunes played by talented locals at the piano bar. You want a chocolate- or pineapple-tini. You wouldn't mind going somewhere where you could have a little after-hours conversation. Martuni's is your destination. The crowd is an eclectic mix both at happy hour and on the weekends. *Daily 4pm-2am.* Four Valencia St. (Market St.), 415-241-0205

Mecca • Castro • Restaurant Bar
Mecca brought the future of restaurant design to San Francisco years ago and many have taken more than a cue from its décor, which is still inviting but no longer as cutting-edge. What other places cannot duplicate is the crowd, a consistently hip, attractive, fashionable, local, affluent, and lively group in its twenties and thirties that arrives en masse for happy hour throughout the week and after dinner on weekends. While there is nothing wrong with the food, the loud music and throngs of cocktailers make it more appealing to join them than to try to enjoy a meal in the din. Mecca has a persistent reputation as a place to meet new people and collect phone numbers. *Sun and Tue-Thu 5-11pm, Fri-Sat 5pm-midnight.* F≡ 2029 Market St. (Dolores St.), 415-621-7000, sfmecca.com

Medjool • Mission • Restaurant Bar
The city's only openair rooftop bar offers cocktails and outstanding North African small plates. *See Hip Restaurants, p.103, for details.* F≡ Elements Hotel, 2522 Mission St. (21st St.), 415-550-9055, medjoolsf.com

Mighty • Mission • Nightclub
Mighty is so old-school, it's new. For those who remember the punk era, Mighty evokes the edgy glory days of underground dance clubs on an epic scale. This is not a Euro-chic lounge. Genuinely lofty and industrial, it's hidden away in a nook between the Mission and Potrero Hill that still has real factories and shipping yards. The exposed brick, heavy timbers, and hardwood floors are original. And the mood? Dark, arty, and anonymous, with a 30-foot steel bar, soaring ceilings, graffiti-style art, a looming chandelier, and floor-to-ceiling mirrors in the bathroom. The space is big (7,000 square feet), so it doesn't get rocking until a good number of people show up. Go late (after 10pm) and expect to drink and dance, but not lounge or chitchat. The music is loud and there are few places to retreat. Check the calendar before heading out, as it frequently hosts private parties and hours and covers vary. On good nights, the hipster crowds will come out in force and the dance floor rocks late into the night. *Fri-Sat and for special events.* C≡ 119 Utah St. (15th St.), 415-626-7001, mighty119.com

Milk • Haight • Nightclub
Best DJ Bars Hip-hop, reggae, dancehall, old school, soul, and funk predominate at this no-frills dance club that attracts a casually hip twenty-something crowd more interested in listening and dancing to great music than posing in designer fashions. There's something on most nights of the week, with Tuesdays and Thursdays looking especially good. It sometimes hosts live music and sushi on Sundays, but check ahead to be sure it's on. Show up before 9pm to get in free, but wait until 10pm to find a crowd. *Mon-Fri 7pm-2am, Sat-Sun 2pm-2am.* C≡ 1840 Haight St. (Stanyan St.), 415-387-6455, milksf.com

Oxygen Bar • Mission • Theme Bar
Where else can you strap a tube under your nose and chill to the DJ's freshest beats while sucking 85 percent oxygen (up from the anemic 25 percent oxygen mix in the atmosphere)? Where else, indeed, but the Oxygen Bar. And the hospital, where they probably won't offer you the Aphrodisiac blend, with ylang ylang, red mandarin, bergamot, and sandalwood aromatherapy. Oxygen Bar also offers an array of other health-related treats, including hot teas, organic wines, and, best of all, several different elixirs. Try the euphoria-promoting Exotic

Dream with pau de arco, dandelion, kava, and raspberry leaf. It also serves sushi and a variety of sakes, but the souped-up air is the big draw. The crowd tends to locals who just couldn't help themselves. *Tue, Thu, and Sun 5pm-midnight, Fri-Sat 5pm-2am.* 795 Valencia St. (19th St.), 415-255-2102, oxygensf.com

Pilsner Inn • Castro • Nighclub/Bar
Best Gay Bars and Clubs Most bars in the Castro cater to a predominantly gay crowd, and that's true of the Pilsner Inn as well, in this case in the sense of gay and lesbian. However, you certainly don't have to be gay or a lesbian to enjoy the 15 different beers on tap, the great outdoor patio (favored by smokers), the pool table, pinball machine, other assorted games, or the friendly environment. Sunny weekend afternoons are the best out on the patio and very popular. The place gets crowded in a good way most nights, but the scene is generally quite laid back, not meet market. *Daily 10am-2am.* 225 Church St. (Market St.), 415-621-7058

Pink • Mission • DJ Bar/Theme Bar
Best DJ Bars Pink is solidly established in the hipster repertoire. Though the space is small, it's dressed up in style, with an idiosyncratic décor that feels like the rosy boudoir of a very edgy, naughty girl. Those in the know drop in when far-flung DJs with serious talent blow through town, stopping to spin a word-of-mouth night at Pink. If you're not part of the grapevine, pass by around 11pm to see what's brewing. Chances are the crowd will be savvy, easy on the eyes, and ready to mix it up to some fresh beats spun by a long list of great local talent. Expensive drinks keep scruffier Mission types on the outside. The perfect mix of polish and grit, Pink does it all just right. *Fri-Sat 9pm-3am, Sun and Tue-Thu 9pm-2am.* 2925 16th St. (S. Van Ness Ave.), 415-431-8889, pinksf.com

The Public • SoMa • Restaurant Bar
A casual and comfortable industrial-chic gathering spot with DJ music. *See Hip Restaurants, p.103, for details.* 1489 Folsom St. (11th St.), 415-552-3065, thepublicsf.com

Rosewood • North Beach • Bar/Lounge
This sleek and tasteful lounge attracts an appealing local crowd of young, affluent urbanites interested in socializing with same. There are several compelling reasons to stop by. First, the design is a knockout. Rosewood-paneled walls, minimalist furniture, and a clever treatment of bottles behind the bar make for an elegant setting that encourages everyone to turn on the charm. Second, the handsome back garden is a rare treat. Third, the patrons are a solid cut above the droves who hit the bigger venues along Broadway. Drop by at happy hour to unwind to DJs spinning house and trip-hop beats. If you're smooth, you might even score a date for the weekend, when the hip-hop and funk cranks up, the door policies tighten, and the snob factor ratchets up several notches. For a happy medium, try Thursday nights. *Wed, Thu, Sat 7pm-2am, Fri 5:30pm-2am.* 732 Broadway (Stockton St.), 415-951-4886, rosewoodbar.com

Rx Gallery • Downtown • Bar/Art Gallery
A den of hipdom in a neighborhood largely dominated by touristy restaurants, Rx Gallery is a pleasant surprise. It opened in 2003 with the goal of "merging art and life." That seems to translate as a hip place to see cutting-edge art by

day and mix with those in the know by night. Featuring a full bar, a loft-style mezzanine, and DJs who know what they're doing, it makes a nice place to mix and dance with people drawn to a creative environment. It hosts a monthly party called Kontrol every third Saturday that is worth the effort. As with other places where the elusive beautiful people gather, the scene and hours vary, so check the website. *Gallery open Wed-Thu 3-7pm, Fri-Sat 5-9pm; lounge 9pm-2am.* 132 Eddy St. (Mason St.), 415-474-7973, rxgallery.com

SF Badlands • Castro • Nightclub
Best Gay Bars and Clubs Do you want to dance without irony to a Madonna single while you watch the video at the same time? In the middle of the afternoon? Then slather on the tanning lotion, bust out your best muscle T, and head for SF Badlands, the baddest gay video dance club in town. Weekends bring lines and every day brings a crowd for unabashed pop top 40 worship. Think of it as a gay wedding, where you can get funky on the dance floor with your Uncle Ed after an early dinner, then get a beer and relax next to a flower arrangement. Mirrored disco ball definitely included. If lines on Friday and Saturday keep you away, try a Thursday or Sunday night. Even if you're female or not gay, you can still have fun here with the young and hunky. *Daily 2pm-2am.* 4121 18th St. (Castro St.), 415-626-9320, sfbadlands.com

Skylark • Mission • Bar
Dim lighting, strong drinks, no cover, DJs spinning standard-fare dance music. Sometimes, keeping it simple is best. There's always a youngish crowd of local hipsters, and on weekends it spills out into the street. Of the nearby bars, the Skylark is best for drinking, dancing, and meeting new people. Skylark invites you to let your hair down, pick up a total stranger, and have the mother of all hangovers the next day. *Tue-Sat 7pm-2am.* 3089 16th St. (Valencia St.), 415-621-9294, skylarkbar.com

Sneaky Tiki • SoMa • Restaurant Bar
Best Tiki Bars A modern take on the tiki lounge with fruity cocktails and music. *See Hip Restaurants, p.104, for details.* 1582 Folsom St. (12th St.), 415-701-8454, sneakytiki-sf.com

Soluna Cafe & Lounge • Hayes Valley • Restaurant Lounge
A restaurant that turns clubby after 10pm, complete with DJs and dancing. *See Hip Restaurants, p.104, for details.* 272 McAllister St. (Larkin St.) 415-621-2200, solunasf.com

Sublounge • Potrero Hill • DJ Bar
Best DJ Bars Sublounge is that variety of hip that makes one think of Burning Man, tattoos, and counterculture fashion bordering on costume. The big draw, aside from the nicely edgy and futuristic setting, is the music, some of the best and freshest around. The crowd, like the neighborhood, is an amusing mixture of artsy types, scroungers, yuppies sniffing around the wrong side of town, hot young things, and just plain old weirdos. Get in touch with your adventurous side and come on out. *Wed-Fri 6pm-2am, Sat 7pm-2am.* 628 20th St. (Third St.), 415-552-3603, sublounge.com

Swig • Downtown • Bar/Performance

Swig took over a beloved old place to hear live music, called the Blue Lamp. The new owners gave it a modern update, but have continued the old Lamp tradition of the Sunday evening electric blues jam from 9pm to 2am. Weekdays, there's live jazz, blues, and other bands. On the weekend, starting Thursday, DJs man the decks and things get busy. It can be a real scene, packed with thirty-ish beautiful people and those who watch them. The décor has retained its soul, including a huge window up front that slides open, inviting passersby to join the party. Later, the fireplace heats up. Later still, the crowd makes its way upstairs into hidden areas for chatting and nuzzling. *Daily 8pm-1:30am.* C≡ 561 Geary St. (Taylor St.), 415-931-7292, swig-bar.com

12 Galaxies • Mission • Nightclub/Performance

New on the scene in 2003, this spacious club has become a live-venue mainstay. It's big enough to hold a goodly number of indie-scene Mission District super-hipsters, but still small enough to feel like a neighborhood hangout, albeit with a bigger design budget than most. Downstairs is a bar, a few cocktail tables, and, almost at eye level, the band du jour. Because the stage is little more than a slightly raised platform, it's hard to see unless you're right up front. Luckily, you can take refuge upstairs, where there is another bar and several chill areas with comfortable but edgy styling. One even has a pool table and fireplace. And if you must see the band—it might be anything from punk to funk to rock or blues—you can do so from the mezzanine railing. Only a brush with actual starvation should drive you to the nachos or jambalaya. *Daily 7pm-2am.* C B ≡ 2565 Mission St. (21st St.), 415-970-9777, 12galaxies.com

The Velvet Lounge • North Beach • Bar/Nightclub

The Velvet Lounge is a great big dance club with all the de rigueur hipster accoutrements, including dark and velvety lounge spaces in which to chill out, dance floors in which to rev up, and DJs spinning funk, hip-hop, and classic soul. Occasionally it busts out with a '70s and '80s cover band that just won't stop until everyone is dancing. The scene is cruisy, with boys and girls alike looking for the next big crush. The crowd is young and bridge and tunnel. If the scene is not happening when you arrive, fear not. Other clubs are within easy walking distance. Get a stamp, try your luck elsewhere, then come back to see if things have taken off. *Thu-Sat 9pm-2am.* C≡ 443 Broadway (Montgomery St.), 415-788-0228, thevelvetlounge.com

Whisper • Potrero Hill • Bar/Nightclub

An upscale after-hours mega dance club, Whisper has pale-blue walls splashed with colored lighting that liven up the place, making it easier to see whom you're dancing with. Multiple levels and plush lounge areas, outdoor spaces complete with views and tiny alcoves (ideal for those impromptu intimate moments), fish tanks, and a fireplace make Whisper something of a jungle gym cum theme park for grownups, who pack the place every weekend to move to electronic dance music. Full VIP service is available, from private booths to valet parking to bottle service and upscale snacks from the American-style grill. Whisper is across the street from Circolo. Start with a cocktail in Circolo's lounge, have a delicious Asian fusion meal, then step across the road to get funky. *Fri-Sat 10pm-4am.* C F ≡ 535 Florida St. (Mariposa St.), 415-252-9442, whispersf.com

Wish • SoMa • Bar/Lounge
When happy hour calls and you want a strong cocktail, a little flirting, and some intelligent conversation, head to Wish, where a sexy, uplifting energy gets started with the close of the work day. Locals pack into this corridor of a space to mix, mingle, unwind, and talk, all the while keeping an eye on the surrounding action. The good-looking crowd is mixed, from alternative-style hipsters to trendy types out to show off their skimpy new outfit to media professionals and other worker bees in their twenties, thirties, and sprightly forties. The music and drinks are both served with expertise. Décor that's a step up from the norm—plush leather couches, artful lighting, and mahogany woodwork—adds a touch of class. Black and crimson tones and candlelight create a sultry ambiance. Late at night, more DJs spin, though there really isn't room to dance. *Mon-Fri 5pm-2am, Sat 7pm-2am, Sun 8pm-2am.* ≡ 1539 Folsom St. (11th St.), 415-278-9474, wishsf.com

Zuni Café • Hayes Valley • Restaurant Bar
Locals of all stripes gather at the copper bar for champagne and more. *See Hip Restaurants, p.107, for details.* 1658 Market St. (Franklin St.), 415-552-2522

Hip San Francisco: The Attractions

Baker Beach• Presidio National Park • Beach
   Best Sex in the City Once in a great while there's a warm, sunny day in San Francisco. Everybody piles in the car and heads for Baker Beach. While the water is always freezing and dangerous, no matter how spectacular the weather, the views are so breathtaking and the people-watching so intriguing, you will never want for entertainment. Grab a patch of sand and study the Golden Gate Bridge, the Marin Headlands in their rugged glory, the sparkling expanse of the great Pacific, and the waves crashing on shore. San Francisco locals stroll by, sporting pale bare skin. At the northern end of the beach, folks bare all and expect others to keep their eyeballs politely fixed on the horizon. Baker Beach is quite cold but equally beautiful on a foggy day. Presidio National Park

Glide Memorial United Methodist Church • Downtown • Church
   Best Only-in-San Francisco Experiences Sunday mornings at Glide are unique. Few other churches combine a handsome venue with such a cross-section of humanity, generous outpouring of goodwill, and rocking musical experience. Glide has been delivering all that and more for over forty years. Even if—or especially if—you haven't set foot in a church in twenty years, Glide will light you up with 1,000 watts of soul. *Services Sun 9am and 11am.* 330 Ellis St. (Taylor St.), 415-674-6000, glide.org

Golden Gate Park—Skating and Biking • Richmond • Activity
   While skaters and bicyclists love the park every day, the roads are all yours on Sundays, when John F. Kennedy Drive between Kezar Drive and Transverse Road is closed to traffic. Spanning over 1,000 acres, from the Pacific Ocean to the Haight-Ashbury, and including miles of paved trails, it's heaven for the wheeled masses. Rent your gear at Skates on Haight, just a block from the park, then roll on up to the Conservatory of Flowers. Just after it, on the right, is a smooth-surfaced skate pad where skaters gather to bust their moves. $$ Rental shops: Skates on Haight, 1818 Haight St. (Shrader St.), 415-752-8376; Golden Gate Park Bike and Skate, 3038 Fulton St. (Sixth Ave.), 415-668-1117; Surrey Bikes and Blades, 50 Stow Lake Drive, 415-668-6699.

Good Vibrations • Mission • Shopping
   Best Sex in the City Hemingway longed for "a clean, well-lighted place" for books. Good Vibrations is that place, only for sex toys and feminist-friendly pornography. The feminine take on things may account for the friendly, non-creepy vibe. While they sell plenty of great big dildos, fanciful vibrators, and candy-colored butt plugs, the bondage gear, for example, tends to the tame and even decorative. If you want hardcore, bust out the antibacterial wipes and head for a real porn shop. But if you want to feel like sex toys can be a healthy, fun way to explore your own and your partner's sexuality without freaking anyone out, stop into Good Vibrations. *Sun-Wed 11am-7pm, Thu-Sat 11am-8pm.* 603 Valencia St. (17th St.), 415-522-5460, goodvibes.com

Kabuki Springs and Spa • Pacific Heights • Spa
Authentic Japanese baths are hard to come by outside Japan, which is what makes Kabuki Springs so uniquely enjoyable. The communal baths are same-sex on alternating days (Sunday, Wednesday, and Friday for women; Monday, Thursday, and Saturday for men), with both sexes and their bathing suits welcome on Tuesdays. In the baths, a clean, Zen-style minimalism prevails, together with an impressive attention to small but important touches such as free sea salts, chilled cucumber slices, warm towels, and tea. The full-service spa is available to both sexes every day and takes a more decorative approach. If you schedule a treatment, give yourself plenty of time beforehand to hit the sauna and steam rooms, cold plunge, and hot pool, in that order. *Daily 10am-9:45pm.* $$ 1750 Geary Blvd. (Fillmore St.), 415-922-6000, kabukisprings.com

Minnie Wilde • Hayes Valley / Mission • Shop
It's signature motocross jackets in flashy, vintage-esque fabrics; inspiration from French disco and unicorns; and a serious dedication to originality and limited editions. Designer Terri Olson and her partner Ann D'Apice scour flea markets, thrift stores, and fabric showrooms for ideas and materials, then put it all together in the back room of their tiny Hayes Valley boutique. The result is a line of sexy, saucy, slightly '70s clothing that is gaining a Hollywood following. They also carry items from other local and favorite designers, so you never know what you might find. The duo also recently opened a second location in the Mission. *Hayes: Tue-Sat noon-7pm, Sun noon-5pm; Mission: Wed-Sat noon-7pm, Sun noon-5pm.* Hayes: 519 Laguna St. (Hayes St.), 415-863-9453; 3266 21st St. (Valencia St.), 415-642-9453, minniewilde.com

Mission Cliffs • Mission • Health Club
Best Workouts You don't have to be a climber to have a great day or evening on the wall at Mission Cliffs. Subject yourself to a training session with the very friendly and helpful staff, pass the test, rent the gear, then start scaling. You don't even need a partner, though it is preferable, since your safety depends upon the reliability of the guy or girl holding the rope. If heights don't thrill you, you can "boulder" upstairs, where veterans hang out working through the toughest problems at ground level. The crowd is all ages and jovial. Unlike the typical gym scene, where workouts can feel like punishment, the mood at Mission Cliffs is pure excitement. Climbers love to climb, and they're thrilled to have a chance to do it. You will leave feeling pumped. *Mon-Fri 6:30am-10pm, Sat-Sun 9am-7pm.* $$ 2295 Harrison St. (19th St.), 415-550-0515, touchstoneclimbing.com

Mission Dolores • Mission • Church
Officially known as Mission San Francisco de Asis, beautiful Mission Dolores, founded in 1776, is the oldest intact structure in the city, with roots going back to the very beginning. The backyard is crowded with gravestones marking the burial spot of dozens of Costanoan Indians, the city's first residents and the labor pool that built the mission. The padres erected their church next to an inlet called Laguna Dolores, now filled in and part of picturesque Dolores Park. The mission's thick adobe walls have withstood several major earthquakes and nearly everything within its cool, dim interior is authentic, including the original redwood ceiling beams. Fans of *Vertigo* will recognize the Mission's tower. *Daily 9am-5pm.* $- 3321 16th St. (Dolores St.), 415-621-8203, missiondolores.org

Paxton Gate • Mission • Shop
If you are in search of rare plants, an alligator head, unusual jewelry, or a beautiful garden tool, Paxton Gate is sure to delight. This exceptionally eclectic shop now carrying a wide range of offerings originally grew out of its owners' interest in gardening and the natural world. It gradually evolved to include more unusual fare—taxidermy and fossils—and later continued to expand into home furnishings, personal beauty products, candles, teas, and other assorted unpredictable items. The owners' keen eyes and interesting perspective are in evidence everywhere. The unifying theme is a celebration of the unexpected. *Daily noon-7pm.* 824 Valencia St. (19th St.), 415-824-1872, paxton-gate.com

Rolo • Castro • Shop
Not everyone can get the personal makeover attention of *Queer Eye for the Straight Guy*. For those on their own, a visit to Rolo should advance the cause considerably. The small selection, for men only, includes an impeccably tasteful assortment of jeans, sweaters, luxury T-shirts, underwear, jackets, personal grooming products, and more. The look is European, hip, and fit, so bring your body. And don't forget the wallet. You could spend more on clothes, but you'd have to make an effort. *Mon-Sat 11am-8pm, Sun 11am-7pm.* 2351 Market St. (Castro St.), 415-431-4545, rolo.com

Twin Peaks • Castro • Sight
Look for the big radio tower, visible throughout the city and from the Marin Headlands all the way to the East Bay and beyond, and you will be staring at Twin Peaks, named thusly for reasons that are obvious from most perspectives. The only point in going to Twin Peaks is to see the view, which is entirely panoramic. From the top, the city stretches out like a great map of itself, offering up all its landmarks for easy reference. The best time of day to visit is at dusk, when you can watch the sunset blend into stars, or at night, when you're sure to get that Inspiration Point feeling. By day, tour buses line the parking lot, choking off the good vibe. Go, soak up the view, and retreat to 24th Street in Noe Valley for refreshment. Top of Twin Peaks Blvd.

West Coast Live • Various • Performance
San Francisco has hosted the witty and beloved Saturday morning radio show *West Coast Live* for more than a decade. A variety show with music, humor, interviews with authors and other thinkers, and more, it's always smart and entertaining, and frequently very funny. While the venue varies, it is often staged at the Freight and Salvage Coffee House in Berkeley, the Empire Plush Room in the York Hotel (940 Sutter St.), the Magic Theater at Fort Mason (Building D, 3rd floor), and SFMoMA. Other venues include some of the best restaurants in the Bay Area. Check the website for upcoming venues and guests. *Doors open at 9:30am, broadcast live 10am-noon coast to coast.* $ 415-664-9500, wcl.org

Yerba Buena Center for the Arts • SoMa • Art Museum
Across the street from SFMoMA, Yerba Buena Center for the Arts has carved out an artistic niche separate from its more conventional neighbor. Billed as a venue for adventurous art, it lives up to the description. The center features leading-edge presentations of visual arts, performing arts, film, and video. The visual exhibitions focus on contemporary art and popular culture with an emphasis on local exploratory artists. The annual Bay Area Now exhibition is one of the most

popular draws. Meanwhile, performing arts programs include year-round theater, dance, and music presented in a state-of-the-art theater. The film and video schedule includes everything from obscure cult revivals to boundary-pushing new works by emerging filmmakers. A variety of arts-themed soirees and openings attract the young and single with food, wine, music, and an artistic experience hard to find elsewhere. In addition, the center hosts a lecture series in design and the arts that brings in the city's creative professionals. Yerba Buena Center also has a handsome garden, host to lunchtime concerts May through October. 701 Mission St. (Third St.), 415-978-2787, yerbabuenaarts.org

Classic San Francisco

It's hard to believe San Francisco didn't get its name until 1847, when there were fewer than 700 inhabitants. Things have come a long way. Today, San Francisco has more than enough history, glamour, local color, and enduring icons to make a classic tour absolutely essential. Do you really intend to visit without raising a martini at the Top of the Mark or hopping onto a trolley just as it crests Nob Hill? Of course you don't. While you're at it, tour the de Young Museum, stop into Masa's for a memorable meal, and gaze at the sailboats tacking across the bay from the Golden Gate. The scent of sourdough, the bark of sea lions, the sound of a fresh shot of espresso being pulled in the Caffe Trieste ... This is your guide to classic Fog City good times.

Note: Venues in bold are described in detail in the listings that follow the itinerary. Those with an asterisk are recommended for both drinks and dinner.

Classic San Francisco:
The Perfect Plan (3 Days and Nights)

Your Hotel: **Campton Place Hotel** Because you can walk out your door and be in Union Square or the Financial District in the time it takes to button your coat.

Thursday

The Perfect Plan Highlights

Prime Time: Thu-Sat

Thursday
Morning	Cable Car
Breakfast	The Buena Vista
Morning	Alcatraz
Lunch	Ana Mandara, Moose's
Afternoon	North Beach, Chinatown
Cocktails	Tosca Café, Enrico's
Dinner	Aqua, Boulevard
Nighttime	Biscuits & Blues, AsiaSF

Friday
Breakfast	Sears Fine Food
Morning	Legion of Honor
Lunch	Greens, Balboa Café
Afternoon	Palace of Fine Arts
	Golden Gate Bridge
Cocktails	Tonga Room
Dinner	Bix, Postrio
Nighttime	Punch Line Comedy Club
	Vesuvio
Late-Night	Starlight Room

Saturday
Morning	Ocean Beach
Lunch	Sutro's at the Cliff House
Afternoon	de Young Museum
	Golden Gate Park
Cocktails	G Bar, Trader Vic's
Dinner	Garibaldi's, Masa's
Nighttime	*Beach Blanket Babylon*
	Boom Boom Room
	Top of the Mark

9am Grab your sunscreen and an extra layer or two in case it gets cold and hop on a passing Powell-Hyde **cable car** on Powell Street. Jump off when you reach Hyde and Beach Streets in front of **The Buena Vista**, where you can fill up on a traditional breakfast and their specialty, an Irish coffee (first served in the US here).

11am When leaving the BV, many are tempted to turn left to spend some time at Ghirardelli Square, the original historic-buildings-turned-shopping-mall. Instead, turn right past Fisherman's Wharf to Pier 39, where you can observe the sea lions and grab a ticket for the **Alcatraz Island** tour.

1pm Lunch Especially if you went to Ghirardelli, settle in at **Ana Mandara** for an elegant culinary sojourn in Colonial Southeast Asia. Or get a head start on your afternoon by making your way to North Beach, San Francisco's Little Italy. Ease into the afternoon with lunch at **Café Zoetrope**, offering excellent Italian cuisine, an intriguing wine list, and a festive mood. For more room, live piano accompaniment, and a

CLASSIC

123

view of Washington Square Park, hit **Moose's**.

3pm After lunch, fortify yourself with an espresso or glass of wine at the Steps of Rome or head to nearby **Caffe Trieste**. Stroll the idiosyncratic shops of Grant Avenue. If you're up for a climb, make the steep trip up to **Coit Tower** to admire the view and the murals. Descend on the eastern side of Coit Tower's Telegraph Hill via the Filbert Steps, lined with cottages and gardens clinging to the precarious slope. Then return to the heart of North Beach. Check out Biordi Art Imports, a long-established source of Italian pottery, and **City Lights Bookstore**. Be sure to climb up to the poetry room, where Beats like Ginsberg, Ferlinghetti, and Kerouac gathered, and where Ferlinghetti still hangs out. From City Lights, you are just a block from the bustling streets of Chinatown. Grant Avenue is lined with tourist bric-a-brac shops, while Stockton Street caters to hordes of locals doing their grocery shopping at bustling markets.

6pm You can't go wrong with a cocktail at the illustrious **Tosca Café**. Or opt for the terrace at **Enrico's***. If you are looking to mingle with those recently escaped from the office, get a glass of something sparkly at the **Bubble Lounge**.

8pm Dinner Make your way to the exquisite seafood restaurant locals swear by known as **Aqua**. Another option is to indulge in classic French fare at the sumptuously beautiful **Boulevard** on the Embarcadero. For more courses than you can count on one hand, take a cab over to the extravagant **Gary Danko**, located near Pier 39.

11pm Add a soulful finish to the evening at **Biscuits & Blues**, with a set of live roots blues. Or cap off the evening on a more surreal note at **AsiaSF**, where you can watch gender illusionists perform upstairs and work the kinks out of your groove downstairs.

Friday

9am If you are anywhere near Union Square, start the day 1955-style at **Sears Fine Food**, where hearty pancakes, eggs, and bacon haven't changed much in the last half-century.

10:30am Journey across town through the Presidio to take in the latest exhibition and permanent collection at the **Palace of the Legion of Honor**. Be sure to take a short stroll outside the museum to enjoy spectacular views. For golfers who enjoy hills in a beautiful setting, tee off or hit a bucket of balls at the misty **Presidio Golf**

CLASSIC · ITINERARY

Course, one of our nation's great new public treasures.

1pm Lunch Head back to Fort Mason to enjoy a San Francisco institution, **Greens**, which offers a vegetarian feast with a magnificent view of the Golden Gate. In the Marina area, another long-time favorite is the **Balboa Café***, where a non-vegetarian burger reigns supreme.

2:30pm Ambitious walkers can hike along the picturesque Marina Green to the **Palace of Fine Arts**. Pass the sailboats at the very exclusive St. Francis Yacht Club and continue to **Crissy Field**, where the beach offers unobstructed views of the Marin Headlands and the Golden Gate Bridge. At the far end of the beach, stop into the Warming Hut for a hot chocolate.

4pm If you are feeling energetic, make your way to the **Golden Gate Bridge** on foot—it's a steep walk up the hillside from the Warming Hut. By car, the best approach is to cross the bridge and park, then walk back. If you've had enough fresh air and exercise, rejuvenate with a rub and soak at the **Nob Hill Spa**. Another form of relaxation is high tea at the **Laurel Court Restaurant** in the Fairmont Hotel.

6:30pm For a cocktail on Nob Hill you can go upscale tiki kitsch at the Fairmont's **Tonga Room** or have a mellow drink at the **Big 4 Restaurant***. For more of a scene, stop in to **Le Colonial***.

8pm Dinner The after-work bar scene should be thinning by the time you arrive for dinner at **Bix*** in Jackson Square. Other dinner options include Wolfgang Puck's San Francisco outpost, **Postrio**, and **Fleur de Lys**, San Francisco's most enduringly romantic French restaurant.

11pm Head to the 11 o'clock show at the **Punch Line Comedy Club** near the Embarcadero Center. After, if you aren't ready for bed, stop into **15 Romolo**, where a younger crowd mixes to the sounds of the DJ du jour. If comedy isn't your thing and the night is still young, a short cab ride will land you at **House of Shields** for a DJ-style nightcap in a classic setting. You can also head to the top floor of the Sir Francis Drake Hotel to spend a little cheek-to-cheek quality time at **Harry Denton's Starlight Room**. Those in North Beach as the night turns to morning may find a last bit of company in the tiny, eccentric, historic **Vesuvio**.

Saturday

10am Fortified with breakfast at your hotel, turn your sights to the Pacific, bordered by **Ocean Beach**. If you're sand and surf averse, Saturday morning is also fantastic at the Ferry Plaza Farmer's Market (see p.83). But that's a different story....

Noon Lunch Grab your shades and settle in at **Sutro's at the Cliff House**, where an extensive remodel brought the seaside Victorian legend into the modern age. If you can't go another step without a steamed dumpling, stop for dim sum at **Ton Kiang** a few blocks north of the park.

2pm Head to Golden Gate Park and the magnificent new **de Young Museum**. Walking around and through this architectural beauty is worth the trip, and don't miss its famed Oceanic art collection.

4pm Among the many worthy attractions of **Golden Gate Park** are the Japanese Tea Garden, the Strybing Arboretum, the Shakespeare Garden, and the **Conservatory of Flowers**.

6pm Near the park and one block from our dinner choice is **G Bar**. Or, head toward downtown and take your aperitif at **Trader Vic's***.

8pm Dinner Except for the fact that it is located in Presidio Heights, one of San Francisco's most prestigious neighborhoods, you wouldn't think of **Garibaldi's** as classic. This New York–style restaurant attracts a good-looking crowd from the area and beyond. A bit more upscale, **Masa's** delivers the kind of dinner that feels like a series of artworks created for your personal satisfaction. From Trader Vic's, it's just a couple of blocks to **Jardinière***, chef Traci Des Jardins' eponymous and much-lauded restaurant.

10pm For your last night, enjoy the quintessential San Francisco experience—**Beach Blanket Babylon**, the notoriously funny, long-running musical revue. A demure and sultry time can be had at the cocktail show at **Jazz at Pearl's** in North Beach. For beer and live blues in the Fillmore District, crowd your way into Johnny Lee Hooker's **Boom Boom Room**.

Midnight There is no more fitting end to the evening and a great weekend in the City by the Bay than going to Nob Hill for scenic drinks and dancing at the perennially elegant **Top of the Mark**.

The Morning After
San Francisco specializes in Sunday brunch. Two of the very special options are: Sunday jazz brunch at **The Terrace** in the Ritz-Carlton, a fantasy moment worthy of royalty; and brunch on the bay with **Signature Yacht Cruises**.

Classic San Francisco:
The Key Neighborhoods

Downtown is anchored by Union Square, which is surrounded by edifices that date back a hundred years or more. Saks, Neiman Marcus, Macy's, and Gucci, among other heavy hitters, all face the square. Every retail indulgence known to modern humanity is represented within a few blocks. Many of the city's most refined and opulent restaurants are within easy reach.

Fisherman's Wharf, despite the hordes of tourists, can still offer a classic San Francisco moment, complete with cable cars, fresh crab, the fog lingering over the bay, and views of Alcatraz Island.

The **Richmond** is best known for Golden Gate Park and its many charming features, including the de Young Museum, a modern classic; the Conservatory of Flowers; the Japanese Tea Garden; and views of the windswept Pacific Ocean lapping at its western edge.

Nob Hill, famed for its crown of luxury hotels, is synonymous with the posh lifestyle that arrived with the railroad barons. Timeless hotel bars and restaurants can be found perched at the top of these hotels or tucked discreetly in their lobbies.

North Beach, lined with historic cafes, shops, and the scruffy bars of the Beat Generation along its main thoroughfares of Columbus Avenue and Broadway, is an essential place to spend a few hours. Nearby Chinatown is another rich repository of vintage atmosphere.

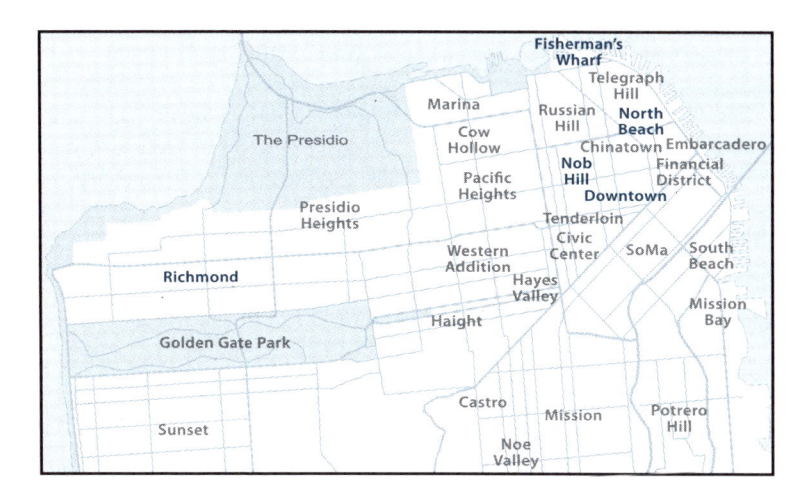

127

Classic San Francisco: The Shopping Blocks

North Beach

From designer denim to custom couture to old-fashioned postcards, North Beach offers a surprising depth of shopping choices.

AB Fits This is the place to come for the jeans of your dreams. 1519 Grant Ave. (Union St.), 415-982-5726

Alla Prima Fine Lingerie A distinctly sexy and upscale selection of European lingerie. 1420 Grant Ave (Green St.), 415-397-4077

Biordi Art Imports Extensive selection of handpainted Italian ceramics. 412 Columbus Ave. (Vallejo St.), 415-392-8096

City Lights Bookstore Legendary bookstore established in 1953 by Beat poet Lawrence Ferlinghetti. (p.153) 261 Columbus Ave. (Broadway), 415-357-4000

Ooma Feminine and colorful women's clothing by local designers. 1422 Grant Ave. (Green St.), 415-627-6963

Sacramento Street

While everything from fine housewares to doggie accessories are on offer here, the main attraction is of-the-moment finery for hot bodies with high credit limits.

The Bar Upscale women's clothing in a lovely setting complete with coffee bar for a shopping pick-me-up. 340 Presidio Ave. (Sacramento St.), 415-409-4901

The Grocery Store European glamour with names like Dolce and Gabbana and Helmut Lang. 3625 Sacramento St. (Locust St.), 415-928-3615

Pamela Mills A tantalizing assortment of designer feminine apparel in a serene and inviting setting. 3375 Sacramento St. (Walnut St.), 415-474-8400

Sarah Shaw Casually trendy and whimsical women's clothing for the decidedly upscale shopper. 3095 Sacramento St. (Baker St.), 415-929-2990

Sue Fisher King A sumptuous selection of European linens and décor for the home and table. (p.156) 3067 Sacramento St. (Baker St.), 415-922-7276

Union Square

San Francisco's premier shopping mecca has something for everyone.

Gumps A San Francisco institution, Gumps carries jewels, housewares, silver and china, vases, linens, and more. (p.154) 135 Post St. (Grant Ave.), 415-982-1616

Wilkes Bashford Company The ultimate address for fine apparel of a lavish but slightly conservative ilk. (p.156) 375 Sutter St. (Stockton St.), 415-986-4380

Classic San Francisco: The Hotels

Campton Place Hotel • Downtown • Modern (117 rms)
Personal service, tranquility, and luxury prevail at Campton Place, a boutique hotel near Union Square with just 117 rooms, including two decadent executive suites and one ultraposh über-sweet suite. A $15 million remodel of all rooms was completed in 2001, and the hotel redid the Campton Place Restaurant in 2002. Both are now in top form, as is the hotel bar, a refuge from the bustle outside. Guest rooms feature fine furniture, pearwood accents, down-filled duvets, and elegantly appointed limestone bathrooms, all in shades of sand, sage, and cinnamon. The two buildings that house the hotel date from the early 1900s and show their historical beauty to advantage. Most downtown points of interest are within walking distance. There is no spa or pool, but the partly outdoor fitness center on the roof maximizes the view. As for who stays here, it's the seasoned travelers, high-end executives, and other sophisticates who appreciate impeccable service bordering on pampering, deep soaking tubs, double-pane windows, and martinis served by waiters in suits. Business king rooms don't have tubs, just showers, so be sure to upgrade to the California king if you plan to soak. Though views are not the forte of the Campton, the corner Superior king room offers a charming look at Union Square. $$$$ 340 Stockton St. (Sutter St.), 415-781-5555 / 800-235-4300, camptonplace.com

The Fairmont • Nob Hill • Timeless (591 rms)
The daughters of "Bonanza Jim" Fair wanted a monument worthy of their late father, who had struck it rich in a Nevada silver mine. So they built the Fairmont. It was nearly complete when the 1906 fire climbed Nob Hill and ravaged the pristine structure just days before its grand opening. It took a year to rebuild. Nearly 100 years and several major renovations later, the Fairmont is still on top, literally and figuratively. Home to the Tonga Room, where a faux monsoon periodically ravages the happy-hour crowd; the ornate Laurel Court Restaurant, where high tea is served daily; and the crystal-chandeliered Venetian Room, where Tony Bennett first sang "I Left My Heart in San Francisco," the Fairmont is redolent with history. Hotel guests have access to the Club One fitness center and spa. (Alas, for a swim, you have to trek to a sister Club One downtown.) Rooms in the six-story main building offer higher ceilings and slightly more traditional décor, while those in the 23-story tower are more modern and boast spectacular views. $$$$ 950 Mason St. (California St.), 415-772-5000 / 800-257-7544, fairmont.com/sanfrancisco

The Huntington Hotel • Nob Hill • Timeless (135 rms)
If you want privacy, a discreet and able staff, and opulence with a 19th-century feel, the still-family-owned Huntington will serve you exceptionally well. Back in the 1800s, C. P. Huntington, a merchant, shipping magnate, and one of the Big Four railroad barons, lived in a mansion across the street in what is now known as Huntington Park. The Huntington Hotel was built in the '20s, a brick-and-steel high-rise said to be the first of its kind in the western United States. Its units were originally residential, and the uniqueness of each has not been

made over. The furnishings are lavish, antique, and idiosyncratic, a good match for the diverse but decidedly monied clientele (Bono stayed here, but so do CEOs and ladies who lunch). Request a room ending in ten for more space and the best views. Two key features are available whether you are a guest of the hotel or not: The Big 4 Restaurant downstairs makes a fine supper of American fare, and the very posh Nob Hill Spa offers a full range of services in addition to an indoor infinity pool and breathtaking views. $$$ 1075 California St. (Taylor St.), 415-474-5400 / 800-227-4683, huntingtonhotel.com

InterContinental Mark Hopkins • Nob Hill • Timeless (380 rms)
Seated on Nob Hill among other grand edifices is the 19-story white monolith that is the Mark Hopkins. Named for the Central Pacific Railroad founder whose mansion stood on the site until the 1906 fire consumed it, the Mark Hopkins offers truly incredible views, to the east in particular. From the higher rooms on the northeast side, you look eye-to-eye with Coit Tower or distant Mount Diablo. (It's worth the extra money to get a deluxe room, meaning those on the eighth to 17th floors.) The accommodations are as luxurious as you might assume from the hotel's exterior, including dark wood furniture, plush seating, the odd tasseled pillow or two, Italian marble in the bathrooms, Frette linens on the bed, and all the other bells and whistles of a well-appointed resting spot. The crowd tends to the expense-account crew and can be a bit staid, but there is no denying the aura of wealth and privilege the walls exude. Be sure to have a cocktail at the Top of the Mark to soak in the panoramic views. $$$ 999 California St. (Mason St.), 415-392-3434 / 888-303-1758, san-francisco.intercontinental.com

The Palace Hotel • SoMa • Timeless (552 rms)
Old World elegance at its finest, the Palace was built in 1875, burned in the great fire of 1906, and was resurrected soon after in opulent style. The hotel joined the Starwood Hotel group and the rooms were remodeled in 2002, adding luxuries and modern essentials while preserving the mood of 19th-century grandeur (think marble vanities and mahogany poster beds). Aside from its convenient location between the Financial District and Union Square, the Palace's many virtues include its fourth-floor skylit pool and spa; rooms with windows that open and 14-foot ceilings; a Maxfield Parrish original in the Pied Piper, the woodsy bar downstairs; and, best of all, the Garden Court, a magnificent construction complete with chandeliers, marble columns, palms, and a 55-foot ceiling comprised of 80,000 panes of glass, giving the room an ethereal, uplifting glow. It is beautiful, and the perfect setting for the Saturday afternoon ritual of high tea (served 2-4pm) and Sunday jazz brunch. Ask for a corner room for more light and space, and if you score the fourth floor you can stroll to the pool without touching the elevator. $$$ Two New Montgomery St. (Market St.), 415-512-1111 / 888-625-5144, sfpalace.com

The Prescott Hotel • Downtown • Modern (164 rms)
Any hotel where the restaurant is as enduringly excellent as Postrio has got to be good, and the Prescott lives up to those breathtakingly high expectations. While it may lose points for flash, it makes them up in unassuming elegance. Neither minimalist nor 19th century, as many of the other luxury hotels in town are, the Prescott eschews fashion trends in favor of enduring contemporary style. Think white wainscoting against mustard walls, cherry wood furniture, fine linens, and subdued stripes, plaids, and florals. The location is tough to beat,

just a block off Union Square, and the lobby makes a nice splash. It's like stepping into an Erté poster, but in a good way. If you get the urge to descend the stairs doing your best Liza Minnelli, Marlene Dietrich, or even Gene Kelly impression, you are to be forgiven. The Prescott is a Kimpton Hotel (like the more whimsical Hotel Monaco and the more luxurious Hotel Palomar), which means it offers plenty of fun little extras, such as free coffee in the living room in the morning, free newspapers, and a complimentary sedan service weekdays to the downtown area. If you want the free cocktail service and breakfast from Postrio, pay $30 to $50 more for a room in the more quiet Club Level. $$ 545 Post St. (Mason St.), 415-563-0303 / 866-271-3632, prescotthotel.com

The Ritz-Carlton • Downtown • Timeless (336 rms)
No other hotel, not even its fellow Nob Hill competitors, says ruling class like the Ritz. Pull into the driveway in front of its six enormous pillars and you get that presidential, inner-sanctum feeling. The 1909 landmark is the city's only hotel boasting both Mobil Travel Guide's five stars and AAA's five diamonds. From Italian-marble bathrooms to afternoon tea, this is traditional European-style pampering at its most sumptuous. Rooms have every imaginable amenity, including puffy down comforters and feather beds, and tremendous views. Ask for a room on the seventh floor or higher to really see forever. You will never want for a good meal while chez Ritz. Nip down to the Terrace Restaurant for Sunday jazz brunch or a morning feast, hit the Lobby Lounge for cocktails and nibbles, or go all out at the Dining Room, one of only three restaurants in California to win five stars from Mobil. Gilded, richly upholstered, and sconce lit, the hotel's flagship restaurant is a white-glove wonderland for culinary classicists looking for contemporary French cuisine. The Equilibrium Massage and Fitness Center features an indoor pool and basic spa services, but in a hotel this elegant, it's not the high point. $$$$+ 600 Stockton St. (California St.), 415-296-7465 / 800-241-3333, ritzcarlton.com/hotels/san_francisco

Westin St. Francis Hotel • Downtown • Timeless (1,200 rms)
St. Francis manages to feel small and charming despite its looming 1,200 rooms. The place crawls with tourists, but is still beloved by locals, many of whom you will find dining at the chic and pretty restaurant Michael Mina. It was first built by the Crocker family with its railroad millions in 1904 and was the social hub for the well-to-do for decades. Today, the Westin company runs the hotel, and the rooms, especially those in the 1970s tower building, have an air of corporate anonymity. Still, much of the San Francisco charm remains, most notably in the main building, where Empire-style furniture prevails, including chandelier lighting, crown molding, armchairs with alligator feet, and mirrors trimmed with gold. All rooms include comfortable new beds and plush bedding. If you opt for the main building, request a traditional room with Union Square view. The tower offers more expensive Grand View rooms, with contemporary furnishings and spectacular views. Avoid the Standard rooms. Business travelers will feel more at home elsewhere. $$$ 335 Powell St. (Geary St.), 415-397-7000 / 888-625-5144, westinstfrancis.com

Classic San Francisco: The Restaurants

Absinthe Brasserie and Bar • Hayes Valley • French Brasserie
As a cocktail, absinthe is a potent, languidly hallucinogenic drug that fueled the Impressionist movement in Paris. It is a fitting name for this medium-sized restaurant, a place that looks like an old Parisian bistro filled with decadent Belle Epoque detail. Velvet, gold, silver, and marble embellish every angle. Absinthe serves a fine oyster, a succulent rabbit, and a creative cocktail. The bar scene, though small, is enjoyable. You won't find the twenty-somethings, but you will find those in their thirties and forties, spruced up, and eager for their Death in the Afternoon, a concoction of Pernod and champagne. The neighborhood galleries and shops offer excellent strolling. *Tue-Fri 11:30am-midnight, Sat 11am-midnight, Sun 11am-10:30pm.* $$ 398 Hayes St. (Gough St.), 415-551-1590, absinthe.com

Acquerello • Nob Hill • Italian (G)
When it comes to Italian restaurants, there's rustic Italian and froufrou Italian. Acquerello, by now a classic fixture in culinary San Francisco, serves froufrou Italian, meaning refined, contemporary, inventive Northern Italian cuisine that is lighter than rustic Italian. The setting in the small dining room is simple and romantic, with butter-colored walls and dreamy watercolors of Venice. You may encounter lobster, a seared carpaccio of halibut, or pasta pappardelle with rabbit. The wine list offers an enormous list of distinguished wines, mostly from small producers in Italy and California. Bring a date to woo because you won't stumble into one here, where the crowd tends to couples who have transcended trendiness. *Tue-Sat 5:30-10:30pm.* $$$ 1722 Sacramento St. (Polk St.), 415-567-5432, acquerello.com

Ana Mandara • Fisherman's Wharf • Vietnamese
Best Chic Asian Restaurants Owned by Don Johnson, Ana Mandara is a Colonial-era Vietnamese fantasy that transports you back in time. Suddenly you are Graham Greene writing *The Quiet American*. You perspire genteelly in your white linen suit. Your companion for the evening wears form-fitting silk with a high-neck blouse buttoned across her slender throat. Go ahead, order the lobster ravioli with mango and coconut sauce. Ana Mandara is white columns, silk cushions, and elegant palms. In other words, high romance, a marvelous setting, and exquisite Vietnamese cuisine. *Mon-Fri 11:30am-2pm, Sun-Thu 5:30-9:30pm, Fri-Sat 5:30-10:30pm.* $$ Ghirardelli Square, 891 Beach St. (Polk St.), 415-771-6800, anamandara.com

Aqua • Financial District • Seafood (G)
Best Seafood Restaurants For fine seafood in an elegant atmosphere, Aqua is the place. The ambiance is classic high-end fine dining, with muted tones, soft light, extravagant floral arrangements, and epic mirrors. The downtown location makes it a first choice for business lunches with a sturdy expense account. In the evening, expect couples, generally of a certain age, conservatively dressed. The extensive wine list is a standout, the desserts are works of art, and the

seafood dishes are some of the best the city has to offer. Look for intricate preparations of scallops, lobster, wild king salmon, ahi tuna, and other favorites. Aqua has transitioned successfully from culinary stars George Marrone and Michael Mina to the current chef, Laurent Manrique. *Mon-Fri 11:30am-2pm and 5:30-9:30pm, Sat-Sun 5:30-9:30pm.* $$$ 252 California St. (Battery St.), 415-956-9662, aqua-sf.com

AsiaSF • SoMa • Tapas
Best Only-in–San Francisco Experiences A unique combination of Asian-fusion cuisine, dancing, and drag queens. *See Classic Nightlife, p.146, for details.* $$ 201 Ninth St. (Howard St.), 415-255-2742, asiasf.com

Balboa Cafe • Marina • Traditional American
Survive long enough and they call you venerable, as they do the Balboa Cafe, established in 1913. It still has that great old San Francisco powerbroker smell to it that makes you want to put your foot on the rail, order a whiskey neat, and tell a story about the way business used to be done. You can take your mother in her pearls and lady suit here for lunch, or turn up for dinner and expect great food and a lively crowd. Save room for crab cakes or the burger with shoestring potatoes. The service can be rude, so don't take any lip. The location is ideal for hitting any of several nearby bars after. This corner is part of what is known as the Triangle, ground zero for yuppie nightlife. *Mon-Wed 11:30am-10pm, Thu-Fri 11:30am-11pm, Sat 9am-11pm, Sun 9am-10pm. Bar open until 2am.* $$ 3199 Fillmore St. (Greenwich St.), 415-921-3944, balboacafe.com

The Big 4 Restaurant • Nob Hill • Traditional American
This clubby restaurant from the '20s has withstood numerous culinary trends and countless fashion assaults. Standing firm with its shining brass, polished mahogany, and leather banquettes, the atmosphere is early 20th-century banker. The room is adorned with historic photographs of California, while the kitchen is known for its wild-game specialties: venison and black bean chili with onion crisps, or organic ostrich steak. If exotic meats aren't your game, there's also a menu of California-inspired fare. On a foggy day, claim a seat next to the fireplace to sip your Scotch on the rocks before dinner. *Mon-Fri 7-10am, 11:30am-3pm, and 5:30-10pm, Sat-Sun 10am-2pm and 5:30-10pm.* $$$ Huntington Hotel, 1075 California St. (Taylor St.), 415-771-1140, big4restaurant.com

Bix • Financial District • Traditional American
Restaurants don't get more San Francisco than venerable Bix. Located in the decorator-chic zone known as the Jackson Square Historical District, Bix has been drawing crowds since 1988. Yep, close to 20 years old and still looking good. There's something magical about diving into the tiny brick alley—where 19th-century San Franciscans brought their gold dust to be weighed and purchased—that evokes the elegance and intrigue of another era. The aptly glittering crowd spills out the door as the valet hands you down and ushers you inside. Part Prohibition speakeasy, part upper-crust eatery, Bix attracts a wide range of diners, from old-school gents puffing over their steak frites to debutantes and their entourages dressed to the nines. Edging up to the mahogany bar, gentlemen may pat their pockets for the nonexistent cigar; ladies are sure to feel daring and order a martini. If you need to watch the action, rather than be part of it, ask for an upstairs table. The best starter is still the Firecracker Shrimp, the

chicken hash is the perennial favorite, and few places serve a better steak. Those who can should wear their highest heels, the jacket with the fur collar, and the fishnets, please. *Mon-Thu 4:30-11pm; Fri 11:30am-midnight, Sat 5:30pm-midnight, Sun 6-10pm.* $$ 56 Gold St. (Sansome St.), 415-433-6300, bixrestaurant.com

Boboquivari's • Marina • Steak House

The team that brought us the Stinking Rose and Calzone's in North Beach opened Boboquivari's (Italian for court jester). The name suits both the theatrical Venetian atmosphere—black-and-white striped tablecloths, red walls and booths—and the playful approach to dining common to all three restaurants. (The chef's website is sexandthekitchen.com.) What it does take very seriously is its steak, crab, and side dishes. The big star is the steak. Bobo's may well serve the best in town, namely corn-fed USDA Certified Prime beef, dry-aged for a month or more to perfection. The rest of the cuisine is Asian-Italian fusion. *Daily 5pm-11pm.* $$$ 1450 Lombard St. (Van Ness Ave.), 415-441-8880, boboquivaris.com

Boulevard • Embarcadero • Californian (G)

Best Romantic Dining Boulevard sits on a busy corner at the edge of the Financial District across from the Ferry Building and facing the water, with views of Treasure Island and the Bay Bridge. It beckons with its Belle Epoque signage evocative of one of Hector Guimard's Paris Metro stops. Inside, the warm interior features lavish Art Nouveau–style details, plenty of dark woods, and a team of servers known for their poise and expertise. The dining room is large—145 seats—but still intimate enough to be romantic. The food is inspired by classic French cuisine, interpreted in the modern style, meaning it bears the influence of any number of world cuisines. Look for succulent meats such as wood-oven–roasted rack of lamb, but also lighter, California-style starters. The crowd tends to be older, including plenty of expense account diners. *Mon-Thu 11:30am-2pm and 5:30-10pm, Fri 11:30am-2pm and 5:30-10:30pm, Sat 5:30-10:30pm, Sun 5:30-10pm.* $$$ One Mission St. (Steuart St.), 415-543-6084, boulevardrestaurant.com

The Buena Vista • Fisherman's Wharf • Traditional American

The Buena Vista stakes its claim to fame on having brought the elusive Irish Coffee to San Francisco back in the early '50s. As it turns out, the combination of whiskey, coffee, sugar, and cream was exactly what San Francisco needed. Perched above Fisherman's Wharf with a handsome view of the Bay and Alcatraz Island, The Buena Vista retains a certain magic even a half-century later. If you've dreamed of San Francisco, this is one of the places that will make you feel like you've arrived, especially if you get there via cable car, which drops you at the door. Do indulge in the house specialty, regardless of the hour. The food, basic diner fare covering breakfast, lunch, and dinner, isn't bad either. *Mon-Fri 9am-2am, Sat-Sun 8am-2am.* $– 2765 Hyde St. (Beach St.), 415-474-5044, thebuenavista.com

Café Claude • Downtown • French Bistro

Café Claude is an authentic French cafe right down to its zinc bar and casually sexy airs. The oft-told tale has it that owner Stephen Decker purchased Le Barbizon cafe in Paris and shipped it over one piece at a time. The result is a slice of France, nestled in a little alleyway. From the table settings to the always dashing but sometimes aloof service, it's like you've been suddenly plopped down in the sixth arrondissement. Signature dishes such as cassoulet maintain the delightful illusion. Live jazz completes the scene Thursday through Saturday. *Mon-Sat 11:30am-4:30pm and 5:30-10:30pm, Sun 5:30-10:30pm.* $ Seven Claude Ln. (Bush St.), 415-392-3515, cafeclaude.com

Café de la Presse • Downtown • French Bistro
The French love San Francisco. For more than a decade, Café de la Presse has been the hub of their stomping grounds, and a good place to unwind after a stressful trip to the French Consulate, more or less across the street. The new new menu is an improvement, but it may still be best to pick up a copy of the *International Herald Tribune* or *L'Uomo Vogue* and order an espresso. Like other nearby Frenchy hangouts, namely Café Claude and Café Bastille, Café de la Presse is a great place to meet swarthy and sultry-accented visitors. Freshly renovated in 2005, it's looking forward to another decade of welcoming European expatriates and those who admire them. *Daily 7am-11pm.* $ Hotel Triton, 352 Grant Ave. (Bush St.), 415-398-2680

Café Jacqueline • North Beach • French
Best Romantic Dining North Beach puts you in the mood for romance and Café Jacqueline closes the deal. The dining room is tiny and unassuming, boasting a handful of tables. It's quiet in there, all the better to get to know your companion and await the specialty of the house: soufflés. Start with a simple salad, share a savory soufflé with mushroom or prosciutto for dinner, and polish off the meal with a chocolate soufflé for two. Café Jacqueline is as unique, personal, and passionate as dinners out get. Hurry before the chef artiste decides she's had enough of cooking every night. Be sure to make a reservation; there's no wiggle room in a place this small. *Wed-Sun 5:30-11pm.* $$ 1454 Grant Ave. (Green St.), 415-981-5565

Café Zoetrope • North Beach • Italian
Francis Ford Coppola had a dream. He wanted a place where artists and writers and other creative people could come together to talk, share ideas, feast, and partake of the good life. His dream comes to life here, a tiny Italian restaurant in North Beach. Situated in the historic Sentinel Building, the café serves the best of the Mediterranean basics. Look for delectable cheese and olive starters, a great Caesar salad and Old World–style pizzas, calzones, and impeccable pastas. Wash them down with a sturdy glass of red from the director's winery, and browse the wall of publications spawned by his literary endeavors, namely *Zoetrope: All Story* magazine. If you're lucky, you may arrive on a night when it's hosting a reading, when the literati crowd in to sip free wine before heading across the street for a serious drink at Tosca. *Tue-Fri 11am-10pm, Sat noon-10pm, Sun noon-9pm.* $ 916 Kearny St. (Columbus Ave.), 415-291-1700, cafecoppola.com

Caffe Trieste • North Beach • Cafe
North Beach has somehow maintained its authenticity after all these years; one of the most authentic spots is Caffe Trieste. Said to be the first espresso cafe opened on the West Coast, it was established in 1956 to fuel the crush of bohemian poets and beatniks overrunning the hill. Nothing much has changed

since then. Say what you will about the scruffy décor, this is the true San Francisco. Grab your macchiato and croissant, open a European novel in translation or the *New York Times,* strike a thoughtful pose, and wait for a good moment to join the inevitable debate among the locals, who seem to have hours to contemplate their cappuccino. The mood is convivial and intellectual, and chatting up your neighbor is definitely allowed. *Sun-Thu 6:30am-11pm, Fri-Sat until midnight.* $– 609 Vallejo St. (Grant Ave.), 415-392-6739, caffetrieste.com

El Raigon • North Beach • Steak House

This stylish little steak house is so small that it can get pretty noisy, but that doesn't detract from the romance of the place. You won't need to talk much, anyway, with your mouth full of perfectly raised, cut, and aged Montana beef, expertly grilled over wood and charcoal the Argentine way. The wine list is plump with Argentine reds, and the sides, sauces, and desserts all have a distinctly South American flavor. Order you favorite cut and a glass of something unapologetically chewy, play a little footsy, and let the conversation devolve into nods of satisfaction. *Mon-Wed 5:30-10pm, Thu-Sat 5:30-11pm.* $$ 510 Union St. (Grant Ave.), 415-291-0927, elraigon.com

Elite Café • Pacific Heights • Cajun-Creole

The newly remodeled Elite remains unabashedly old school. Tiny mahogany booths with curtains offer privacy of the Prohibition Era ilk, while an oyster bar and Art Deco tile and fixtures suggest Belle Epoque Paris. So when the Cajun-influenced cuisine arrives, it may be slightly disorienting. Think New Orleans pre-Katrina and it will all make sense. In the evenings, the bar gets packed with upper-crust beautiful people from the surrounding posh neighborhood letting their hair down, but the best thing on offer is still the blackened steak, done with plate-scraping–good Southern butter sauce. Be sure to indulge in the biscuits, a house favorite, in addition to such specialties as crayfish bisque, hominy-crusted catfish, and fried green tomatoes. *Tue-Thu 5:30-10pm, Fri 5:30-10:30pm, Sat 10am-2:30pm and 5:30-10:30pm, Sun 10am-2:30pm and 5:30-10pm.* $ 2049 Fillmore St. (California St.), 415-346-8668, theelitecafe.com

Ella's • Pacific Heights • Traditional American

Best Brunches When you hear the siren call of the calorie-packed brunch, head down to Ella's, where you'll find a casually attired Gucci-loafered crowd perusing the *New York Times* as they wait for a table. Bring your own newspaper and hang in there for a table, you'll get one eventually. The food is standard egg, omelet, and pancake stuff, always tasty and done here with style. The breads, muffins, and pastries are made on the spot and a serious cut above the norm. Lunch is equally good, and dishes up American-style comfort food, a euphemism for pot pies, burgers, and chicken salad. *Mon-Fri 7am-9pm and Sat-Sun 8:30am-2pm.* $ 500 Presidio Ave. (California St.), 415-441-5669, ellassanfrancisco.com

Fleur de Lys • Downtown • French (G)

Best Romantic Dining As ornate and luxe as its name implies, Fleur de Lys is fancy with a capital F. If you know an elegant lady or gentleman in the mood for a quiet, sophisticated, expensive meal, brush them off and throw them in the cab because this is the place for them. It's also prime expense account fodder for you and your fellow suits. It is not a good place to meet Mr. or Ms. Right hanging out at the bar sipping Chardonnay. Fleur is an establishment in Fog City, having weathered early '90s stagflation, the dot-com bust, and a roaring fire that leveled the place in 2001. It bounces back better than ever each time. How? Extremely good French cuisine in a classically opulent setting. *Mon-Thu 6-9:30pm, Fri 5:30-10:30pm, 5-10:30pm.* $$$ 777 Sutter St. (Jones St.), 415-673-7779, fleurdelyssf.com

Garibaldi's • Pacific Heights • Californian
Best Always-Hot Restaurants The ambiance at Garibaldi's is elegant but inviting, an uplifting home away from home for the legions of devoted locals who create a convivial atmosphere. On the menu is a wide range of Cali-Mediterranean dishes, such as wild morel mushroom and fava bean risotto, fennel and black pepper crusted ahi tuna salad, and pan-seared scallops. Wash it down with any of the extensive list of wines by the glass. Bustling any night of the week with casually well-dressed locals who all seem to go way back, Garibaldi's makes you wish you lived around the corner. Come early for a drink at the small bar. *Mon-Thu 11:30am-2:30pm and 5:30-10pm, Fri 11:30am-2:30pm and 5:30-10:30pm, Sat 5:30-10:30pm, Sun 5:30-9pm.* $$ 347 Presidio Ave. (Sacramento St.), 415-563-8841, garibaldisrestaurant.com

Gary Danko • Fisherman's Wharf • New American (G)
Best Fine Dining The location is a bit out of the way, and it is possible to walk away from a five-course French-inspired tasting menu ready to hit the local diner for a burger. Nevertheless, this special-occasion destination restaurant has reached new heights in the culinary world. Gary Danko has four points in its favor: a dedicated, meticulous, highly creative chef; a quietly elegant setting; ingredients and flavor combinations you won't easily find elsewhere; and service worthy of truly fine dining. It's not food, it's tiny art you can eat. It's not dinner, it's a culinary experience. Prepare for your mouth to be amused, even if your wallet is not. *Daily 5:30-10pm. Bar open 5pm-midnight.* $$$ 800 North Point St. (Hyde St.), 415-749-2060, garydanko.com

Grand Cafe • Downtown • French Brasserie
The Grand Cafe lives up to its name, in part because of the late–19th-century architecture, double-high gilded ceiling, and enormous windows. If you've been to La Coupole in Paris, you may get a sense of déjà vu. The whole scene makes you feel as though you should be carrying a parasol and wearing a bustle, or else wearing a top hat and talking up that unstoppable 1920s stock market. Yes, it feels part Victorian gentlemen's club, part flapper-girl watering hole. If you can walk through the door without ordering a cocktail, you have either tremendous discipline or incredibly poor instincts. Dinner has been unsteady in the past, but may find solid ground under new chef Fabrice Roux. Breakfast is particularly transporting, like a voyage to the Continent. *Mon-Thu 7am-10pm, Fri 7am-11pm, Sat 8am-11pm, Sun 9am-10pm.* $$ Hotel Monaco, 501 Geary St. (Taylor St.), 415-292-0101, grandcafe-sf.com

Greens Restaurant • Marina • Vegetarian
Best Restaurants with a View Run by the San Francisco Zen Center and opened near the end of the hippie heyday in the '70s, Greens is a landmark establishment for highbrow vegetarian cuisine. The décor features incredible woods simply fashioned and presumably harvested without harm to the tree, or at least the for-

est. While the food is reliably good and features the best locally grown produce—much of it from the Zen Center's own garden in Marin—the real attraction here is the spectacular, ground-level view of the water, Golden Gate Bridge, and Marin Headlands. *Mon 5:30-9pm, Tue-Fri noon-2:30pm and 5:30-9pm, Sat noon-2:30pm and 5:30-9pm (prix fixe dinner), Sun 10:30am-2pm.* $$ ⬜ Fort Mason Center, Bldg. A (Marina Blvd.), 415-771-6222, greensrestaurant.com

Harris' Restaurant • Pacific Heights • Steak House
Big-time indulgence is the order of the day at Harris', an elegant (think leather booths) steak house in a venue practically as old as the city. It goes like this: You want your martini, then your prawn cocktail and Caesar salad, then a bottle of California's finest red, then your steak—dry-aged for 21 days and cut on the premises—then your baked potato, and then, after a bite of chocolate mousse, you want a glass of the world's finest single malt Scotch whisky or vintage port. It may sound like the cardiac crisis special, but for the right occasion, a traditional steak house is exactly what the doctor ordered. *Mon-Thu 5:30-9:30pm, Fri 5:30-10pm, Sat 5-10pm, Sun 5-9:30pm.* $$$ ⬜ 2100 Van Ness Ave. (Pacific Ave.), 415-673-1888, harrisrestaurant.com

Hawthorne Lane • SoMa • Californian
Best Power Lunch Spots Ambitious, well-established Hawthorne Lane is tucked into an eponymous alley in the middle of SoMa. Part of its charm is the surprise of turning off gritty, loud Howard Street to find a lush culinary oasis. The motif is that of a refined garden hideaway done in pastels, warm woods, and floral accents—a far and refreshing cry from the modernist standard that prevails elsewhere. A large island bar sits in the middle of the front room; more intimate dining areas adjoin. The crowd is businessy; the food is distinctly Californian with a fusion of world flavors and an emphasis on quality ingredients. Stop in 4 to 6pm weekdays for a happy hour with high-class nibbles and drinks. They even have free wireless at the bar. *Mon-Thu 11:30am-1:30pm and 5:30-9pm, Fri 11:30am-1:30pm and 5:30-10pm, Sat 5:30-10pm, Sun 5:30-9pm. Hors d'oeuvres at the bar weekdays 3pm-midnight.* $$$ F⬜ 22 Hawthorne Ln. (Howard St.), 415-777-9779, hawthornelane.com

Hayes Street Grill • Hayes Valley • Seafood
Best Seafood Restaurants Patricia Unterman opened her restaurant in the late '70s, at the beginning of the local food revolution, and it has been a mainstay of the San Francisco foodie scene ever since. Easy, reliable, and comfortably worn in, Hayes Street Grill is the favorite sweater of the restaurant scene. Expect fresh seafood prepared simply to let the natural flavors shine through, delicious pastas, and expertly grilled meats. Browse the shop-laden streets of Hayes Valley until you feel your appetite bite, then head to the Grill for a masterful repast. Since it is frequently a destination of the pre-symphony or opera crowd, it's worth calling ahead to reserve a table. *Mon-Thu 11:30am-2pm and 5-9:30pm, Fri 11:30am-2pm and 5-10:30pm, Sat 5:30-10:30pm, Sun 5-8:30pm.* $$ F⬜ 320 Hayes St. (Franklin St.), 415-863-5545, hayesstreetgrill.com

Jackson-Fillmore • Pacific Heights • Italian
You will feel like a Pac Heights local when you squeeze in the door of Jackson-Fillmore, a lively, diminutive eatery serving basic, well-executed Italian fare. The setup is better suited to singles—who are seated at the tiny bar—or three or four

people, the magic number to lay claim to one of the densely arranged tables. Couples generally end up at the bar. Gregarious types should have good luck striking up conversations over the free round of bruschetta that starts off the meal. A long-standing local institution, Jackson-Fillmore captures the simpatico camaraderie of those who live nearby. *Tue-Thu 5:30-10pm, Fri-Sat 5:30-10:30pm, Sun 5-9:30pm.* $ 2506 Fillmore St. (Jackson St.), 415-346-5288

Jardinière • Hayes Valley • Californian (G)
A favorite stop before and after the opera and symphony, both a short walk away, Jardinière maintains a festive scene loaded with sparkle that more than lives up to the champagne theme. A two-story setup with a central bar draws everyone together, especially on nights when live jazz plays upstairs, which is often. Those in their twenties who grace this venue are likely to be showing their parents a good time or stepping out with an older lover. Owner Traci Des Jardins' French-California cuisine, now executed by others in the kitchen, is excellent. The extensive wine list should cover anything you'd like to go with it. *Sun-Mon 5-10pm, Tue-Wed 5-10:30pm, Thu-Sat 5-11:30pm.* $$$ 300 Grove St. (Franklin St.), 415-861-5555, jardiniere.com

Jazz at Pearl's • North Beach • Spanish
Enjoy an assortment of tapas before settling in to savor the fabulous jazz. *See Classic Nightlife, p.149, for details.* $ 256 Columbus Ave. (Broadway), 415-291-8255, jazzatpearls.com

Julius' Castle • North Beach • Italian
Best Restaurants with a View Sometimes weird is weird, and sometimes weird is fantastic. Julius' Castle is weird fantastic. The place is trapped in amber, circa 1849. Settle into the Wild West saloon downstairs and take in the view. No one will be surprised if you pretend to be a railroad tycoon, a wealthy merchant outfitting Gold Rush hopefuls, or a painted lady expert at fleecing new money. The food is surprisingly good, considering how far such a place could get on historical cachet and a million-dollar view. Plan your approach carefully. The area is so rich with history and sights, it's a shame to just pull up out front. A stroll in North Beach and a look at the Coit Tower murals (footwear permitting) will put you in the mood. This is a special-occasion restaurant frequented by visitors from across the bay and around the world. *Daily 5-9:30pm.* $$$ 1541 Montgomery St. (Union St.), 415-392-2222, juliuscastlerestaurant.com

Kokkari Estiatorio • Financial District • Greek
Imagine, an ambitious new restaurant that doesn't serve French-inspired California cuisine. From the moment it opened, Kokkari has been embraced for its warm, woodsy, sepia-toned atmosphere, its delicious food, and above all, its fresh perspective on the culinary scene. Greek restaurants conjure images of group dancing and tables lofted in the air à la Zorba. Not at elegant Kokkari. It claims to serve "the food of the gods," and one is tempted to agree. The emphasis is on hospitality, not attitude, as demonstrated by the 20-foot family table. Enter the rustic setting—Arts and Crafts meets Shaker, plus modern sophistication—and you enter a fantasy where the artisan foods runneth over. Feta, olives, lamb, filo pies, stuffed grape leaves, meatballs, octopus, and crab are all of the best quality and done to perfection. Such a romantic setting attracts diners of

all ages in the mood for love. *Mon-Thu 11:30am-2:30pm and 5:30-10pm, Fri 11:30am-2:30pm and 5:30-11pm, Sat 5-11pm.* $$ ≡ 200 Jackson St. (Front St.), 415-981-0983, kokkari.com

Kyo-Ya • SoMa • Japanese
Best Sushi Restaurants If you want to experience a Japanese meal the way Japanese connoisseurs like it, visit Kyo-Ya. The setting is subdued and quiet, a fitting complement to the highly traditional and precisely rendered cuisine. By cuisine, we mean more than sushi, though the sushi is excellent. Order a noodle soup, tempura, or teriyaki and you will understand why this is considered one of the city's premier Japanese restaurants. Try a set dinner to get the chef's take on a meal, complete with Japanese-style pickles. Japanese businessmen frequent Kyo-Ya, as do other expense account executives who take their sushi seriously. *Tue-Fri 11:30am-2pm and 6-10pm, Sat 6-10pm.* $$ ≡ Palace Hotel, Two New Montgomery St. (Jessie St.), 415-546-5090, kyo-ya-restaurant.com

Laurel Court Restaurant • Nob Hill • High Tea
The recently restored Laurel Court lobby at the Fairmont, with its trio of ornate domes, pristine marble floors, and Corinthian columns trimmed in gold, makes an opulent setting for afternoon tea, a ritual certain to evoke your better self. Lift a cucumber sandwich to your lips, dab the last bit of caviar from your chin, and you will know you have arrived. *Afternoon tea served daily 2:30-4:30pm.* $$$ ≡ The Fairmont, 950 Mason St. (California St.), 415-772-5260

Le Central • Downtown • French Bistro
A French brasserie serving consistently well-rendered classics for more than three decades, Le Central is a staple of the business people who work nearby. Generally crowded and noisy, the zinc bar makes for good people-watching. At lunchtime, the city's power brokers and Parisian expats come for their fix of roast chicken with frites, onion soup, steak au poivre, and cassoulet with white beans and sausage. *Mon-Sat 11:30am-10:30pm.* $$ ≡ 453 Bush St. (Grant St.), 415-391-2233

Le Colonial • Downtown • Vietnamese
Le Colonial evokes Southeast Asia of the early 20th century, meaning white pillars, plantation shutters, palms, ceiling fans, and white linen suits—the days when Ho Chi Minh City was a sweltering paradise called Saigon. It stands on hallowed ground, having taken over where the infamous Trader Vic's left off. Le Colonial has lived up to the legacy. The French-Vietnamese fusion food is excellent, and the scene is energetic, one might even say sexy. Although not the sizzling spot it once was, a nightcap at Le Colonial can still produce connections with the young and hot. *Sun-Wed 5:30-10pm, Thu-Sat until 11pm.* $$ ⛵≡ 20 Cosmo Pl. (Taylor St.), 415-931-3600, lecolonialsf.com

LuLu • SoMa • Provençal
This classic and perennially popular San Francisco eatery turns out consistently delicious, rustic, Italian-influenced fare, including wood-fired oven, rotisserie and grilled specialties, pizzas, pasta, and shellfish. Dishes come on platters that are meant to be shared family-style. The industrial-looking space is usually filled to capacity, so book a table in advance, or take your chance at the bar. Be warned, conversation is difficult in the noisy and crowded room. LuLu's wine bar

next door is a more intimate alternative, with some 70 wines available by the glass. *Mon-Thu 11:30am-10pm, Fri 11:30-11pm, Sat 11am-11pm, Sun 11am-10pm.* $$ 816 Folsom St. (Fourth St.), 415-495-5775, restaurantlulu.com

Mama's on Washington Square • North Beach • Traditional American
The swear-by dish is the crab omelet, but the French toast made with homemade breads such as cinnamon swirl brioche and paired with homemade jams and freshly squeezed juice will knock your socks off. Other omelets arrive perfectly flipped, with no brown, and stuffed with succulent fillings such as Italian bacon, fresh herbs, and roasted tomatoes. And the location, on the corner of Washington Square in North Beach, can make you want to belt out a little Tony Bennett number. What's the catch? Horrible, long, slow lines; little in the way of atmosphere; and parking, or the distinct and painful lack of it. So, if you are up with the birds and traveling by foot, bus, or taxi, head straight to Mama's. *Tue-Sun 8am-3pm.* $– 1701 Stockton St. (Filbert St.), 415-362-6421

Masa's • Downtown • French (G)
Best Wine Lists Masa's is the place for a formal dining experience of the sort that consistently merits a gold star in your long-term memory. The setting is elegant and refined, with a streak of modernism. Dark walls set off abstract artworks beautifully in the open dining room, where the ambiance is subdued and romantic but not terribly private. With the focus on the culinary experience, this is a great restaurant for married couples and business associates. (It also seats groups in the wine cellar, which feels like a secret clubhouse.) Expect multiple courses of perfectly rendered, exquisite French-Japanese-California cuisine, an acclaimed wine list, an amuse-bouche or two, and glorious desserts. The tasting menu might include such delicacies as ahi tartare with gold leaf nori and curry oil; chilled foie gras with peach and lavender honey jam, and Gewürztraminer gelée; crab with tangerine and avocado with orange-infused oil; or duck with shallots in a port reduction. *Tue-Sat 5:30-9:30pm.* $$$ 648 Bush St. (Powell St.), 415-989-7154

Moose's • North Beach • Californian
Aside from the blue neon moose head out front, the draws here are a full bar, an open kitchen serving consistently good California cuisine (in spite of a revolving chef door), and an extensive wine list. Regardless of changes to the menu over time, the storied Mooseburger persists, as does the excellent Sunday brunch. From the tables in front, you can admire the view of grassy Washington Square. The scene is heavy with politicians and the Financial District crowd. Remember that large cap mutual fund you bought? Someone in this room is spending your transaction fee on a nice dry Chardonnay right now. In the evening, come for dinner or drinks and hear live jazz every night. By day, stroll around the area, hitting any of the great Italian cafes for a post-déjeuner espresso. *Mon-Wed 5:30-10:30pm, Thu 11:30am-2:30pm and 5:30-10:30pm, Fri-Sat 11:30am-2:30pm and 5:30-11pm, Sun 10am-2:30pm and 5-10pm.* $$$ 1652 Stockton St. (Filbert St.), 415-989-7800, mooses.com

Park Chalet • Richmond • Traditional American
The airy, skylit Park Chalet draws a relaxed crowd to its bar and outdoor patio. *See Classic Nightlife, p.149, for details.* $ 1000 Great Hwy. (Fulton St.), 415-386-8439, parkchalet.com

PlumpJack Cafe • Marina • Californian
Associated with investors from the Getty family and Mayor Gavin Newsom, PlumpJack properties tend to the inhabitants of Pacific Heights and Cow Hollow—that is, the posh bits—and have a certain mood to them, like a wealthy but fun-loving patron's living room. At the cafe, the wine list is a standout, with a consistent flow of soon-to-be-hot discoveries and bargains by the glass. The California-style menu changes frequently. A spring menu featured dishes such as green garlic soup, crab and endive salad, roasted quail, vegetable risotto, and porterhouse steak, for example. *Mon-Fri 11:30am-2pm and 5:30-10pm, Sat-Sun 5:30pm-10pm.* $$ ▭ 3127 Fillmore St. (Filbert St.), 415-563-4755, plumpjack.com/cafe_main.html

Postrio • Downtown • Californian
When you want to party like it's 1989, head to Postrio, Wolfgang Puck's long-running success story. Postrio is another Pat Kuleto–designed interior, identifiable by its elaborate blown-glass light fixtures, ambitious scale, and general effusiveness. The impressive main dining room boasts quite a bit of modern art, including a terrific Rauschenberg, and a number of truly enormous flower arrangements. The quality dipped in the late '90s, but seems to be back on track these days. In the end, Postrio still goes the extra mile, serving house-made breads, pastas, smoked salmon, and just about everything else. *Sun-Wed 5:30-10pm, Thu-Sat 5:30-10:30pm.* $$$ TB▭ Prescott Hotel, 545 Post St. (Mason St.), 415-776-7825, postrio.com

The Rotunda at Neiman Marcus • Downtown • Californian
The same qualities that make a Chanel suit sexy on a woman of any age keep the Rotunda on top of the lunchtime heap year after year. This is especially true now that it has been refurbished and updated, without, thankfully, changing its classic approach to good taste. Décor to menu, it retains its character from a more genteel era. The tables seem to float up against the golden, glass-paneled, and ornate rotunda drifting above the light-filled foyer of the department store. This is not a place to do business, it is a place to discuss frivolous, privileged dilemmas, such as which Hermès scarf to buy or whether dusty rose is the new black. The crab cakes and lobster bisque are tried-and-true favorites. You may take your mother. You may take your sister. But in such a bastion of tradition, it may be most fun to take your favorite naughty girl or boy toy. Not a place to meet people, it's also not the place to dine solo. *Mon-Sat 11am-5pm, Sun noon-5pm.* $$ ▭ 150 Stockton St. (Geary St.), 415-362-4777, rotundarestaurant.com

Rubicon • Financial District • Californian
Best Wine Lists Not a newcomer, not a trendy hangout, and not a big flashy joint, Rubicon is like your favorite jazz standard. Artful, sophisticated, and yet not stodgy, it's refreshingly enjoyable each time you go back to it, perpetually revealing some new nuance of skill and insight. While the French-California cuisine is top-notch, the wine list is even more of a standout. Those dedicated to great food and wine make a visit to Rubicon a priority whenever they're in town. Nestled in the thick of the high-rises downtown, it attracts plenty of suits on weekdays. The exposed brick walls bear the creative work of Robert DeNiro, who co-owns the place with Francis Coppola, Robin Williams, and others. *Mon-Tue 5:30-10:30pm, Wed 11:30am-2pm and 5:30-10:30pm, Thu-Sat 5:30-10:30pm.* $$ ▭ 558 Sacramento St. (Sansome St.), 415-434-4100, sfrubicon.com

CLASSIC · RESTAURANTS

Scala's Bistro • Downtown • French/Italian
The Sir Francis Drake Hotel, not to be confused with the nearby Westin St. Francis, opened in 1928 just off Union Square. Its street-level dining room, Scala's Bistro, maintains the aura of the roaring '20s in grand style with dark wood booths, amber walls, an expansive mural, chandeliers, and plenty of Parisian-bistro ambiance. Not a trendy spot, although eating in the bar area can be lively, it has earned its reputation the hard way: by serving consistently good meals in a highly enjoyable setting. This is the place for a post-shopping refuel or pre-theater dinner. The food is French-Italian, with dishes like roasted chicken with braised broccoli rabe, fried calamari, pastas, and beef bourguignon. It's also great for a high-minded breakfast, meaning French toast made with orange brioche and blueberry sauce. After dinner, try the Bostini, a decadent cream and chocolate experience, then take the elevator to the 21st floor to shake it up at Harry Denton's Starlight Room. *Daily 8-10:30am and 11:30am-4pm, bistro menu 4-5:15pm, dinner 5:15pm-midnight.* $$ Sir Francis Drake Hotel, 432 Powell St. (Sutter St.), 415-395-8555, scalasbistro.com

Sears Fine Food • Downtown • Diner
Founded in 1938, Sears stopped evolving sometime in the mid-'50s. And why not? Once you've achieved the perfect pancake and the bottomless coffee cup, there's not much to improve. An enjoyable antidote to the chichi madness of Union Square, Sears is as wholesome as a cool glass of milk. A recent remodel spruced the place up without stripping away the character. Late sleepers will be happy to know that it serves breakfast until 2:30pm. *Daily 6:30am-10pm.* $– 439 Powell St. (Sutter St.), 415-986-0700, searsfinefood.com

South Park Café • SoMa • French Bistro
By day, the South Park Café serves an excellent morning cappuccino—French newspapers included—and white-linen French lunch. In the evening, the tiny dining room, done in hues of cream and white and adorned with fresh flowers, shines like the secret gem that it is. Windows open on sidewalk tables facing the lawn and towering trees of the park. Sip aperitifs at the zinc bar and watch the table action reflected in the mirror behind the bar. The steak frites is one of the best in town, and the rest of the menu is excellent. Thumbs up for the profiteroles. The patrons are a blend of upper-crust media types and slightly older fans of French food. *Mon-Fri 11:30am-2:30pm and 5:30-10pm, Sat 5:30-10pm.* $$ 108 South Park (Second St.), 415-495-7275

Sutro's at the Cliff House • Richmond • Californian
Best Restaurants with a View If the Cliff House were a cat, it would definitely be living its ninth life. Built on a rocky bluff in 1863, the first Cliff House was a playground for prominent San Francisco families, who would drive their carriages out to Ocean Beach for horse races. It has burned to the ground twice. The current structure, extensively modified, was built in 1909. The restaurant recently completed a sleek, modern renovation. Arrive before dusk, grab a seat at a crisply set table by one of the soaring floor-to-ceiling windows overlooking the Pacific, and watch the sun go down while you sip cocktails. Finally, a reason—other than the view and a chance to dip one's toes in the water—for urban pleasure-seekers of all ages to make the journey to the western edge of the city. *Daily 11:30am-3:30pm and 5-9:30pm.* $$ 1090 Point Lobos Ave. (Balboa Ave.), 415-386-3330, cliffhouse.com

Swan Oyster Depot • Nob Hill • Seafood

A San Francisco institution since 1912, the Depot is half fish market and half counter-service hole-in-the-wall. The best time to visit is between November and June, when the local Dungeness crab is in season. But at any time of year you'll find the selections are straight-from-the-water fresh. Specialties include classic clam chowder, the smoked salmon plate, and an obscenely large variety of oysters. The staff is boisterous and friendly and makes everyone feel like a regular. For the full classic San Francisco effect, order a side of sourdough bread and a locally brewed Anchor Steam beer. Be prepared, it only takes cash. *Mon-Sat 8am-5:30pm.* $ 1517 Polk St. (California St.), 415-673-1101

Tadich Grill • Financial District • Seafood

Opened in 1849 as a coffee stand, the Tadich Grill is San Francisco's oldest restaurant. Its specialty is seafood. Favorites include the sand dabs and the clam chowder, simple classics it has been doing well for decades, both of which go beautifully with crusty sourdough bread (made on the spot daily) and butter. A long counter offers extensive seating for singles, who will feel right at home, especially at lunchtime, when the Financial District hits the place in force. Two or more can tuck into one of the semiprivate wooden booths. During the week, diners arrive straight from their offices. On weekends, couples and small groups visiting the city prevail. *Mon-Fri 11am-9:30pm, Sat 11:30am-9:30pm.* $$ 240 California St. (Front St.), 415-391-1849

The Terrace • Downtown • Californian

Best Brunches If P. Diddy rolled out of bed one bright morning with the itch for Sunday brunch, he would summon his posse and nip right down to the Ritz. The garden is lovely, the view is spectacular, and the buffet covers every breakfast impulse imaginable. On Sunday there is live jazz; other days you can still breakfast or lunch while you wonder how the little people are struggling through the day. If you're feeling peckish in the afternoon, nothing is more genteel than high tea. Ladies, the Chanel suit is not required, but it's a nice touch. The Ritz also boasts the Dining Room, its exquisite dinner destination. *Mon 6-11am, 11:30am-2:30pm, and 6-9:30pm, Tue-Sat 6:30-11am and 11:30am-2:30pm, Sun 6-10am, 10:30am-2:30pm, and 6-9:30pm.* $$$ Ritz-Carlton Hotel, 600 Stockton St. (California St.), 415-773-6198, ritzcarlton.com

Ton Kiang • Richmond • Dim Sum

Best Dim Sum The avenues of San Francisco have seen as many waves of immigrants as Ocean Beach has seen waves, among them Hong Kong Chinese arrivals bearing dim sum know-how. Ton Kiang, with its big, noisy dining areas, bad chairs, and bland décor, is typical of dim sum restaurants. The difference is the quality of the dumplings, clay pot dishes, and other fare, all of which is a serious cut above the norm. It's most popular at lunch when the dishes are wheeled around on carts. Don't be dismayed by the always long lines outside the door—they tend to move quickly. *Mon-Thu 10am-10pm, Fri 10am-10:30pm, Sat 9:30am-10:30pm, Sun 9am-10pm.* $ 5821 Geary Blvd. (22nd Ave.), 415-387-8273, tonkiang.net

CLASSIC • RESTAURANTS

Trader Vic's • Hayes Valley • Polynesian
Get your umbrella drinks and pupus (full dinners, if you like) at this reborn classy tiki. *See Classic Nightlife, p.151, for details.* $$ ⅩF⩵ 555 Golden Gate Ave. (Van Ness Ave.), 415-775-6300, tradervics.com/rest-sanfran.html

Yank Sing • SoMa • Dim Sum
Best Dim Sum Yank Sing is perkier than the usual dim sum eatery. There is a nicely crisp, snappy, energetic feel to the place that is not entirely accounted for by the steady stream of customers. The same zing is apparent in the food, which is flavorful and arrives swiftly. You will no sooner unfold your napkin than the first cart will roll by, offering steamed dumplings filled with pork, chicken, or shrimp; succulent vegetables; or any of dozens of other treats. Say yes to the asparagus. Both locations draw a big business crowd at lunchtime. *Mon-Fri 11am-3pm, Sat-Sun 10am-4pm.* $ ⩵ One Rincon Center, 101 Spear St. (Mission St.), 415-957-9300; 49 Stevenson St. (Second St.), 415-541-4949, yanksing.com

Classic San Francisco: The Nightlife

Absinthe Brasserie and Bar • Hayes Valley • Restaurant Bar
A Belle Epoque scene catering to the pre-symphony crowd. *See Classic Restaurants, p.132, for details.* 398 Hayes St. (Gough St.), 415-551-1590, absinthe.com

AsiaSF • SoMa • Nightclub/Performance
Best Only-in-San Francisco Experiences Dinner, dancing, and drag queens—what more could you want? The Asian fusion cuisine is served by gender illusionists who take turns taking to the runway that juts into the dining room. The performances are titillating and very polished. When you've sated your hunger aboveground, descend to the sunken dance floor to work a little of your own magic. The décor is Asian glam with ample Chinese-red features; the crowd is upscale. Dress your sexy best. While the theatrically enhanced dinner is great fun, the dance club downstairs makes a worthy weekend destination on its own merit. *Mon-Wed 6:30pm-2am, Thu 6pm-2am, Fri 5:30pm-2am, Sat 5pm-2am, Sun 6pm-2am.* 201 Ninth St. (Howard St.), 415-255-2742, asiasf.com

Balboa Cafe • Marina • Restaurant Bar
An upscale saloon with a fine long bar that's been a buzzing scene for well over 90 years. *See Classic Restaurants, p.133, for details.* 3199 Fillmore St. (Greenwich St.), 415-921-3944, balboacafe.com

Beach Blanket Babylon • North Beach • Performance
A North Beach institution and the longest running musical revue in American history, *Beach Blanket Babylon* opened in 1974. More than 30 years later, it still sells out nearly every show. The secret may be the constant addition of new material. *BBB* adds new spoofs, parodies, and references to current events and popular culture, so the show is always fresh and relevant. The music is infectious, the costumes outrageous, the jokes silly, and of course the preposterous hats keep getting bigger and bigger. *BBB* is all in good fun. Most of the seats are first-come, first-seated, so arrive early. *Wed-Thu 8pm, Fri-Sat 7 and 10pm, Sun 1pm and 4pm.* Club Fugazi, 678 Beach Blanket Babylon Blvd. (Green and Powell Sts.), 415-421-4222, beachblanketbabylon.com

The Big 4 Restaurant • Nob Hill • Restaurant Bar
A clubby and exclusive atmosphere reigns at this traditional hotel bar. *See Classic Restaurants, p.133, for details.* Huntington Hotel, 1075 California St. (Taylor St.), 415-771-1140, big4restaurant.com

Biscuits & Blues • Downtown • Blues Club
Live acts play nightly at this subterranean Southern speakeasy near Union Square, now more than a decade old. In 2005 it added a full-service restaurant upstairs, serving down-home staples such as jambalaya, catfish, its illustrious biscuits, and fried chicken. Downstairs, blues artists of every stripe rock the house. The setting is intimate, with tables squeezed into a small, dimly lit space. The whole club is sit-down, so you can relax with a beer and enjoy the

show. Don't plan to socialize once the music starts, it's far too loud. Generally, it's traditional blues and bluegrass on Mondays, women in the spotlight on Tuesdays, Chicago-style blues on Wednesdays, roots on the weekends, gospel on Sundays. *Tue-Sat 5:30pm-1am; Sun-Mon 6:30pm-1am.* C F ≣ 401 Mason St. (Geary St.), 415-292-2583, biscuitsandblues.com

Bix • Financial District • Restaurant Bar
A sophisticated place to order a martini and chat with a stylishly attired crowd. *See Classic Restaurants, p.133, for details.* F ≣ 56 Gold St. (Sansome St.), 415-433-6300, bixrestaurant.com

Boom Boom Room • Pacific Heights • Blues Club
The Fillmore corridor boasts an incredibly rich musical history, especially considering it really only started in the '30s. In those days, the clubs were all about bebop. Soon blues and jazz moved in. In the '40s and '50s it was known as the "Harlem of the West." Today Johnny Lee Hooker's Boom Boom Room carries the torch, booking blues and jazz of the highest quality seven nights a week. Fans of every stripe turn up to worship their blues roots and get funky, and the range of attire is equally accepting. Everybody likes a sharp-dressed man, or woman, but this is one venue where nobody will complain if you show up in jeans and work boots. The sound system belts it out; don't expect to chat up your neighbor while the band is playing. *Check the website for show times.* C ≣ 1601 Fillmore St. (Geary Blvd.), 415-673-8000, boomboomblues.com

Bubble Lounge • Financial District • Lounge/Wine Bar
Located in Jackson Square, the Bubble Lounge makes for an easy stop after work or a convenient nightcap after dinner nearby (Bocadillos is next door). Exposed brick, overstuffed seating, candlelight, and more than 300 varieties of champagnes and sparkling wines create a relaxed ambiance in which to get to know your neighbor. The cave-like downstairs rooms offer privacy, a bit of dancing, and a pool table. This is no longer the place to find cutting-edge scenesters, but if you're looking for a romantic glass of something to tickle your nose or a chance to meet an investment banker, you're in business. *Mon 5:30pm-1am, Tue-Fri 5:30pm-2am, Saturday 6:30pm-2am.* B ≣ 714 Montgomery St. (Washington St.), 415-434-4204, bubblelounge.com

The Buena Vista • Fisherman's Wharf • Restaurant Bar
This San Francisco institution is where the Irish Coffee was first served in America. *See Classic Restaurants, p.134, for details.* ≣ 2765 Hyde St. (Beach St.), 415-474-5044, thebuenavista.com

Café Claude • Downtown • Restaurant Bar
A traditional French cafe with live jazz Thursday through Saturday. *See Classic Restaurants, p.134, for details.* F ≣ Seven Claude Ln. (Bush St.), 415-392-3515, cafeclaude.com

Café Zoetrope • North Beach • Restaurant Bar
Snag a streetside table at Francis Ford Coppola's cafe and watch the world go by. *See Classic Restaurants, p.135, for details.* F ≣ 916 Kearny St. (Columbus Ave.), 415-291-1700, cafecoppola.com

Enrico's • North Beach • Restaurant Bar
Is this Milan or San Francisco? Starting in the late afternoon, the front patio at Enrico's is a European-style scene for watching the eclectic foot traffic on Broadway and making friends from every walk of life. Outdoor heaters warm the air and, in the later evening, *le jazz hot* warms up the mood. A glass of red wine, a cocktail, an appetizer, or dinner—it's all good, and you can even light up on the patio. While not glam or new, Enrico's has an air of well-deserved confidence. Like North Beach in general, it may be slightly worn around the edges, but that's part of its charm. *Sun-Thu 11:30am-11pm, Fri-Sat 11:30-midnight.* C F 504 Broadway (Kearny St.), 415-982-6223, enricossidewalkcafe.com

15 Romolo • North Beach • DJ Bar
Hidden away in a steep alley in North Beach, 15 Romolo is the bar associated with the Hotel Basque, information you really only need in order to find the place, which is otherwise unmarked. The décor is Euro-lounge chic, done a few years ago so it's not white and it's not brand new, but it is stylish and self-confident. It was lounge (slightly) before lounge was cool. The bar makes a beautiful display of backlit bottles, the light menu items are tasty, and the DJ is often quite good, especially on Sunday night. The scene is young and more stylish than the crowds hitting the bigger North Beach venues. Beware, the small space is packed to its nightclub gills on weekends. *Mon-Fri 5:30pm-2am, Sat-Sun 7pm-2am.* C Hotel Basque, 15 Romolo Pl. (Broadway), 415-398-1359

G Bar • Pacific Heights • Hotel Bar/Lounge
An unexpected find in an otherwise sleepy neighborhood, G Bar has a sophistication not typically associated with a motor lodge (it's attached to the Laurel Inn). It began as a true locals-only draw, catering to the area Laurel Heights elite. But the ultramodern fireplace and other cutting-edge elements made a stir and, as word of mouth spread, it began bringing in trend-seekers from all parts. The line out the door eventually scared the original crowd away. Lately things have rebalanced, and there's usually a good mix of locals and visitors. The small, modern room has an energetic vibe, with good-looking, well-dressed singles jockeying for a little cheese fondue and eye contact before heading off for late-night parts unknown. This is the perfect place to pop in for a nightcap after dinner at Garibaldi's. *Tue 7pm-midnight, Wed-Sat 6pm-2am.* B Laurel Inn, 488 Presidio Ave. (California St.), 415-409-4227, gbarsf.com

Harry Denton's Starlight Room • Downtown • Piano Bar
Best Lounges with a View They call it "glamour with a view." From the top of the Sir Francis Drake Hotel, you can see for miles in almost every direction. The Starlight Room is a nightly party in opulent Vienna opera house–style surroundings, serenaded by the Starlight Orchestra and its dance-friendly jazz, Motown, disco, and soul hits. Few places invite couples past their twenties to shake their proverbial booties, let alone snuggle up for a romantic slow dance. Harry's does both with style. Seize the opportunity to try a Cable Car, its signature concoction with cinnamon and brandy. The dress code—no jeans, no sports attire—is strictly enforced. Though couples will feel more than welcome, the mix-and-mingle action is lively and inviting as well. *Daily 5pm-2am.* C Sir Francis Drake Hotel, 450 Powell St. (Sutter St.), 415-395-8595, harrydenton.com

CLASSIC • NIGHTLIFE

House of Shields • SoMa • Restaurant Bar
Since 1908, the House of Shields has been a popular gathering spot, whether for jazz, hearty meals, or a happy-hour cocktail. The Victorian and Art Nouveau detail, tile floor, mirrored bar, blown-glass light fixtures, and wooden booths are all original. It's abuzz at lunchtime, serving burgers, meatloaf, Caesar salad, and other mainstays. While suits and live jazz rule the afternoons and evenings, after 9pm the DJs come out every night to play new wave, house, funk, and jazz in the room upstairs, bringing the dance club scene along with them. *Mon-Sat 2pm-2am.* C≡ 39 New Montgomery St. (Market St.), 415-975-8651

Jardinière • Hayes Valley • Restaurant Bar
The perfect destination pre- and post-opera. *See Classic Restaurants, p.139, for details.* F≡ 300 Grove St. (Franklin St.), 415-861-5555, jardiniere.com

Jazz at Pearl's • North Beach • Jazz Club
Pearl's was an institution for years, until Pearl decided to hang it up. Luckily, sultry jazz vocalist Kim Nalley and her husband stepped in to remodel, upgrade, and generally save the day. They offer a Byzantine array of details about ticket options, and many stern warnings about arriving late. It boils down to this: If you want to feel like you are in a Fred Astaire flick circa 1934, sign up for dinner and a show. You will be seated, served surprisingly good food, and later, when the plate clattering and fork pinging is over, the show will begin. Arrive late, and you won't get to eat because the show must go on. Or choose the 10:30 cocktail show, where again, you must arrive well in advance to enjoy tapas, dessert, and cocktails. Choose a night when Kim is singing and you will not be disappointed. *Dinner show Sun-Thu 8:30, Fri-Sat 9pm. Arrive an hour early for dinner. Cocktail show Sun-Thu 10:30pm, Fri-Sat 11pm. Arrive an hour early for tapas and dessert.* CF≡ 256 Columbus Ave. (Broadway), 415-291-8255, jazzatpearls.com

Julius' Castle • North Beach • Restaurant Bar
This elegant restaurant bar is perched on Telegraph Hill overlooking the bay. *See Classic Restaurants, p.139, for details.* ≡ 1541 Montgomery St. (Union St.), 415-392-2222, juliuscastlerestaurant.com

Le Colonial • Downtown • Restaurant Bar
A sexy setting for an exotic cocktail among attractive locals. *See Classic Restaurants, p.140, for details.* F≡ 20 Cosmo Pl. (Taylor St.), 415-931-3600, lecolonialsf.com

Park Chalet • Richmond • Restaurant Bar
The Park Chalet is a 3,000-square-foot glass-enclosed extension onto the back of the landmark Beach Chalet structure, sheltered from the offshore winds and facing the lush grass, Monterey pines, and old Dutch windmill of Golden Gate Park. The weekend can be a crush, but it's worth it. The two-story stone fireplace and floor-to-ceiling retractable windows make a cozy setting on a foggy day and a marvelous place to bask on warm ones. The food is basic but good, with items such as pizzas, hamburgers, crab cocktail, shepherd's pie, and banana splits. Of the few places in San Francisco to eat outside, the Park Chalet is among the best. *Mon-Thu 11am-10pm, Fri 11am-11pm, Sat 9am-11pm, Sun 9am-10pm.* CF≡ 1000 Great Hwy. (Fulton St.), 415-386-8439, parkchalet.com

Punch Line Comedy Club • Financial District • Comedy Club
Now legendary, the Punch Line has been around for more than a quarter of a century, having helped launch such talents as Robin Williams, Ellen DeGeneres, Rosie O'Donnell, Drew Carey, Chris Rock, and Dana Carvey. The yucks may be top-of-the-line, but the food is basic at best. Luckily, you probably won't have to eat it. A dozen great restaurants are within walking distance. On the weekends, plan to enjoy a great meal, then walk over for the 11:00 show. *Shows at 9pm daily with an additional 11pm show Fri-Sat.* 444 Battery St. (Washington St.), 415-397-0644, punchlinecomedyclub.com

Scala's Bistro • Downtown • Restaurant Bar
The perfect place to take a break from the rigors of Union Square shopping. *See Classic Restaurants, p.143, for details.* Sir Francis Drake Hotel, 432 Powell St. (Sutter St.), 415-395-8555, scalasbistro.com

Tonga Room • Nob Hill • Theme Bar
Best Tiki Bars No kidding, the drinks come in a ceramic mug shaped like a tiki totem and topped with pineapple and a paper umbrella. You may need the umbrella, because the fantastically kitschy draw of the Tonga Room is its indoor monsoon. Thunder precedes the melodious downpour, the perfect backdrop to your enjoyment of this faux Polynesian paradise complete with faux thatch roof, faux bamboo, and plenty of real fruit juice–based cocktails served in very large, island-themed containers. *Sun-Thu 6-10pm, Fri-Sat 6-11pm.* Fairmont Hotel, 950 Mason St. (California St.), 415-772-5278, tongaroom.com

Top of the Mark • Nob Hill • Hotel Bar
Best Lounges with a View You can't help but feel nostalgic when you make your way up to the 19th floor of the Mark Hopkins. This is the old San Francisco, full of history, romance, and high style. Choose one of the 100 martinis, settle in at a window seat anywhere along the 360-degree view, and watch the city and bay unfold before your eyes. The Black Market Jazz Orchestra plays on Fridays and Saturdays, and there's salsa on Wednesday, harp on Sunday. It also serves Sunday brunch and breakfast and lunch every day. In World War II, the soldiers would come here for one last toast before shipping out. Dress up in honor of those who have come before you. *Mon-Thu 6:30-11am, noon-2:30pm, and 5pm-midnight, Fri-Sat 6:30-11am, noon-2:30pm, and 4pm-1am, Sun 10am-2:30pm, and 5pm-midnight.* InterContinental Mark Hopkins Hotel, 999 California St. (Mason St.), 415-392-3434, sanfrancisco.intercontinental.com

Tosca Café • North Beach • Bar
Where do you go to meet Russian ballerinas, famous writers and film directors, visiting starlets, and leaders of the local intelligentsia? Tosca. Serving since 1919, it's one of the city's oldest bars. Its beautiful chrome espresso machines, imported from Italy and dating from 1920, are said to have been the first to arrive in the city. The red vinyl booths transport you back to the time of Prohibition, when asking for a "cappuccino" got you a shot of brandy in your hot chocolate. Order a martini or a Manhattan, put a quarter in the opera jukebox, and think about Michael Douglas thinking about Sharon Stone in *Basic Instinct*. Yep, this is the bar. The best bet for mingling with the big shots is Wednesday and Thursday nights after happy hour. *Tue-Sat 5pm-2am, Sun 7pm-2am.* 242 Columbus Ave. (Broadway), 415-986-9651

CLASSIC · NIGHTLIFE

Trader Vic's • Hayes Valley • Theme Bar
Best Tiki Bars If there is such a thing as classy tiki bar, this is it. You'll find your quality tiki torches, your better paper umbrellas, and your finer pupus. Come at happy hour or for dinner (but not later, when the crowd dissipates) and voyage to the South Seas. The crowd is parent-friendly but not stodgy. *Restaurant Mon-Fri 11:30am-2:30pm and 5-10pm, Sat 5-10pm, Sun 4-10pm. Bar 11:30am-12:30am.* F 555 Golden Gate Ave. (Van Ness Ave.), 415-775-6300, tradervics.com/rest-sanfran.html

Vesuvio • North Beach • Bar
The still-beating heart of North Beach, Vesuvio opened in 1948 and has been a haven for writers, artists, sailors, students, and saucy-eyed tourists ever since. Immortalized in the classic *On the Road*, it's an ideal place to find the spirit of the Beat Generation. The mood is lively and loud in these tight quarters, as beer by the pitcherful is poured and literary pretense starts to spew. Bookish arguments can be settled just a stone's throw away at City Lights Bookstore. *Daily 6am-2am.* 255 Columbus Ave. (Broadway), 415-362-3370, vesuvio.com

View Lounge • SoMa • Lounge
Best Lounges with a View From the sidewalk, you wouldn't think there'd be much to see from this convenient downtown hotel, but take the elevator up to the 39th floor and you're in for a pleasant surprise. The enormous, three-story windows evoke grand urban thoughts, framing a spectacular semi-circle view spanning the southern half of the city from the Bay Bridge to Twin Peaks. Don't expect a big crowd of hipsters crowding the bar—you'll generally find more suits than anything else. If you're in a quiet mood, View Lounge makes a great pre-dinner stop after shopping or business meetings. *Mon-Wed 5:30-10pm, Thu-Sat 5:30-11pm.* B Marriott Hotel, 55 Fourth St. (Jessie St.), 415-896-1600

Classic San Francisco: The Attractions

Alcatraz Island • Fisherman's Wharf • Activity
Talk to locals and they've never been to Alcatraz Island. Talk to visitors, and they can't recommend it enough. The ferry ride out is exhilarating and the views from the island are worth the trip, but it's the tour that fascinates year after year. From its days as a maximum security prison to its time in the hands of Native American protesters who briefly reclaimed the island in 1969, Alcatraz has a colorful history, much of which has left its mark. Walk among the ruins of the notorious prison and you feel chills, pondering what it might mean to live in isolation with the joys of the city so close and yet so far. Bird watchers love the island and the beauty of its Agave Trail leading up to the highest ground. The trip takes about three hours and the ferry ticket includes the audio tour. For a moonlit kick, consider touring at night. $ Blue and Gold Ferry, Pier 39, 415-705-5555, nps.gov/alcatraz and blueandgoldfleet.com

Audium • Pacific Heights • Performance
Best Only-in-San Francisco Experiences Just weird enough to be really fun, the Audium is an experiment in sound that will expand your mind. Take a seat in any of the chairs set up in concentric rings and let the work of composer Stan Shaff wash over you from all directions. Soon the vibrations become mind-altering, or at least mood-altering, taking you on a sensory journey guided only by sound. Shaff may be a genius or merely a man obsessed. Either way, it makes for a unique theatrical experience and solid food for thought—and dinner conversation. *Performances every Fri and Sat 8:30pm (arrive early).* $$ 1616 Bush St. (Franklin St.), 415-771-1616, audium.org

Cable Cars • Scenic Route
In these litigious times, when we're lucky kneepads and crash helmets aren't mandatory anytime we leave the house, hanging on the outside of a cable car as it trundles precariously up and over the pitch of a serious grade, with the wind tossing your hair and astonishing bay views all around, is nothing short of exhilarating. And all for $3! Pick your route and start whistling the Rice-A-Roni theme. Three routes traverse the city: the Powell-Hyde line, the Powell-Mason line, and the California line. The two Powell lines begin at the turntable at Powell and Market. The Mason line runs up Powell, over Nob Hill, and down to Fisherman's Wharf. The Hyde line heads over Nob Hill and Russian Hill to land at Aquatic Park. The California line starts at Market and Main, runs east-west from the Financial District, through Chinatown, over Nob Hill, and stops at Van Ness Avenue. Take the Hyde if you can for the most scenic route. Lines at the turntable and at Fisherman's Wharf can be ugly. Jump on mid-route if possible (watch for the brown cable car signs along the route). $– sfcablecar.com

Chinatown: Wok Wiz Tour • Chinatown • Tour
San Francisco is home to a thriving Chinese community (especially notable on Chinese New Year, when Chinatown is a wonder of spectacles). The jumble of foot traffic, exotic vegetables, herb shops, teahouses, roast ducks, and silk

pajamas on offer bewilders the senses. One of the most interesting ways to experience this neighborhood is through one of the specialty tours given by expert Shirley Fong-Torres, whose numerous tour offerings give insider insights into the food, culture, and history of the area. Some even include cooking classes. Otherwise, start at the Chinatown Gate at Grant Avenue and Bush Street and stroll up Grant and Stockton to Broadway, where Chinatown and predominantly Italian North Beach overlap. If the clamor of the produce vendors overwhelms you, take cover in Tru Spa at 750 Kearny for a manicure or massage. *Tour times vary. See website for specific times.* $$$ 654 Commercial St. (Kearny St.), 212-209-3370, wokwiz.com

City Lights Bookstore • North Beach • Shop

As much a hallmark of North Beach cool as Café Trieste and Vesuvio's, City Lights will fire up the most reluctant reader with book lust. Three floors of hand-selected books cover all the greats of world literature. Up the creaky, antique stairs is an entire room of poetry, befitting a bookstore that was born of and helped launch America's Beat Generation, including Allen Ginsburg, Jack Kerouac, Kenneth Rexroth, and Lawrence Ferlinghetti, who still runs City Lights Publishers out of the same location. Established in 1953, this is one of the great independent bookstores in the country, where the walls hum with history and a passion for the printed word. *Daily 10am-midnight.* 261 Columbus Ave. (Broadway), North Beach, 415-362-8193, citylights.com

Coit Tower • North Beach • Sight

What's 210 feet tall and erected in honor of the firefighters who defended the city after the 1906 earthquake? That's right, San Francisco's own Art Deco pillar perched on top of Telegraph Hill. The design, said to be reminiscent of an, uh, fire hose nozzle, was controversial during its construction in 1933. Inside, it is decorated with Works Progress Administration murals in the style of Diego Rivera. The top offers unobstructed views in every direction. The tower was commissioned by Lillie Coit, a flamboyant fan of the volunteer fire crews. Feeling jaunty? Walk down the Greenwich steps to Montgomery Street, turn right, and take the Filbert Steps past a multitude of gardens all the way to Sansome Street. *Daily 10am-6:30pm.* $– One Telegraph Hill Blvd. (Pioneer Park), 415-362-0808, coittower.org

Conservatory of Flowers • Richmond • Sight

San Francisco's beautiful conservatory—like an overgrown greenhouse—located regally on a slope on the eastern side of Golden Gate Park, has been sumptuously restored to its former grandeur after a devastating wind storm damaged its ornate glass-and-steel structure. Built in 1878-89, it is the oldest public conservatory in the western hemisphere. Today it houses some 2,000 plant species in its five galleries. Plant experts and laypeople alike will enjoy the wide-ranging displays, which include an aquatic area with water cascading into lotus-filled pools; the Lowland Tropics area with its displays of chocolate, coffee, and vanilla; and plant-themed temporary exhibits. *Tue-Sun 9am-4:30pm.* $– John F. Kennedy Dr. (Golden Gate Park), 415-362-0808, conservatoryofflowers.org

Crissy Field • Presidio • Park
Despite the expansive view of Golden Gate Bridge and Marin, the mile and a half or so of waterfront strolling, the beach, the windsurfing, and the fantastic people-watching, the best thing about Crissy Field is actually the parking. Drive right up, get right out, don't even touch your wallet. And there are even clean bathrooms. What other tourist-worthy destination can say as much? There are warm, sunny days at Crissy Field, but usually it's cold and sunny, and often freezing cold and foggy, and almost always breezy. Regardless, it is always overwhelmingly beautiful. You must make the walk to Fort Point at the foot of the bridge—where Madeleine threw herself into the waves in *Vertigo*. On the beach route, you will arrive at the Warming Hut Café near the end *(Thu-Mon 9am-5pm)*. It's a charming place to have a hot chocolate and a scone or sandwich. End of Marina Blvd. (Lyon St.), 415-561-7690, crissyfield.org

de Young Museum • Richmond • Art Museum
Opened in late 2005, the new de Young, by the same designers responsible for the Tate Modern in London, is a stunner inside and out. The exterior is a new landmark, the extensive collection of art and artifacts from cultures around the world is displayed to perfection in the handsome new space, and the chic new cafe makes a perfect setting in which to reflect. The de Young attracts world-class traveling exhibitions, but its permanent collection is definitely worth exploring. It includes one of the finest collections of American paintings in the United States, from colonial times through the 20th century; extensive collections of Oceanic artworks and artifacts from the Pacific; African art; art of the Americas; American craft and sculpture; and more. Not to be missed. *Tue-Thu 9:30am-5pm, Fri 9:30am-8:45pm, Sat-Sun 9:30am-5pm.* $ 50 Hagiwara Tea Garden Dr. (Golden Gate Park), 415-863-3330, thinker.org/deyoung

Golden Gate Bridge • Presidio • Sight
Best Outdoor Activities Unlike the Bay Bridge, the majestic Golden Gate allows foot and bike access during daylight hours. It's a brisk 1.7 mile walk each way with a view of the bay, the city, and the surrounding landscape that is worth the effort. Bring a jacket; it's often windy and can be cold. The parking at the northeast end of the bridge is free for four hours. It can be hard to get a spot on sunny summer weekends, but it's worth the wait and the five-dollar southbound toll. Hwy. 101 N., 415-921-5858, goldengatebridge.org

Golden Gate Park • Richmond • Park
Best Outdoor Activities Like Central Park in Manhattan, Golden Gate Park offers a multitude of wonderful ways to amuse yourself outdoors in the heart of the city, whether you stroll the many paths through lush gardens and towering trees or visit one of the main attractions. The park's highlights include the de Young Museum, the Japanese Tea Garden, the Fragrance Garden, Strybing Arboretum, the Conservatory of Flowers, the Shakespeare Garden, and dozens of other treats. *Daily dawn-dusk.* Bounded by Stanyan, Fulton, and Lincoln Streets, and the Great Highway, 415-831-2700, parks.sfgov.org

Gump's • Downtown • Shop
There is no dress code at Gump's, but wear a suit anyway. It's just that sort of place, where you want to feel dignified, even old money, as you browse for imported fragrances, luxury towels, art glass, fancy paper, Italian leather desk

CLASSIC · ATTRACTIONS

accessories, frou-frou candles, silverware that's actually silver, elegant dinnerware, and antique Chinese boxes. Like Tiffany's but with a broader selection, a box from Gump's says you've bought something special. *Mon-Sat 10am-6pm, Sun noon-5pm.* 135 Post St. (Grant Ave.), 415-982-1616, gumps.com

Nob Hill Spa • Nob Hill • Spa
Best Spas You don't have to stay at the hotel to enjoy this luxurious day spa and wellness zone, complete with a beautiful indoor infinity pool overlooking the city. Choose a treatment from the wide range of options, take a yoga or tai chi class, hang out in the eucalyptus steam room, and lounge by the pool. With 11,000 square feet of spa to roam around, this kind of relaxation could take all day. *Daily, facility 6am-9pm, for treatments 8am-8pm.* $$$$ Huntington Hotel, 1075 California St. (Taylor St.), 415-474-5400, nobhillspa.com

Ocean Beach • Richmond • Beach
The western edge of San Francisco is as straight and neatly trimmed as the edge of a cake. Its beach, exposed to the open Pacific, offers dramatically varied conditions. In the summer, bright, hot days with tidy rows of waves are possible, and so are frigid, fogbound afternoons with the sea roiling in an angry chaos. In winter, the waves are often big, sometimes as big as 15 feet or more, attracting a diehard group of skilled, wet-suited surfers who swear by the ever-changing ride. To watch them practice their art, park near Taraval Street toward the north end of the beach. For a picturesque hike along the dunes, head for Fort Funston at the southern end. Dress in layers and finish off with a microbrew at the historic Beach Chalet at 1000 Great Highway. Great Highway (Balboa Ave.)

Palace of Fine Arts • Marina • Sight
Celebrated Berkeley architect Bernard Maybeck designed the Palace of Fine Arts for the 1915 Panama Pacific Exposition, an event celebrating the completion of the Panama Canal, and the rebirth of San Francisco following the disastrous 1906 earthquake. Not a palace or a museum, as the name implies, it is a Classical-style ruin complete with an enormous rotunda and colonnade. Surrounded by a lagoon, it makes an ideal spot to stroll. It also houses the Exploratorium, an interactive science museum that's immensely popular with kids, and the Palace of Fine Arts Theatre, which hosts a range of concerts, films, and other events. 3301 Lyon St. (Marina Blvd.), 415-567-6642, palaceoffinearts.org

Palace of the Legion of Honor • Richmond • Art Museum
The Legion of Honor is one of four major museums in San Francisco. The setting alone is worth the journey. Perched atop a bluff in Lincoln Park, it is nestled among towering pines and eucalyptus with a direct view of the Golden Gate and a peekaboo look at the Presidio Golf Course and the Pacific. The permanent collection covers 4,000 years of ancient and European art, beautifully displayed in the vast Beaux Arts structure, the archway approach to which makes a perfect setting for one of Rodin's "Thinker" statues. Traveling exhibitions have included everything from ancient Mayan art to a retrospective of Georgia O'Keefe's paintings. *Tue-Sun, 9:30am-5pm.* $ Lincoln Park, 100 34th Ave. (Clement St.), 415-863-3330, thinker.org/legion

Presidio Golf Course & Clubhouse • Presidio National Park • Golf
One of the oldest courses on the West Coast, the Presidio Golf Course is also one of its most handsome, renowned for its spectacular views and 100-year-old eucalyptus and pine forest. Once restricted to military officers and members of a private club, it became part of the Presidio National Park in 1995 and was opened to the public. Now, for next to nothing, you can golf where Teddy Roosevelt and Dwight Eisenhower played. Colorful Victorians pop up in the distance and wisps of fog slink in from the nearby shore. Practice your swing, hit a bucket of balls at the grass tee-practice center. It's hard to imagine a prettier setting. A new clubhouse offers excellent California cuisine for lunch Monday through Saturday and Sunday brunch. *Course open daily dawn until dusk.* $$$ 300 Finley Rd. (Presidio at the Arguello Gate), 415-561-4661, presidiogolf.com

Signature Yacht Cruise • Embarcadero • Sailing
You want to feel like a player? Grab a few of your favorite friends (or that special lady or gentleman) and rent the *Yacht Lady* for the afternoon from Signature's fleet of luxury yachts. The outside is 80 feet of sleek white hull, built for speed. Inside looks like a suite at the Bellagio, with four bedrooms. Other amenities include a devoted crew, gourmet meals, and a couple of Seadoos for jetting around. Cruise the bay, take in the views, and relax in supreme privacy. Or go for the Sunday champagne brunch ($59) serving waffles, eggs, and even beef Wellington aboard the *San Francisco Spirit*, Signature's 150-foot flagship. $$$$ Pier 9 (Embarcadero), 415-788-9100, signaturesf.com

Sue Fisher King • Pacific Heights • Shop
A landmark in chic Pacific Heights, Sue Fisher King is a fantasy of a place, where every object seems to shine with some inner light. It's not just a candle, it's *the* candle. You thought you knew pillow cases, vases, Venetian glass, Provençal soap, and teacups? Please, think again. If sumptuous table linens or silk cushions in exactly the right shade of cardamom or puce make your heart beat a little faster and your palms grow moist, you will need a defibrillator before you leave this place. *Mon-Sat 10am-6pm.* 3067 Sacramento St. (Baker St.), 415-922-7276, suefisherking.com

Wilkes Bashford • Downtown • Shop
Forbes called it, "San Francisco's answer to Bergdorf Goodman." Serving the high society of San Francisco for three decades and counting, Wilkes Bashford is the place to gear up for opening night at the opera, to buy that extra Brioni suit you've been needing, and drop a few thou on a pair of jeans and a sweater. No teeny-bopper trends here, the style is fashionable, elegantly European, and most decidedly upper crust. *Mon-Wed, Fri-Sat 10am-6pm, Thu 10am-8pm.* 375 Sutter St. (Stockton St.) 415-986-4380, wilkesbashford.com

PRIME TIME SAN FRANCISCO

Everything in life is timing (with a dash of serendipity thrown in). Would you want to arrive in Pamplona, Spain the day *after* the Running of the Bulls? Not if you have a choice, and you relish being a part of life's peak experiences. With our month-by-month calendar of events, there's no excuse to miss out on any of San Francisco's greatest moments. From the classic to the quirky, the sophisticated to the outrageous, you'll find all you need to know about the city's best events right here.

Prime Time Basics

Eating and Drinking

San Francisco starts lunch between noon and 1pm, dinner between 7:30 and 9pm, and Sunday brunch at 10am. Cocktails before dinner are most popular at 7pm, unless we're talking about happy hour in the Financial District, which gets going around 6pm. While bars fill up by 10pm, nightclubs don't rock until midnight. Recent years have brought more restaurants serving dinner late, but most places still close the kitchen at 10pm, and getting lunch after 2:30 can be a challenge. Though there have been legislative efforts to extend it, last call for alcohol is still 2am. At the after-hours clubs, Red Bull and water are the beverages of choice.

Weather and Tourism

San Francisco's weather is mild but notoriously unpredictable. The weather is a strong argument for traveling in the shoulder seasons, and you'll be competing with fewer tourists since summer is the most crowded time to visit. (Unlike seasonal destinations like, say, Miami, San Francisco generally has the same hotel rates year-round).

Dec.–Feb.: These months tend to have the most wind and rain, although due to the changeable conditions you can end up with a glorious beach day when the rest of the country is experiencing ice storms.

Mar.–May: Spring generally brings glorious clear blue skies, with somewhat warmer temperatures.

June–Aug.: During the summer, when thick, damp fog closes in on the city, it can be downright chilly; such conditions can prevail all day long. At other times, sunshine breaks by afternoon and the weather warms up.

Seasonal Changes

Month	Fahrenheit High	Fahrenheit Low	Celsius High	Celsius Low
Jan.	56	43	13	6
Feb.	59	46	15	8
Mar.	61	47	16	8
Apr.	64	48	18	9
May	67	51	19	11
June	70	53	21	12
July	71	55	22	13
Aug.	72	56	22	13
Sept.	73	55	23	13
Oct.	70	52	21	11
Nov.	62	48	17	9
Dec.	56	43	13	6

Sept.–Nov.: If fair weather is an absolute must for your trip, the safest bet is to arrive in the early to mid-fall, which typically has the highest temperatures and longest all-day sunshine.

The city also has several microclimates: Parts of the Mission District are sometimes referred to as San Francisco's "banana belt" because the sun will shine brightly there even while cold fog shrouds the Sunset and Richmond neighborhoods set closer to the Pacific Ocean. You shouldn't be discouraged from a hike in the Marin Headlands just because the weather in the city is gray—the East Bay and Marin are often enjoying warm sun. Above all, be sure to dress in layers so you can keep pace with the ever-changing conditions. Any time of year, a day that begins with fog, wind, and temperatures in the 40s and 50s might clear to sun and temperatures in the 60s and 70s by the afternoon, and the reverse.

The only natural phenomenon that may affect your visit—aside from earthquakes, which are impossible to predict—is the weather cycle known as El Niño, which brings heavy rains and flash floods that have caused mud slides and closed highways. But weather forecasters know in advance when El Niño is on its way, allowing you to plan accordingly while on your trip.

National Holidays

New Year's Day	January 1
Martin Luther King Day	Third Monday in January
Valentine's Day	February 14
President's Birthday	Third Monday in February
Memorial Day	Last Monday in May
Independence Day	July 4
Labor Day	First Monday in September
Columbus Day	Second Monday in October
Halloween	October 31
Veterans' Day	November 11
Thanksgiving Day	Fourth Thursday in November
Christmas Day	December 25
New Year's Eve	December 31

Listings in blue are major celebrations but not official holidays.

The Best Events Calendar

January
- San Francisco International Art Exposition

February
- Chinese New Year Festival

March
- Bouquets to Art

April
- Cherry Blossom Festival
- San Francisco International Film Festival

May
- Bay to Breakers Race
- Carnaval
- Cinco de Mayo Festival

June
- Haight-Ashbury Street Fair
- LGB&T Pride Parade and Celebration
- North Beach Festival
- SF International LGBT Film Festival

July
- Fillmore Jazz Festival
- Up Your Alley Fair (Dore Alley Fair)

August

September
- Folsom Street Fair
- San Francisco Blues Festival

October
- ArtSpan's SF Open Studios
- Castro Street Fair
- Fleet Week
- Halloween Night
- LitQuake
- SF Jazz Festival

November
- Día de los Muertos

December

Night+Day's Top Five Events are in blue.

The Best Events

January

San Francisco International Art Exposition
Fort Mason Center, San Francisco, 312-226-4700, sfiae.com

The Lowdown: Well-heeled arts patrons attend the elegant opening night gala that kicks off this annual high-profile art expo, but it opens to the public the day after. The work of over 2,000 modern and contemporary artists is presented, and includes every medium from painting, drawing, photography, and printmaking to sculpture, video, and mixed media. Fort Mason Center, with the spectacular backdrop of the bay, gives the exhibit a uniquely San Francisco flair. *Four days in the middle of January, beginning on a Friday. Opening night preview benefit takes place on the Thursday before the first day.* $12 admission.

February

Chinese New Year Festival
San Francisco's Chinatown; for more information, contact the Chinese Chamber of Commerce, 415-391-9680, chineseparade.com

The Lowdown: The San Francisco Chinese New Year Festival and Parade is the largest celebration of its kind in the world, attracting over 3 million spectators and television viewers throughout the United States, Canada, and Asia. Related events include the parade's finale with a 200-foot-long Golden Dragon and 600,000 firecrackers; and the Chinese New Year Treasure Hunt, a popular adventure in seeking out obscure landmarks and vestiges of San Francisco's colorful past. Many restaurants in Chinatown host special Chinese New Year dinners. *Two weeks in February (sometimes begins in late January), culminating in the parade on the last day.* Free.

March

Bouquets to Art
de Young Museum, 50 Hagiwara Tea Garden Dr., 415-750-3504, bouquetstoart.org

The Lowdown: The museum galleries at the de Young fill up with extravagant floral arrangements created by more than 100 of California's top floral designers. Each designer's floral creation is inspired by a work from the museum and is showcased alongside the artwork. Activities during this week-long event include lectures on flower arranging, luncheons, and teas. *Four days, Tuesday through Friday, during the second week in March. Opening night gala takes place on the Monday before the first day.* Gala tickets approximately $100-750; daily program tickets approximately $30-75.

PRIME TIME

April

Cherry Blossom Festival
Japantown (at Post and Buchanan Streets)

The Lowdown: This colorful spectacle includes a busy street fair with performances by Japanese classical and folk dancers, martial artists, and taiko drummers, as well as a food bazaar with traditional Japanese cuisine and cooking demonstrations. Over 1,500 participants including kimonoed dancers and traditional musicians join in the festive Grand Parade, which begins at Civic Center and winds its way through Japantown. *Two consecutive weekends in April.* Free.

San Francisco International Film Festival
Castro Theatre, AMC Kabuki Theaters, and other venues, 415-561-5000, sfiff.org

The Lowdown: Get the cinematic leg up on the world's best movies before everyone else does. This San Francisco institution has presented the best in world cinema since its inception in 1957. Call ahead to find out about films with a special celebrity appearance from the director or actors involved. The festival usually showcases at least 200 new feature films and documentaries from as many as 50 countries, with its emphasis on current trends and international films that have not yet secured U.S. distribution. *Two weeks beginning on a Thursday in late April and continuing into early May.* $12 admission per program.

May

Bay to Breakers Race
Starts at the Embarcadero at 8am, 415-359-2800, baytobreakers.com

The Lowdown: Attended by more than 80,000 runners and walkers each year, many sporting wild costumes and body paint, the Bay to Breakers is more of an urban adventure than your average workout. An audience of thousands gathers at the sidelines to cheer and gawk as the event—the world's largest footrace—unfolds, as it has each year for more than 90 years. The 12-kilometer (7.46-mile) course begins at sea level at the Embarcadero, rises steeply along Hayes Street's "Heartbreak Hill," and then descends through Golden Gate Park to the ocean. *On Sunday in mid-May.* $$. Approximately $30 to register to run.

Carnaval
Harrison Street, between 16th and 23rd Streets, 415-920-0125, carnavalsf.com

The Lowdown: Exotically costumed Carnaval dancers and live music are highlights of this popular San Francisco version of Mardi Gras. Bringing together traditions from countless countries, including Bolivia, Brazil, Cuba, Jamaica, Puerto Rico, and Trinidad, events include the main Carnaval Parade, as well as booths with food, arts and crafts, and activities on several stages. *Last weekend in May, culminating on Sunday with the Carnaval Grand Parade.* Free.

Cinco de Mayo Festival
Mission District

> The Lowdown: It only makes sense that the celebration of Mexican Independence Day happens in the Mission District, San Francisco's predominantly Hispanic neighborhood, known for its great taquerias, Mexican bakeries, fresh produce markets, and specialty shops, as well as the historic Mission Dolores, the oldest structure in San Francisco. The festivities include mariachis, food, children's activities, and a live salsa orchestra. *May 5.* Free.

June

Haight-Ashbury Street Fair
Haight Street, 415-863-3489, haightstreetfair.org

> The Lowdown: You'll be having your own summer of love when you join the tens of thousands who descend on San Francisco's most famous crossroads—Haight and Ashbury—to celebrate the neighborhood's hippie heritage. You'll find festive crowds, live music, and arts and crafts, including Haight Street Fair posters and T-shirts featuring the instantly recognizable designs and drawings of the psychedelic '60s. *One day, mid-June.* Free.

Lesbian, Gay, Bisexual, and Transgender Pride Parade and Celebration
Civic Center (celebration area) and Embarcadero (parade starting point), 415-864-3733, sfpride.org

> The Lowdown: Theatrical parade floats, iconic drag queens, inspirational gay activists, as well as celebrities, politicians, and hundreds of thousands of other wildly costumed participants gather for this proud and raucous festival, which in some years has drawn more than a million revelers. The party kicks off on Saturday in Civic Center Plaza, where the Celebration Area has live music stages and booths that sell everything from food and drink to sex toys; the Sunday parade along Market Street is the most high-profile event. *Last Saturday and Sunday in June, culminating in the Pride Parade on Sunday morning.* Free.

North Beach Festival
Washington Square Park (Grant Avenue) and adjacent streets in North Beach, 415-989-2220, sfnorthbeach.org/festival/

> The Lowdown: A tradition in the Italian neighborhood of North Beach for more than 50 years and the oldest outdoor arts and crafts festival in the country, this event has something for everyone. The eclectic grab bag of fun events includes juried arts and crafts exhibitions, "Arte di Gesso" (the competition of Italian street chalk art, on the 1500 block of Stockton), plus a cooking stage, celebrity chef appearances, and a competitive pizza toss. The entertainment stages have live music, everything from reggae and blues to salsa and swing. *Saturday and Sunday in mid-June.* Free.

San Francisco International LGBT Film Festival
Castro Theatre and other venues, 415-703-8650, frameline.org/festival/

The Lowdown: The world's oldest and largest celebration of lesbian and gay cinema, this event brings even more excitement to the already-bustling Castro neighborhood. Past festivals have drawn over 80,000 attendees, and you can expect to see short films and nearly 80 features, including many world and US premieres. Book your tickets in advance, or consider the Castro Pass, which allows admission to all Castro Theatre screenings aside from the gala opening and closing nights. *Eleven days, Thursday through Sunday, in mid-June.* Price varies.

July

Fillmore Jazz Festival
On Fillmore Street between Jackson and Eddy Streets, fillmorejazzfestival.com

The Lowdown: It makes sense that this event, the largest free jazz festival on the West Coast, takes place in the Fillmore, where dozens of World War II–era jazz clubs hosted the major musical talents back in the day, including Ella Fitzgerald, Duke Ellington, Count Basie, and Billie Holliday. Now, current jazz stars grace the three musical stages while 90,000-plus visitors groove in the streets, sample gourmet food, and browse fine arts and crafts booths. *4th of July weekend.* Free.

Up Your Alley Fair (Dore Alley Fair)
Dore Alley between Folsom and Howard Streets and Ninth and Tenth Streets, folsomstreetfair.com/alley

The Lowdown: If you want all the great people-watching and bondage-leather culture of San Francisco's infamous Folsom Street Fair, but want to avoid the masses, this event will be right up your alley. The Folsom Street Fair's notorious little brother is a smaller-scale festival, with a more local crowd. The numbers still impress—estimates are that over 12,000 leather-folk attend. Needless to say, everyone here is right at home wearing chaps. *The last Sunday in July.* Free.

September

Folsom Street Fair
Folsom Street between Seventh and 12th Streets, 415-861-3247, folsomstreetfair.com

The Lowdown: It's easy to get a safe S&M spanking at this fetish-friendly festival—all you need to do is stand in line at a booth. In fact, there's little you can't see or experience at this bacchanal that concludes San Francisco's Leather Pride Week, where leather hot pants, leashes, and tassled floggers are standard attire for many. The entertainment stages and food booths take a backseat to people-watching—after all, this is the third largest event in California (behind the Rose Bowl and San Francisco Pride). *The last Sunday in September.* Free.

San Francisco Blues Festival
Fort Mason's Great Meadow, 415-979-5588, sfblues.com

The Lowdown: With the Golden Gate Bridge and sparkling San Francisco Bay as its backdrop, the longest continuously running blues festival in the US unfolds to ecstatic crowds each year. Since its beginnings in 1973, the event has featured some of the biggest names in the blues, including B.B. King, John Lee Hooker, Stevie Ray Vaughan, Bonnie Raitt, Albert Collins, Robert Cray, Albert King, Buddy Guy, Taj Majal, Dr. John, and Carlos Santana, to name just a few. Each year brings a new all-star lineup. *Third or fourth weekend in September. Price varies.*

October

ArtSpan's San Francisco Open Studios
Locations vary by weekend, 415-861-9838, artspan.org

The Lowdown: Founded in 1975 by a small group of enterprising artists, San Francisco Open Studios is now a popular citywide program through which emerging and established artists invite the public into their studios. The neighborhoods involved change with the dates; for example, studios in North Beach and Russian Hill might be open the first weekend, while the fourth weekend might give access to studios in the Hunter's Point area. Open Studios is a completely unique and fun way to meet artists, see where they create artwork, explore San Francisco's diverse neighborhoods, and build collections. *Four weekends in October. Free.*

Castro Street Fair
Intersection of Market and Castro Streets, castrostreetfair.org

The Lowdown: It's fun in the sun at this popular fair in the Castro, where the entertainment includes nonstop outdoor dancing pavilions, food and drink booths, male beauty contests like Cutest of the Castro, and even a country Western dance stage. It's been a neighborhood tradition for more than 30 years, and it's a good cause, too, with profits going to charitable groups that are important to the Castro Community. *First Sunday in October. Free.*

Fleet Week
San Francisco, 800-367-5833, airshownetwork.com

The Lowdown: It's impossible to miss this window-rattling two-day air show in which daredevil Navy pilots fly in formation over the city. If you consider meeting sailors a fun pastime (did you see that episode of *Sex and the City*?), head to North Beach, where the clubs look like Navy-themed dance parties during Fleet Week. San Francisco's Municipal Pier and Pier 39 are popular places to view the aerial shows. *One weekend in October, dates vary. Free.*

Halloween Night
Civic Center and the Castro

> The Lowdown: Halloween is San Francisco's holiday, and the city celebrates it with unparalleled enthusiasm. These days, the photo-snapping tourists outnumber the elaborately costumed participants; but still, the memorable group outfits—for example, a group dressed in exact replica of the original *Star Trek* cast—and the famously extravagant drag queens are highlights. Long held in the Castro, the festival takes place at Civic Center simply because of the size of the crowd, although spill-over into the Castro still makes the neighborhood feel like party central. *Street closure every October 31, and generally a big bash the weekend before.* Free.

LitQuake
Various locations around San Francisco, litquake.org

> The Lowdown: Ever since the Beats claimed North Beach and Jack Kerouac inspired a generation with books like *On the Road*, San Francisco has been filled with writing luminaries. Now everyone can join in the fun at this freeform festival that represents a lively overview of San Francisco's thriving literary scene. A mix of readings, panel discussions, and themed events with established and new rising stars in the Bay Area writing community gives fans the opportunity to hear high-quality literature straight from the author's mouth and participate in general literary mayhem. The LitCrawl is a highlight, when a rolling sequence of live readings takes crowds from bar to bar in the Mission. *Nine days in October.* Some events free, others vary.

San Francisco Jazz Festival
Music venues around San Francisco and the Bay Area, 415-398-5655, sfjazz.org

> The Lowdown: This two-week celebration is widely considered one of the best jazz festivals in the world. The phenomenal array of jazz concerts, from the classic to the avant-garde, gathers the legends of today and the rising stars of tomorrow. Dozens of other events include commissions of new works by some of the most creative contemporary artists, unique "Jazz on Film" presentations, family matinee concerts, dance performances, and photography exhibits. *Two weeks at the end of October.* Price varies.

November

Día de los Muertos
San Francisco Mission District, dayofthedeadsf.org

> The Lowdown: The traditional Mexican holiday of Día de los Muertos celebrates death and the cycle of life, and San Francisco's celebration is one of the oldest and most spectacular in North America. The colorful Day of the Dead Procession is along 24th Street, and starts in the evening; bring candles, photos, food, or something that reminds you of a person who has passed away to place at the altars, striking community art installations exhibited at Garfield Park in the Mission District. *November 2.* Free.

HIT the GROUND RUNNING

There will be moments that test your "I'm not a tourist" credentials. Every city has a "right look"—*how do you avoid being cited by the fashion police?* You get to go to the city for business—*what do you bring home for your spouse?* You arrive at SFO early and the security lines are short—*where are the airport's best restaurants?* Here are the *City Essentials* and *Cheat Sheet* that will practically put your picture on a San Francisco driver's license.

City Essentials

Getting to San Francisco: By Air

San Francisco International Airport (SFO)
650-821-8211, flysfo.com

San Francisco International is located 13 miles south of San Francisco, near the junction of Highways 101 and 380.

SFO is a polished, high-tech airport that reflects the city's identity as a design and technology hub. Top industry awards for its sophisticated airport security and an outstanding wireless technology service show off its new-millennium savvy, as does the highly efficient and eco-friendly public transportation system featuring a sleek AirTrain. The airport is a major gateway to and from Asia, with nonstop flights to Japan and China, as well as frequent flights to Europe and all major points on the East Coast.

At the end of 2000, as part of its $2.4 billion expansion project, SFO unveiled its shiny, futuristic new international terminal, making it the largest international air terminal in North America. The revamp includes a dramatic architectural gesture on the outside and loads of creature comforts on the inside.

Happily, hungry travelers will find more than the typical fast food offerings, including SFO versions of many leading Bay Area eateries. In the International Terminal, sample sushi at Ebisu, visit the Firewood Grill, or try dim sum at the Harbor Village Kitchen. In Terminal Three, you can get an Irish coffee from the airport edition of The Buena Vista Cafe, a microbrew at Anchor Brewing, and garlic fries at Gordon Biersch. There are several Peet's Coffee and Tea venues serving seriously strong coffee and three Just Desserts. Terminal One has a branch of Perry's, where San Franciscans have been drinking and schmoozing for decades.

Flying Times to San Francisco

From	Time(hr.)
Chicago	4
Honolulu	5
London	10
Los Angeles	1½
Mexico City	4½
Miami	5½
New York	5
Tokyo	10
Vancouver	2
Washington, D.C.	5½

Airlines Serving San Francisco Airport

Airlines	Website	800 Number	Terminal
Air Canada	aircanada.ca	888-247-2262	1
Air China	airchina.com	800-986-1985	G
Air France	airfrance.us	800-237-2747	A
Air New Zealand	airnewzealand.com	800-262-1234	G
AirTran Airways	airtran.com	800-247-8726	A
Alaska Airlines	alaskaair.com	800-426-0333	1
America West	americawest.com	800-235-9292	1
American Airlines	aa.com	800-433-7300	3
ANA (All Nippon Airways)	fly-ana.com	800-235-9262	G
Asiana Airlines	us.flyasiana.com	800-227-4262	G
ATA Airlines	ata.com	800-435 9282	1
British Airways	britishairways.com	800-247-9297	A
Cathay Pacific	cathaypacific.com	800-233-2742	A
China Airlines	china-airlines.com	800-227-5118	A
Continental Airlines	continental.com	800-525-0280	1
Delta Airlines	delta.com	800-221-1212	1
EVA Air	evaair.com	800-695-1188	G
Frontier Airlines	flyfrontier.com	800-432-1359	1
Hawaiian Airlines	hawaiianair.com	800-367-5320	1
Horizon Air	horizonair.com	800-547-9308	1
Japan Airlines	japanair.com	800-525-3663	A
KLM Royal Dutch Airlines	klm.com	800-225 2525	A
Korean Air	koreanair.com	800-438-5000	A
LACSA	grupotaca.com	800-225-2272	A
Lufthansa	lufthansa.com	800-645-3880	G
Mexicana	mexicana.com	800-531-7921	G
Midwest Airlines	midwestairlines.com	800-452-2022	1
Northwest Airlines	nwa.com	800-225-2525	1
Philippine Airlines	philippineair.com	800-435-9725	A
Singapore Airlines	singaporeair.com	800-742-3333	G
TACA	grupotaca.com	800-535-8780	A
United Airlines	united.com	800-241-6522	3
US Airways	usairways.com	800-428-4322	1
Virgin Atlantic	virgin-atlantic.com	800-862-8621	A
WestJet	westjet.com	888-937-8538	A

SFO takes airport art to the next level, hosting an impressive series of international displays throughout all terminals, which might include anything from Japanese parasols to ancestral figures from Papua New Guinea. Terminals also feature a $10 million permanent collection, including a number of works by notable local artists. In the International Terminal, the new Louis A. Turpen Aviation Museum offers memorabilia from aviation history, including wacky-looking old uniforms, in a setting reminiscent of the original 1936 waiting room. Upstairs is the extensive San Francisco Airport Commission Aviation Library. Still waiting for that flight? Check out the aquarium in Terminal One.

The International Terminal boasts plenty of high-quality browsing. Highlights include Coach, the SFMoMA Museum Store, and several places to buy gourmet foods, wine, and gifts with a local spin. Don't miss Compass Books in Terminal Three, a good independent bookstore selling more than the usual fare. For showers and more, visit the SFO Hairport. Manicures and spa treatments are available at XpressSpa.

SFO makes business travel easy. Seventy self-service business center kiosks throughout the airport let you make copies and send faxes. Most phones have data ports for going online with your laptop, and Starbucks offers Wi-Fi Internet access via T-Mobile.

San Francisco International is about 20 minutes by car from downtown San Francisco, depending on traffic. As you might expect, traffic is steady most of the day, with rush hours between 7-9:30am (north, south and eastbound into downtown San Francisco) and 3-7pm or so

Rental Cars: All of the following major rental car companies have counters inside the airports.

Agency	Website	800 Number	Local Number
Alamo	alamo.com	800-327-9633	415-701-7400
Avis	avis.com	800-331-1212	415-885-5011
Budget	budget.com	800-527-0700	415-433-3717
Dollar	dollar.com	800-800-4000	415-999-1111
Enterprise	enterprise.com	800-325-8007	415-441-2100
Hertz	hertz.com	800-654-3131	415-986-2319
National	nationalcar.com	800-227-7368	415-693-0191
Thrifty	thrifty.com	800-367-2277	415-788-8111

Limos
- City Limousine, citylimosf.com — 800-956-5466
- San Francisco Limo, sanfranciscolimo.com — 800-851-4294

CITY ESSENTIALS

(north, south, and eastbound out of downtown). Going to the city during either rush hour period will likely extend the trip up to an hour. Hours of operation for carpool lanes are clearly marked, and you must have three people in the car to qualify as a carpool.

Into Town by Taxi: Rates from the airport are metered and range from $29 to $44, depending on your destination.

Into Town by Airport Shuttle Service: Quake City Shuttle (415-255-4899) and SuperShuttle (415-558-8500 / 800-258-3826; supershuttle.com) vans are available via the upper (departure) level. Fares are cheaper than those for taxis, with typical fares to the downtown area about $15 per passenger.

Into Town by Public Transit: AirTrain links SFO to BART (Bay Area Rapid Transit), providing easy public transportation access to points in downtown San Francisco and beyond. The AirTrain operates on two lines: the Red Line, which connects all terminals, garages, and the BART station; and the Blue Line, which connects all terminals, garages, and the BART station with the Rental Car Center (a one-stop–shopping five-story rental car facility).

Oakland International Airport (OAK)
Hegenberger Rd. off Hwy. 880, 510-563-3300, oaklandairport.com

OAK has three advantages over SFO, as well as several drawbacks. The advantages are simple: it's smaller and less congested, making it easier to get in and out; fares are often lower; and there is plenty of convenient parking. The disadvantages include a lack of amenities, comparatively speaking (a major upgrade, including expanding concessions, will be completed in 2006) and a journey into the city 25 miles away that includes crossing the Bay Bridge. Without traffic, driving time into the city is roughly the same as coming from SFO. But the Bay Bridge usually has heavy traffic, especially during commute rush hour. Low-fare carriers including JetBlue and Southwest, and major carriers such as Delta, United, and Continental, operate out of Oakland.

Into Town by Taxi: Rates from the airport are metered and run about $55 to downtown San Francisco. Confirm a price before you leave.

Into Town by Airport Shuttle Service: Numerous van services are available at the curb outside baggage claim. Fares run about $25 per person.

Into Town by Public Transit: AirBart links the airport to BART (Bay Area Rapid Transit), providing easy public transportation access to points in downtown San Francisco and beyond. AirBart runs every 10-20 minutes, costs $2, and takes about fifteen minutes.

Getting to San Francisco: By Land

By Car: You can get to San Francisco on a number of major highways. From the east, I-80 runs from Berkeley and Oakland (the East Bay) via the Bay Bridge (bridge toll is $3). From the north, Highway 101 runs from Marin County via the Golden Gate Bridge (bridge toll is $5). From the south, Highway 101 and Highway 280 are the two major routes into the city, and both link San Francisco to the neighboring city of San Jose (Silicon Valley). If you're coming from the south along the coast, the route is along California's famously scenic Highway 1, also known as the Pacific Coast Highway. The fastest route between San Francisco and Los Angeles is the inland route along I-5; the long, flat, boring drive takes approximately six hours but is much faster than taking Highway 101 along the coast, which can take approximately 11 or 12 hours.

Driving Times to San Francisco

From	Distance (mi.)	Approx. Time (hr.)
Las Vegas	570	9
Los Angeles	380	6
Portland	630	10
Sacramento	190	1½
San Diego	500	8
Seattle	805	12

By Train: Amtrak (800-872-7245, amtrak.com) offers service up and down the West Coast on its Coast Starlight route, which stops in Los Angeles, San Francisco (East Bay), Seattle, and points in between, as well as trains connecting to cities such as Chicago. The Amtrak stations are in the East Bay; for San Francisco, disembark at the Emeryville station and catch the free connecting Amtrak shuttle to the San Francisco Ferry Building. Note: These are not high-speed trains. It takes tk hours to get from Los Angeles to San Francisco.

Caltrain (415-546-4461 or 800-660-4287, caltrain.com) is the commuter transportation system that connects San Jose and other smaller towns in the South Bay, such as Palo Alto (Stanford University), to the city. All trains terminate at the San Francisco Depot (700 Fourth St.), conveniently located near SBC Park (there aren't many train seats on game days).

San Francisco: Lay of the Land

Located on a famously picturesque and hilly peninsula surrounded by water—the Pacific Ocean to the west and San Francisco Bay to the east—this city packs its dense population into a mere 47 square miles. All the city's most visited neighborhoods, such as North Beach, Fisherman's Wharf, the Castro, the Mission, Pacific Heights, and the Marina, are easily accessible by taxi or public transportation from downtown. The Bay Bridge connects San Francisco to the East Bay, while the Golden Gate Bridge provides the link to Marin County; both bridges afford views of Alcatraz Island, Angel Island, and Treasure Island as you cross the bay.

Getting Around San Francisco

By Car: San Francisco is hemmed in by bridges and busy highways that draw commuters from all over the Bay Area, and this contributes to the notoriously bad traffic. The rush-hour madness on I-80 and Highway 101 often causes gridlock around major exits and entry points to the city; this, combined with congestion on major city streets and intimidating steep hills in some neighborhoods, makes public transportation and your own two feet the most appealing ways to get around. It's especially efficient to skip driving if you're staying downtown, where cable cars, BART, and MUNI provide easy access around the city, as do taxis. This will save you hefty parking and valet fees.

Parking: Parking is notoriously hard to come by in San Francisco, both downtown and in nearly every residential neighborhood from Pacific Heights to North Beach to the Mission. Watch for signs in these residential zones; parking is usually limited to two hours unless you're a resident with a bona fide permit. Along major shopping streets such as Fillmore Street in Pacific Heights, or in parts of SoMa (South of Market), old-fashioned meters are still in effect, so it's good to keep some quarters on hand. Also, always be on the lookout for street cleaning signs; if you neglect to move your car in time, expect a ticket. And don't even think about parking in a bus zone. Above all, don't get tempted into taking that too-small spot that extends your bumper into someone's driveway or you'll end up at City Tow, a place many rueful locals and visitors become all too well acquainted with.

It's virtually impossible to find street parking downtown, and the best option is to park in one of the lots with an hourly rate (usually you pay at a kiosk on the ground floor before returning to your car and exiting).

> **Parking Garages**
>
> Here are some of the biggest and most convenient parking facilities.
>
> - Sutter-Stockton Garage (330 Sutter St., Downtown)*
> - Fifth and Mission Yerba Buena Garage (833 Mission St., SoMa)
> - Union Square Garage (333 Post St., Downtown)
> - Embarcadero Center Garage (Embarcadero Center, Financial District)
> - Fisherman's Wharf Parking (665 Beach St., Fisherman's Wharf)
> - Civic Center Garage (355 McAllister St., Civic Center/Hayes Valley)
> - 75 Howard Street Garage (75 Howard St., SoMa)*
>
> *Note: There are great views from the rooftop parking.*

By Taxi: You'll find taxis in front of major hotels downtown. In busy residential neighborhoods such as the Mission, it's possible if not always easy to catch (they're available if the light on top of the cab is on). When in doubt, have the restaurant call for a cab. Taxis are a preferred way to get around to clubs and restaurants on the weekends, so there can be a delay while calling at peak times on Saturday nights.

- American Cab 415-614-2000
- Citywide Taxi Dispatch 415-920-0700
- Luxor Cab 415-282-4141
- Yellow Cab 415-626-2345

By Subway: BART (415-989-2278 or bart.org) links San Francisco to the East Bay, with stops in Berkeley, Oakland, and beyond, and is used by more commuters than visitors. However, the trains can be an efficient way to travel from San Francisco's downtown to the Mission District (16th Street Station). Fares range from $1.50 to $5, depending on your arrival and departure points; BART provides public transit from the AirTrain at SFO to downtown.

By Train and Bus: Locals pride themselves on getting around by train, bus, and cable car or streetcar, and the city's transportation system works for visitors as well as locals. Within the city, the most extensive public transportation system is MUNI (415-673-6864, sfmuni.com), the trains that travel above- and underground to link many of the city's outlying neighborhoods to downtown. MUNI also runs the city buses, as well as the beautifully restored vintage streetcars that run along Market Street between downtown and the Castro. MUNI is generally reliable, although it's not unusual to encounter lengthy delays during commute times, so plan accordingly if you need to be somewhere at a specific time. The MUNI trains and BART are quite efficient, especially compared to the buses, which can be slow. MUNI fare is $1.50 and exact fare is required. You can save money with a three- or seven-day pass.

Cable Cars: They might seem charmingly antiquated now, but when they made their debut in San Francisco in the early 1870s, cable cars were acclaimed as a modern miracle. Their arrival affected the very landscape of the city; now that people could ascend even the steepest heights easily, vertiginous neighborhoods such as Nob Hill emerged. (The cars also brought an end to terrible accidents resulting from the attempt of horse-drawn carriages to scale such heights in rainstorms.) It was the world's first successful cable car line, and other cities, such as Sydney and London, followed suit. In 1964, the cable car was designated the nation's only mobile historic landmark. Today, tourists flock to the cable car turnaround at Powell and Market Street to line up for a scenic ride over Nob Hill to Fisherman's Wharf; a ticket costs $3. MUNI (415-673-6864, sfmuni.com) has more-detailed information on cable cars. The Cable Car Museum (415-474-1887), located at the cable car barn at Washington and Mason Streets, shows off the transit's proud history, with displays depicting the huge drive wheels and electric motors that move the cables used to propel the cable cars, as well as cable cars that operated in 19th-century San Francisco.

Other Practical Information

Money Matters (Currency, Taxes, Tipping and Service Charges): It's dollars ($) and cents (100 to the dollar). For currency conversion rates, go to xe.com/ucc/. There is no national sales (value-added) tax. However, the sales tax within the city limits (includes both state and city taxes) is 8.5 percent, 14 percent for hotels, and is added onto the bill (not included in the price). Service charges are not included in prices but, depending on the venue, may be added to the bill. Hotels generally do not include breakfast in their prices. Tipping for taxis and restaurants should be in the 15 to 20 percent range. Leaving $3 per day for the hotel housekeeper is becoming standard practice.

Metric Conversion

From	To	Multiply by
Inches	Centimeters	2.54
Yards	Meters	0.91
Miles	Kilometers	1.60
Gallons	Liters	3.79
Ounces	Grams	28.35
Pounds	Kilograms	0.45

Safety: It's important to keep your street smarts about you in San Francisco as you would in any major metropolitan area, but overall, the city is a relatively safe place to visit. Neighborhoods are densely populated for the most part, and feel well trafficked and safe; the major tourist areas feel equally busy and well protected. Nonetheless, all the usual urban precautions apply: Lock up valuables in hotel safes, don't leave luggage or goods in parked cars, keep your wallets and handbags close to your side, and ask for directions before venturing into unfamiliar neighborhoods.

Gay and Lesbian Travel: San Francisco is world-famous for its vibrant gay community, and for being a community that advocates for gay rights, particularly when it comes to the same-sex marriage debate. Most recently, the city made international news after Mayor Gavin Newsom allowed more than 4,000 gay and lesbian couples to legally marry at

Numbers to Know (Hotlines)

Emergency, police, fire department, ambulance, and paramedics	911
Poison Control	800-876-4766
Rape Crisis Line	415-647-7273
San Francisco Suicide Prevention	415-781-0500
24-Hour Access Mental Health Helpline	415-255-3737 888-246-3333

Along the highways, you'll find call boxes for emergency use.

Medical/Travel Office (nonemergency medical conditions)	415-362-7177
The Dental Referral Service	800-422-8338
San Francisco Dental Society Referral Service	415-421-1435

24-hour emergency rooms:

• San Francisco General Hospital 1001 Potrero Ave.	415-206-8000
• UCSF Medical Center 505 Parnassus Ave.	415-353-1037

24-Hour Walgreens pharmacies:

• Castro Walgreens 498 Castro St.	415-861-3136
• Marina Walgreens 3201 Divisadero St.	415-931-6417

City Hall in what many referred to as the "Summer of Love 2004." (The California Supreme Court later ruled that the mayor had overstepped his legal authority, and voided the marriages.)

The Castro neighborhood is the heart of the city's gay culture—and the huge rainbow flags fluttering at the corner of Market and Castro Streets make clear its intent to provide a safe haven and a vast playground for gays in the city. But even beyond the Castro, San Francisco is gay friendly, with many gay-specific lodgings, restaurants, and nightclubs. Among the more famous events hosted here are the legendary Halloween celebrations and the Folsom Street Fair. For information on the local scene, pick up the *San Francisco Bay Guardian*. Visit the Convention and Visitors Bureau's website, sfvisitor.org, for resources for the gay and lesbian market.

Traveling with Disabilities: Check accessnca.com for the basics and icanonline.net for travel tips and ideas.

Print Media: The *San Francisco Chronicle* (sfgate.com), the local daily, covers entertainment in depth in the Sunday pull-out "Pink Pages" section. The *San Francisco Bay Guardian*, a free alternative weekly, provides the latest scoop on what's hot in town and pursues a liberal agenda that's well suited to the city; it also has detailed nightclub and restaurant listings. Another excellent resource for art, dining, and music listings is the *San Francisco Weekly*, the city's other alternative weekly. *San Francisco* is a glossy and stylish city magazine. Its competitor, the hip and glossy *7x7 Magazine*, aims to be an arbiter for the urban lifestyle.

Radio Stations (a selection)

FM Stations

88.5	KQED	NPR
91.1	KCSM	24-hour Jazz
91.7	KALW	NPR, BBC
94.1	KPFA	Alternative News, Music
94.9	KYLD	Urban Top 40
95.7	KZBR	Country
96.5	KOIT	Adult Contemporary
97.3	KLLC	Adult Contemporary
98.1	KISQ	Classic Soul, R&B
101.3	KIOI	Adult Contemporary
103.7	KKSF	Smooth Jazz
104.5	KFOG	Adult Alternative Rock
105.3	KITS	Alternative Rock
106.1	KMEL	Hip Hop, R&B

AM Stations

610	KFRC	Oldies, Sports
740	KCBS	All News
810	KGO	Sports, News

Shopping Hours: Most downtown shops and department stores are open 10am-6pm, with many shops extending hours on Saturday. During the holiday season, Union Square bustles until 9pm or later.

Attire: Given San Francisco's mix of fog, rain, wind, and sunshine, it's more challenging to find the right weight of clothing than the right look. Always carry a light sweater or jacket, in case the fog rolls in suddenly and the weather turns chilly. Dress is generally stylish yet relaxed—this is the West Coast after all, so there's not a lot of formality in terms of suits and ties, and only a handful of the most expensive restaurants require a jacket. When in doubt, lots of black, a chic trench coat, and fashionable footwear will give you the local look. Given the hills, comfortable shoes are a must—unless you're taking cabs all over town for a night hitting the clubs, in which case you can go strappy and sky-high with the heels. In January and February, be prepared for temperatures that can dip into the 40s at night, and keep umbrellas and raingear handy for rainstorms. Sunglasses are a must, even if it's foggy when you leave the hotel, since sunshine often arrives by afternoon.

Size Conversion

Dress Sizes

US	6	8	10	12	14	16
UK	8	10	12	14	16	18
France	36	38	40	42	44	46
Italy	38	40	42	44	46	48
Europe	34	36	38	40	42	44

Women's Shoes

US	6	6½	7	7½	8	8½
UK	4½	5	5½	6	6½	7
Europe	38	38	39	39	40	41

Men's Suits

US	36	38	40	42	44	46
UK	36	38	40	42	44	46
Europe	46	48	50	52	54	56

Men's Shirts

US	14½	15	15½	16	16½	17
UK	14½	15	15½	16	16½	17
Europe	38	39	40	41	42	43

Men's Shoes

US	8	8½	9½	10½	11½	12
UK	7	7½	8½	9½	10½	11
Europe	41	42	43	44	45	46

CITY ESSENTIALS

When Drinking Is Legal: The legal drinking age is 21. Bars, nightclubs, and lounges close at 2am. (See Eating and Drinking, p.158)

Smoking: If you're thinking of lighting up, don't. Starting in 2005, it became illegal to smoke outdoors at all city-owned venues, including parks and plazas. It is also illegal to smoke indoors in almost all public venues, including bars and restaurants. Some night spots have smoking patios.

Drugs: Back in 1870, San Francisco was one of the first cities to pass a law against smoking opium. Today you'll score time in the pokey for possession, sale, or use of all the usual suspects, including cocaine, marijuana, and ecstasy. Don't let the medicinal marijuana hubbub fool you, it's still illegal and stiff penalties apply.

Time Zone: San Francisco falls within the Pacific time zone. A note on daylight saving: Clocks are set ahead one hour at 2am on the first Sunday in April and set back one hour at 2am on the last Sunday in October.

Additional Resources for Visitors

San Francisco Convention & Visitors Bureau Pick up brochures, maps, and tour information. Check online for information on over 200 Bay Area hotels, or call the bureau's hotel reservation service (888-782-9673) for assistance. *Mon-Fri 9am-5pm, Sat-Sun 9am-3pm* Lower level of Hallidie Plaza at Market and Powell Streets, 415-391-2000, sfvisitor.org

Foreign Visitors
Foreign Embassies in the U.S.: state.gov/misc/10125.htm
Passport requirements: travel.state.gov/travel/tips/brochures /brochures_1229.html
Cell phones: North America operate on the 1900Mhz frequency. Cell phones may be used while driving. For buying or renting a phone go to telestial.com/instructions.htm.
Toll-free numbers in the U.S.: 1-800, 1-866, 1-877, and 1-888.
Telephone directory assistance in the U.S.: 411
Electrical: U.S. standard is AC, 110 volts/60 cycles, with a plug of two flat pins set parallel to one another.

The Latest-Info Websites
Go to sfstation.com and sfgate.com for events and restaurant reviews, nitevibe.com for the scoop on nightlife. And, of course, pulseguides.com.

HIT THE GROUND

Party Conversation—A Few Surprising Facts

- The Golden Gate Bridge has 24-hour cameras with detailed surveillance of bridge sidewalks and crisis telephones because so many people try to jump off it.

- Jack Kerouac is responsible for the term "Beat Generation," but Herb Caen, the famous columnist for the *San Francisco Chronicle*, coined the term "Beatnik" in 1958. Asked where he got the "nik," Caen explained that he'd been inspired by the recently launched Sputnik satellite.

- Cable cars are the nation's only mobile National Landmarks. Cable cars run at a constant 9.5 miles per hour.

- The inspiration for the fictional Barbary Lane in Armistead Maupin's *Tales of the City* series is a real place; it's called Macondray Lane, and you'll find it between Union and Green Streets (stretching from Leavenworth to Taylor Streets).

- The Bay to Breakers race is the biggest foot race in the world, with over 75,000 participants, many of whom are in costume.

- Fortune cookies were invented at the Japanese Tea Garden in Golden Gate Park in the 1890s. Not long afterwards, the city's Chinese restaurants embraced them, starting a trend that has not fallen from favor since.

- The average rate of motion across the San Andreas Fault Zone during the past 3 million years has been 56 millimeters per year. This is about the same rate at which your fingernails grow. At this rate, scientists project that Los Angeles and San Francisco will be adjacent to one another in 15 million years.

- San Francisco has provided the setting for countless films, including classics such as *Bullitt*, *The Maltese Falcon*, *Vertigo*, *The Birds*, and *The Graduate*.

- Don't fret if a local describes unseasonably warm or humid conditions as "earthquake weather." There is no such thing. Statistically, there is an equal distribution of earthquakes occurring in cold, hot, and rainy weather.

The Cheat Sheet
(The Very Least You Ought to Know
About San Francisco)

It's always a good idea to know a bit about the places you're going. Here's a countdown of everything you need to feel like a consummate insider in the San Francisco scene.

10 Neighborhoods

- **The Castro**, the hub of the city's (and some might say the world's) gay community, is a vibrant neighborhood with a lively nightlife and shopping scene. Beautifully preserved Victorian homes, the Castro Theatre, built in 1922, and steep thigh-burning hills are a few of the highlights.
- **Downtown** San Francisco's heart is Union Square, a gleaming shopping mecca anchored on a scenic plaza and surrounded by the city's grandest hotels and finest theaters. It extends to the streets of the Financial District, lined with glass-and-steel skyscrapers, and adjoins the city's vibrant Chinatown.
- **Haight-Ashbury**—the infamous intersection that symbolizes Flower Power—still shows vestiges of its hippie roots, but is mainly characterized these days by its funky clothing stores, tattoo parlors, and youthful grunge-and-alternative crowd. Beautiful Victorians, plus its proximity to Golden Gate Park, make it a quintessentially San Franciscan area.
- **The Marina** and **Cow Hollow**, two adjoining neighborhoods, are populated by preppy, well-dressed, and affluent professionals, and filled with high-gloss shops and restaurants. The Marina's chic shopping is on Chestnut Street; in Cow Hollow, the action goes down on Union Street. And we mean action—the bars around Fillmore and Greenwich Streets are a destination for singles on weekend nights.
- **The Mission District**'s cultural identity is predominantly Hispanic, and city landmarks like the Mission Dolores, constructed in the late 1700s, speak to its Spanish and Mexican origins. But the old exists alongside the new here, and in the vicinity of 16th Street you'll find legions of hipsters and some of the city's most stylish bars and restaurants.
- **Nob Hill**, an affluent hilltop neighborhood adjacent to downtown and North Beach, has a noble grandeur. Cable cars climb its steep streets, and landmarks include Grace Cathedral, inspired by 13th-century French Gothic architecture, as well as some of the city's best-known luxury hotels.

Noe Valley is a hillside neighborhood anchored by 24th Street, lined with charming shops, restaurants, and cafes, and often trafficked by "stroller patrols," as locals fondly refer to the groups of mothers perambulating with babies. The steep surrounding streets lined with beautiful Victorian homes rank among the city's most sought-after real estate.

North Beach, originally settled by Italians during the Gold Rush era, is famous for the authentic Italian restaurants and sidewalk cafes lining Columbus Avenue. The neighborhood also boasts lively bars and artsy bookstores from the days when this was the epicenter of the 1950s Beat Generation. Fisherman's Wharf, at the foot of Columbus Avenue on the bay, is anchored by Pier 39 and functions as San Francisco's tourist hub.

Pacific Heights, a ritzy neighborhood of steep streets lined with exquisitely preserved mansions, is anchored by the beautiful hilltop Alta Plaza Park which affords some of the finest views of the city. Fillmore Street is one of the city's most whimsical and distinctive shopping districts.

SoMa is the acronym for South of Market, where urban renewal has transformed a former warehouse district into a hot destination. Crowds migrate to the nightclubs and trendy restaurants on the weekend. Other draws include Yerba Buena Gardens, a park with sophisticated landscape architecture, theaters, and galleries set just across the street from the San Francisco Museum of Modern Art.

9   Landmarks

City Hall Recently restored to its original glory inside and out, this Beaux Arts–style building topped by a massive dome was a bustling hub of San Francisco's 2004 "Summer of Love," when thousands of gay couples married after the city's Mayor Gavin Newsom signed a bill allowing it. One Carlton B. Goodlett Pl. at Polk Street, 415-554-4858

Coit Tower The legacy of a famously flirtatious and fireman-friendly 19th-century socialite named Lillie Hitchcock Coit, this 180-foot fluted pillar set on a hilltop in North Beach is designed to resemble a firehose (although other off-color comparisons have been made). The views from the tower's high point, and even from the parking lot, are spectacular. One Telegraph Hill Blvd., 415-362-0808

Ferry Building This beautiful historic building, the hub of San Francisco's bustling ferry terminal in the early 1900s, is an example of urban renewal at its finest. After years of neglect, it has become the white-hot center of San Francisco's sophisticated culinary scene, with sought-after restaurants and an upscale Farmers Market several times a week that draws celebrity chefs. On the Embarcadero at the end of Market Street.

Golden Gate Bridge Hailed as an architectural feat when it was constructed in the 1930s, this bright-orange bridge spanning the waters between the city and the Marin Headlands is a beloved icon. Walk across it for an exhilarating vantage point on the city's famous hills and skyline. Hwy. 101 North out of the city toward Marin County.

CHEAT SHEET

Mission Dolores Handwrought ironwork and thick adobe walls characterize this historic mission; mass is still held in the 175-seat chapel, and the adjoining small white building is the city's oldest, dating back to the 1780s. The mission's cemetery appeared in the Hitchcock film *Vertigo*. 16th St. at Dolores Street.

Painted Ladies These seven beautifully preserved Victorians, set like gems against the backdrop of San Francisco's city skyline, are a picturesque and iconic San Francisco sight. The famous homes are best admired from the adjacent Alamo Square Park. Steiner between Hayes and Grove Streets.

Palace of Fine Arts Corinthian columns that evoke a Roman ruin, surrounded by green lawns and anchored by a swan-filled reflecting pond, characterize this Marina District landmark preserved from the Panama-Pacific International Exposition of 1915. 3301 Lyon St.

Sentinel Building Construction of this ornate and distinctive wedge-shaped building set on the southern edge of historic North Beach began before the 1906 earthquake and fire. The steel frame survived the tragedy, and the building was completed in 1907. Corner of Kearny Street and Columbus Avenue.

Transamerica Pyramid This iconic building soars up 853 feet, including the 212-foot spire, and is set adjacent to a small redwood park, a surprising oasis in the midst of the steel-and-glass surroundings of the Financial District. 600 Montgomery St.

8 Great Parks

Alta Plaza Park This hilltop park with sweeping views across the city is where well-groomed Pacific Heights residents walk their equally well-groomed pets; it's surrounded by exquisitely kept mansions and located just blocks from bustling Fillmore Street. At Steiner and Clay Streets.

Buena Vista Park This green space with terraced hillsides and treelined paths is the city's oldest park. The lawn along Haight Street can draw ne'er-do-wells, so it's best to walk with a friend. At Haight and Baker Streets.

Dolores Park This hillside park draws an eclectic crowd to its grassy slopes. Soccer teams and tennis players recreate side-by-side with loungers and sunbathers; Speedo-clad Castro residents arrive in droves in warm weather. At 18th and Dolores Streets.

Golden Gate Park Vast picnic lawns, flower gardens and lakes, and a beautifully restored Victorian conservatory are just a few highlights of this 1,013-acre park, San Francisco's center of outdoor recreation. Bound by Fulton Street, Lincoln Street, Stanyan Street, and the Great Highway.

The Presidio Once a U.S. military base but now owned by the National Park Service, these vast eucalyptus-scented grounds by the water are dotted with white clapboard buildings and draw visitors for scenic bike rides and walks. Enter on Presidio Avenue.

South Park A tiny gem in SoMa, this urban postcard-stamp–sized park is busy during the weekday lunch hour, when office workers take refuge from downtown and picnic on the grass—several excellent take-out cafes and restaurants line the park. On South Park between Second and Third Streets.

Washington Square Park Located in the historic Italian North Beach neighborhood and anchored by Saints Peter and Paul Church, this park is a hub of local activity, with loungers, dog-walkers, tourists, and Tai Chi practitioners from Chinatown all sharing space on the small green lawn. At Powell and Columbus Streets.

Yerba Buena Gardens A sleek fountain and emerald lawns provide a place of rest and tranquility in SoMa. The park is bordered by the Metreon, an entertainment complex of movies, restaurants, and shops; and SFMoMA, as well as the Yerba Buena Center for the Arts' galleries and theaters. At Third and Howard Streets.

7 Hills

Well, actually there are some 40 hills around here, but wanting to be like Rome, San Francisco has adopted the sobriquet "The City of Seven Hills."

Lone Mountain Also referred to as Laurel Hill, and considered part of the now-sophisticated neighborhood of Laurel Heights, this area around California and Masonic Avenues was home to the city's largest cemeteries in the mid-1800s.

Mount Davidson At 938 feet above sea level, Mount Davidson is the highest of San Francisco's hills. While not a famous tourist destination, it has a landmark towering cross at its summit—which is located near the geographic center of the city, southwest of the crossroads of Portola Drive, O'Shaughnessy, and Laguna Honda Boulevards.

Nob Hill The city's mining and railroad millionaires built lavish mansions on this gorgeous hilltop in the 1870s; although many of the spectacular homes were lost in the 1906 earthquake and fire, the hill retains its grandeur thanks to beautiful Grace Cathedral and several historic hotels.

Rincon Hill Set south of Market Street, this area was considered the city's most desirable neighborhood in the 1850s because it receives less wind and fog—until Nob Hill supplanted it 20 years later as the city's most fashionable address. Eventually, this area between Folsom Street and the Bay Bridge sprouted with factories and warehouses. Today, it's being revitalized, with developers planning glitzy new high-rises.

Russian Hill Near-vertical streets, narrow dead-ends, steep staircases, and towering retaining walls give this densely populated hilltop in the northern part of the city a quiet tranquility.

Telegraph Hill Most famous for the iconic landmark of Coit Tower, this high hilltop is set between North Beach and San Francisco Bay; climbing the area's thigh-burning staircases isn't easy, but the views from the top are unforgettable.

Twin Peaks From afar, you can spot this high point by its iconic radio tower, often shrouded in fog with just the highest spires peeking out of the mist. A popular viewpoint at the top, from a grassy meadow, offers a panoramic vista of the city and the East Bay beyond.

6 Party Zones

The Castro It's no surprise that San Francisco's most vibrant gay neighborhood has a world-class nightlife; it's easy to find nonstop dance floors at hot spots such as SF Badlands, or to join the crowds of locals at see-and-be-seen cocktail bars along Market Street.

Downtown Contemporary lounges, classic hotel bars, chic cafes, buzzing dance clubs, and upscale restaurants draw all sorts for a big night out. No matter what you seek, you are sure to find a fun crowd to revel with here.

The Marina and Cow Hollow This is one of San Francisco's most popular singles pickup scenes on the weekends, populated by post-collegiate and well-dressed young professionals who like to party spring break–style in the bars along Chestnut and Union Streets. You'll find busy sports bars here, too.

The Mission This neighborhood is knee-deep in hipsters on weekends, particularly in the vicinity of 16th and Valencia Streets. Come prepared to crowd into the small, intimate bars with arty types in outfits that are even trendier than the trendy cocktails served at the bar.

North Beach The eclectic nightlife in North Beach ranges from singles-scene dance clubs and the hot-date champagne bar at the Bubble Lounge to infamous strip clubs like the Lusty Lady. Other popular bars include Vesuvio, a former hangout of famous Beatnik writer Jack Kerouac.

SoMa San Francisco's largest dance club meccas cater to both straight and gay in this industrial part of the city; Folsom Street is a main nightlife corridor.

5 Big Museums

Asian Art Museum One of the largest museums devoted exclusively to Asian art, with holdings that include nearly 15,000 treasures. 200 Larkin St., Civic Center Plaza, 415-581-3500, asianart.org

de Young Museum The de Young opened its long-awaited new museum to the public in October 2005, providing access to its priceless collection of American art from the 17th through the 20th centuries, in addition to art of the native Americas, Africa, and the Pacific. 50 Hagiwara Tea Garden Dr., Golden Gate Park, 415-682-2481, thethinker.org/deyoung

Exploratorium Frequently hailed as the finest science museum in the United States, this 100,000-plus square-foot destination is distinctly down-to-earth, with hundreds of hands-on displays for kids and adults. 3601 Lyon St., 415-397-5673, exploratorium.edu

Palace of the Legion of Honor This neoclassical building inspired by the Legion of Honor in Paris stands on a cliff above the Pacific's pounding surf and displays the works of artists such as Monet, Cézanne, Rembrandt, and Rodin. Near 34th Avenue and Clement Street, 415-863-3330, 415-750-3600, thethinker.org

San Francisco Museum of Modern Art This striking modernist museum designed by Mario Botta houses an extensive collection of modern paintings, sculptures, and photography, and regularly hosts must-see traveling art shows. 151 Third St., 415-357-4000, sfmoma.com

4 Linguistic Mistakes to Avoid

Frisco Only tourists, and lame ones at that, call it anything but San Francisco (or "The City").

Gough Street Pronounced "goff," not "gow" or "go."

Kearny Street Pronounced "ker-nee," not "keer-nee."

Trollies They might be called trollies in other cities, but in San Francisco, it's cable cars that transport you up and down the hills.

3 Performing Arts Centers

San Francisco Symphony The sleek glass-enclosed Louise M. Davies Symphony Hall, presided over by music director Michael Tilson-Thomas, has hosted many of the world's most important conductors and composers. 201 Van Ness Ave., 415-864-6000, sfsymphony.org

War Memorial Opera House The magnificent French Renaissance–style building hosts the internationally renowned San Francisco Ballet and world-class operatic performances that have drawn San Francisco's best-dressed and most cultured crowds since the 1920s. 301 Van Ness Ave., ballet: 415-865-2000, sfballet.org; opera: 415-864-3330, sfopera.com

Yerba Buena Center for the Arts A multimedia center that promotes cutting-edge visual arts, performing arts, film and video, and educational programs. 701 Mission St., 415-978-2787, ybca.org

CHEAT SHEET

Sports Teams

San Francisco 49ers Wondering what your colors are? Gold and red! The famous football team, which has taken home five Super Bowl trophies, plays here at Monster Park (previously named Candlestick Park). sf49ers.com

San Francisco Giants The city is proud of their Giants, as well as the home-run-friendly SBC Park; the ballpark food includes sophisticated pan-Asian options and the views encompass the skyline and the Bay. sfgiants.com

Cardinal Rule

In Fog City, always carry an **extra** layer.

Coffee (quick stops for a java jolt)

Atlas Cafe A Mission hub with an outdoor garden, live music, great coffee, and food. 3049 20th St. (Alabama St.), 415-648-1047

Boulange de Cole A popular gathering spot in Cole Valley with delicious French pastries. 1000 Cole St. (Parnassus Ave.), 415-242-2442

Boulange de Union This lovely French cafe is the ideal place to regroup after a morning of shopping. 1909 Union St. (Laguna St.), 415-440-4450

Caffe Centro Meeting spot at the heart of Multimedia Gulch. (p.100) 102 South Park (Second St.), 415-882-1500

Caffe Trieste The first espresso bar established on the west coast and still going strong. (p.135) 609 Vallejo St. (Grant Ave.), 415-392-6739

Farley's The center of the Potrero Hill scene with a devoted following of hipsters drinking strong coffee. 1315 18th St. (Texas St.), 415-648-1545

The Grove A prime location, outdoor seating, and a wide selection make this a local favorite. 2250 Chestnut St. (Avila St.), 415-474-4843

Martha and Brothers A Noe Valley hub with great coffee and outdoor benches for prime socializing. 3868 24th St. (Sanchez St.), 415-641-4433

Peet's This beloved local chain started the gourmet coffee revolution in the Bay Area and serves up a particularly potent brew. 2197 Fillmore St. (Sacramento St.), 415-563-9930, and throughout the city.

Steps of Rome A charming sidewalk cafe in North Beach that serves up excellent espresso. 348 Columbus Ave. (Vallejo St.), 415-397-0435

The Warming Hut Set at the edge of the bay, this is a breathtaking place to stop for a coffee, hot chocolate, or sandwich. Across from fishing pier on the way to Fort Point from Crissy Field in the Presidio, 415-561-3042

HIT THE GROUND

Just for Business & Conventions

San Francisco is an incredibly easy town to do business in, especially if your business takes you to Moscone Center or the Financial District. From upscale boutique hotels to high-rises with spectacular bay views, there are plenty of hotels within walking distance of both, as well as countless fantastic restaurants. Across the street from Moscone is SFMoMA, and directly above it is Yerba Buena Center for the Arts, flanked by a glorious, sun-bathed park. The Financial District is within an easy stroll of the Ferry Building Marketplace. Even an hour or two of free time can be enough to enjoy a waterfront stroll, have a great meal, or relax over a cocktail.

Addresses to Know

Convention Centers

- Concourse Exhibition Center and Trade Show Facility
  635 Eighth St. (Brannan St.), SoMa, 415-487-3293, sfvenues.com
- Moscone Center
  747 Howard St. (Third St.), SoMa, 415-974-4000, moscone.com

City Information

- San Francisco Convention and Visitors Bureau
  Visitor Information Center
  Downstairs at 900 Market St. (Powell St.), Downtown, 415-391-2001 recorded events listing, 415-391-2000 live help, sfvisitor.org
- Official San Francisco City and County Website, sfgov.org

Business and Convention Hotels

A number of the hotels that we recommend in our San Francisco Black Book (see p.212) cater to business travelers and are near Moscone Center and the Financial District. Some additional choices include:

The Argent Hotel Artful high-rise hotel in the middle of downtown. $$ 50 Third St. (Market St.), 415-974-6400 / 877-222-6699, argenthotel.com

Marriott San Francisco Plenty of room, convenient location, and a bar with a view. $$ 55 Fourth St. (Mission St.), 415-896-1600 / 800-228-9290, marriott.com

Omni San Francisco Hotel Boutique chic, four-diamond hotel. $$ 500 California St. (Montgomery St.), 415-677-9494 / 888-444-6664, omnihotels.com

Park Hyatt San Francisco Spectacular views and a boutique hotel atmosphere. $$$ 333 Battery St. (Embarcadero), 415-392-1234 / 877-557-5368, sanfranciscoparkhyatt.com

Business Entertaining

The following San Francisco Black Book recommended restaurants fit the bill for sealing the deal over a drink or meal:

Bix A longtime favorite with plenty of character, glamour, and great martinis. $$ (p.133) 56 Gold St. (Sansome St.), 415-433-6300

La Suite Impeccable French food on the Embarcadero waterfront. $$ (p.67) 100 Brannan St. (Embarcadero), 415-593-5900

Myth A handsome newcomer serving French-inspired California cuisine. $$ (p.67) 470 Pacific Ave. (Montgomery St.), 415-677-8986

Ozumo Fine Japanese cuisine in an elegant, contemporary setting. $$ (p.68) Harbor Court Hotel, 161 Steuart St. (Mission St.), 415-882-1333

Also see:
Best Fine Dining (p.22)
Best Power Lunch Spots (p.33)
Best Seafood Restaurants (p.38)
Best Wine Lists (p.47)

Ducking Out for a Half-Day

When the opportunity to sneak out of the convention arises, check these out and get back in time before anyone notices.

Ferry Building Marketplace An emporium of gourmet food purveyors carrying California products located on the scenic waterfront. (p.83) One Ferry Building (Market St.), 415-693-0996

Golden Gate Park Visit the de Young Museum or the Conservatory of Flowers. (p.154) Stanyan, Fulton, Lincoln, and the Great Highway, 415-831-2700

San Francisco Museum of Modern Art The nation's second-largest collection of modern art is a stone's throw from Moscone. (p.86) 151 Third St. (Howard St.), 415-357-4000

Also see:
Best Historic San Francisco (p.24)
Best Outdoor Activities (p.32)
Best Spas (p.41)

Gifts to Bring Home

What fun is unpacking if you can't pull out a treasure or two to share with those at home? Get the goods here.

Ferry Building Marketplace From local McEvoy olive oil to Scharffen Berger chocolate. (p.83) One Ferry Building (Embarcadero and Market St.), 415-693-0996

Gumps A local institution carrying fine china, jewelry, linens, silver, fine home accessories, and more. (p.154) 135 Post St. (Kearny St.), 800-766-7628

SFMoMA Museum Store The gift shop has unique jewelry, kids' toys, and stylish accessories. (p.87) 151 Third St. (Howard St.), 415-357-4000

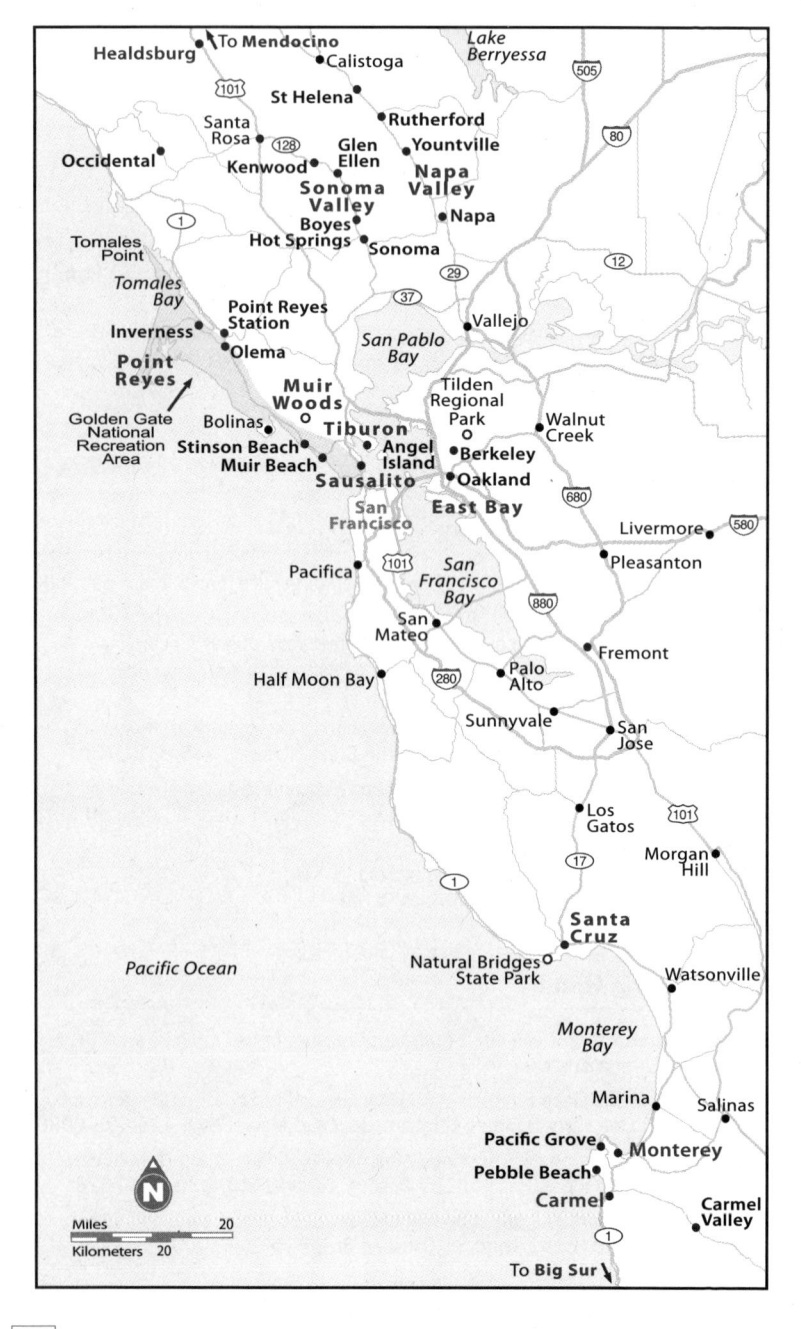

SAN FRANCISCO REGION

LEAVING SAN FRANCISCO

If you want a break from the San Francisco scene, a breathtaking variety of nearby excursions are yours for the choosing—from the refined Napa and Sonoma Valley wine country to the relaxed beaches of Santa Cruz. Consider taking a few days to combine several destinations. A Northern Tour could easily include Sausalito, Tiburon, Sonoma, Napa, and Mendocino (with a stop in Pt. Reyes on your way back to town). A Southern Tour could cover a visit to Santa Cruz, Monterey, Carmel, and Big Sur.

Mendocino

150 miles N

Hot Tip: Summer is the height of tourist season, so try spring or early fall. Off-season discounts don't start until November.

The Lowdown: This quaint northern town set on scenic bluffs above the turbulent Pacific is the gem of Northern California's rugged coast. Its natural beauty is such that the four-hour drive from San Francisco doesn't seem to deter urbanites from flocking here, despite the high room prices and summer crowds. Fortunately, whether you arrive via the dramatic Highway 1 that hugs the coast or the pastoral Anderson Valley wine region along Highway 128, the trip here is a wildly scenic experience. When you arrive, the picturesque views continue; founded in 1852, Mendocino has the appeal of a New England–style seaside village complete with a white-spire church. It's the town's location on the renowned Mendocino Headlands that truly sets it apart, however. Emerald green in spring, golden in summer, or dramatically cloaked in fog in the winter, these scenic open bluffs beg for exploration. After you've strolled along the flat, easily accessible trails, spend a lazy afternoon exploring the town's bookstores, boutiques, and bakeries, or visit one of several beautiful state parks nearby for a more vigorous hike.

Best Attractions

Anderson Valley Wine Region Most of the wineries in this beautiful 35-mile-long valley are found along a narrow and winding stretch of Highway 128, around the town of Philo. Highlights include Husch Vineyards, Pacific Echo Cellars, and Roederer Estate. 707-468-9886, mendowine.com

Mendocino Coast Botanical Gardens Set eight miles north of the village of Mendocino, this well-groomed wonder is comprised of 47 beautiful acres. 18220 Hwy. 1, 707-964-4352, gardenbythesea.org

Mendocino Headlands State Park This coastal headlands park surrounds the town on all sides, and the heather-covered bluffs are criss-crossed with flat, wide paths that offer spectacular ocean views. A stroll along the bluffs is not to be missed. 707-937-5804

Best Hotels

Brewery Gulch Inn This gorgeous lodge-style inn set high on a bluff a mile south of Mendocino is the region's newest (opened in 2001) and most luxurious lodging. 9401 Coast Hwy. 1, Mendocino, 707-937-4752 / 800-578-4454, brewerygulchinn.com

Heritage House Inn Supremely located along the cliffs and beaches on the ocean side of Hwy. 1, this rambling resort divides its 66 rooms among a variety of houses. 5200 North Hwy. 1, Little River, 707-937-5885 / 800-235-5885, heritagehouseinn.com

MacCallum House Inn and Restaurant Beautifully restored Victorian mansion with ocean views and an ideal location in the heart of town. 45020 Albion St., Mendocino, 707-937-0289 / 800-609-0492, maccallumhouse.com

The Stanford Inn by the Sea An eco-conscious redwood lodge with rustic elegance and home to an award-winning vegetarian restaurant. Hwy. 1 and Comptche-Ukiah Rd., Mendocino, 707-937-5615 / 800-331-8884, stanfordinn.com

Whitegate Inn Elegant and traditional Victorian bed-and-breakfast in a central location with tasteful amenities. 499 Howard St., Mendocino, 707-937-4892/ 800-531-7282, whitegateinn.com

Best Restaurants

Cafe Beaujolais Sleek, sophisticated dining room with creative European-style cuisine and an outstanding selection of desserts. 961 Ukiah St., Mendocino, 707-937-5614, cafebeaujolais.com

MacCallum House Inn and Restaurant Excellent fresh seasonal cuisine in either an elegant, intimate redwood-paneled dining room or a more casual cafe housed in a window-enclosed Victorian sunporch with good views of the ocean. 45020 Albion St., Mendocino, 707-937-0289, maccallumhouse.com

Mendocino Hotel Restaurant The elegant sitting room and bar of this historic hotel built in 1878 is one of the best spots in town for a pre-dinner warm-up (often needed) or an after-dinner drink. 45080 Main St., Mendocino, 707-937-0511/ 800-548-0513, mendocinohotel.com

The Moosse Café A cozy and casual restaurant overlooking the headlands with a seasonal menu that specializes in Mediterranean cuisine. 390 Kasten St., Mendocino, 707-937-4323, theblueheron.com

Contacts

Fort Bragg–Mendocino Coast Chamber of Commerce 707-961-6300 / 800-726-2780, mendocinocoast.com

Mendocino State Park Visitor Center Ford House, 735 Main St., Mendocino, 707-937-5397

Getting There: Exit from Hwy. 101 North after Cloverdale to the Mendocino/Hwy. 128 West. Travel west on Hwy. 128 through Boonville and Anderson Valley to connect to Hwy. 1, and go north 10 miles to Mendocino. For the slower but more scenic route, take Hwy. 1 North the whole way.

Monterey and Carmel

112 miles S

Hot Tip: It's beautiful year-round, but late September brings especially nice weather and (slightly) shorter lines at attractions like the Monterey Bay Aquarium.

The Lowdown: With its rugged coastal beauty, famous destinations including Monterey and Carmel, and world-class attractions like the golf courses at Pebble Beach, this part of California's Central Coast is an internationally known playground. Monterey's historic Cannery Row—once a bustling capital of the sardine industry, and the inspiration for John Steinbeck's 1945 novel by the same name—recalls the town's early days as a fishing and whaling port, but today is lined with restaurants and souvenir shops. This is where you'll find the famous Monterey Bay Aquarium, the largest aquarium in the United States, with unforgettable exhibits like the three-story Kelp Forest, teeming with leopard sharks and other fish. Monterey's downtown has shop-lined streets and sophisticated eateries; each September, music-lovers arrive in droves for the annual Monterey Jazz Festival, the oldest continuous jazz celebration in the world. Attractions such as Pacific Grove, the starting point for the scenic 17-Mile Drive, Pebble Beach, and Carmel are just minutes from Monterey. Carmel's fancy shops, upscale restaurants and hotels, and fabulously scenic white-sand beaches—plus its former mayor, actor Clint Eastwood—have made it justly famous as a weekend getaway. (Bring the dog, too; Carmel is famously dog friendly, with pooches even allowed in many hotels and restaurants.) Drop by to visit the historic and beautiful Carmel Mission, established in 1797, or lose yourself in the winding, storybook streets at dusk—it's easy given that town ordinances prohibit streetlights and even street addresses (find your way by searching out street intersections). East of town is the beautiful wine region of Carmel Valley, where wineries like Chateau Julien Wine Estates offer the pleasures and sights of Napa in an off-the-beaten-path setting.

Best Attractions

Carmel Beach City Park Stroll along this popular silky white-sand beach a half hour before sunset and soak up the best views (and people-watching) Carmel has to offer. At the end of Ocean Ave., Carmel

Monterey Bay Aquarium Nearly 200 galleries exhibiting more than 35,000 animals and plants make up this world-famous attraction. 866 Cannery Row, Monterey, 831-648-4888 / 800-756-3737, montereybayaquarium.org

17-Mile Drive Secluded sandy coves, an iconic lone cypress clinging to a rocky outcropping, and frolicking wildlife at Seal and Bird Rocks are just a few snapshots of the sights along this famously scenic driving route, which also passes through exclusive Pebble Beach. 831-624-3811, pebblebeach.com/17miledrive.html

Tor House Craggy, ocean-view Tor House and Hawk Tower, built almost a century ago by famed poet and writer Robinson Jeffers, are reminiscent of ancient Irish stone towers. 26304 Ocean View Ave., at Stewart Way, Carmel, 831-624-1813, torhouse.org

Best Hotels

Bernardus Lodge This 57-room luxury resort with spa nestled in the spectacularly beautiful Carmel Valley wine country specializes in the finest epicurean experiences (Bernardus is also an acclaimed winery). 415 Carmel Valley Rd., Carmel Valley, 831-659-3131 / 888-648-9463, bernardus.com

Cypress Inn White stucco walls, red tile roof, and Spanish arches characterize this stately, 53-room inn with a central downtown Carmel location, owned by famously pet-friendly actress Doris Day (yes, pets are allowed). Lincoln St. at Seventh Ave., Carmel, 831-624-3871 / 800-443-7443, cypress-inn.com

The Lodge at Pebble Beach This famous golf resort is known for its luxury amenities, including a 22,000-square-foot, full-service spa, as well as its world-famous links. 17-Mile Dr., Pebble Beach, 831-647-7500 / 800-654-9300, pebblebeach.com

Seven Gables Inn and Grand View Inn Choose between Victorian or post-Victorian rooms and cottages at these immaculate sister bed-and-breakfast properties. 555 and 557 Ocean View Blvd., Pacific Grove, 831-372-4341, pginns.com

Spindrift Inn Chic, boutique 42-room hotel with garden room on Monterey's historic Cannery Row directly overlooks the sparkling bay. 652 Cannery Row, Monterey, 831-646-8900 / 800-841-1879, spindriftinn.com

Best Restaurants

Club XIX An intimate high-end dining room overlooking the famous 18th green of Pebble Beach Golf Links and Carmel Bay; extensive wine list with famous and vintage wines draws connoisseurs. The Lodge at Pebble Beach, 831-625-8519, pebblebeach.com

Fresh Cream Three separate dining rooms with floor-to-ceiling windows showcase views of Monterey Bay at this highly respected French restaurant. 99 Pacific St., Monterey, 831-375-9798, freshcream.com

Marinus at Bernardus Lodge The luxury dining room at Carmel Valley's most sophisticated and plush resort. 415 Carmel Valley Rd., Carmel Valley, 831-659-3131 / 888-648-9463, bernardus.com

Red House Café This tiny restaurant in a red brick house is equal parts charm and sophistication; it's wildly popular for breakfast and lunch, but dinner is also a casual and delicious affair. 662 Lighthouse Ave., Pacific Grove, 831-643-1060, redhousecafe.com

Contacts

Carmel Visitor Information Center 831-624-2522, carmelcalifornia.org
Monterey Peninsula Visitors and Convention Bureau 831-649-1770 / 888-221-1010, monterey.com

---

Getting There: Hwy. 1 South provides direct access to Monterey and Carmel. From Hwy. 101 South, take Hwy. 156-Monterey exit, which merges with Hwy. 1, for both destinations. The town of Pacific Grove is a 5-minute drive from Monterey's Cannery Row.

Napa Valley

55 miles N

Hot Tip: Autumn, when the vines are full, is an especially fun time to visit, but many people enjoy Napa's summer heat. Weekend travel means gridlock during high season (March through November).

The Lowdown: The 35-mile-long Napa Valley is a tourist destination extraordinaire, but even tour buses can't take anything away from this famous region's breathtaking natural beauty. Rows of lush vineyards, warm sunshine, scenic back roads, and the chance to indulge in some of the world's finest food and wine easily outweigh the gridlock you might encounter on the county's main wine road, Highway 29. A good (if still busy) driving alternative to this congested thoroughfare is the Silverado Trail, a scenic roadway with exquisite vineyards and access to some of Napa's most memorable tasting rooms. (Come prepared to pay small tasting fees at most wineries; while these can add up, it's a small price to pay to sample the region's famous vintages.) Aside from the wineries, Napa's charming wine towns, most of which are located along Highway 29, are the biggest draw. Set in the heart of the valley, the town of St. Helena has an impressive selection of excellent restaurants, and its historic Victorian boutique-lined Main Street is charming to explore on foot. To the north, the quaint town of Calistoga beckons with its famous historic hot springs and mud baths. Highway 29 also provides access to the quiet little hamlet of Yountville, best known as the home to the world-famous restaurant, the French Laundry; and Rutherford, the address of the luxurious hotel, The Auberge du Soleil. Anchoring the valley's southern end is the town of Napa, the county's working-class hub; although less-visited in previous years, its popularity is ever-increasing thanks to destinations including Copia: The American Center for Wine, Food & the Arts, and the revitalized historic downtown on the Napa River.

Best Attractions

Copia: The American Center for Wine, Food & the Arts Beautiful organic gardens and lush grounds surround this museum and educational center, which offers art exhibitions and classes integrating food, wine, and art; check out the performance calendar for the center's 500-seat concert terrace on the scenic Napa River. 500 First St., Napa, 707-259-1600, copia.org

Indian Springs Historic spa with legendary mud baths and a heated natural mineral pool. 1712 Lincoln Ave., Calistoga, 707-942-4913, indianspringsnapa.com

Napa Valley Wine Train Traverse the floor of Napa Valley in the well-appointed 1915 Pullman cars of this upscale dining train, which offers lunch and dinner daily, and a weekend brunch. 1275 McKinstry St., Napa, 707-253-2111 / 800-427-4124, winetrain.com

Silverado Trail This wildly scenic wine road parallels Highway 29 and runs the length of Napa Valley; for stunning hilltop views of the valley, visit Silverado Vineyards (6121 Silverado Trail, 707-257-1770). silveradotrail.com

Best Hotels

Auberge du Soleil A hilltop retreat with a worldwide reputation as a luxurious, exclusive, and private escape; includes tennis, pool, and spa. 180 Rutherford Hill Rd., Rutherford, 707-963-1211 / 800-348-5406, aubergedusoleil.com

Carneros Inn A unique resort that has applied Napa chic to a farmhouse setting; you'll find guest cottages, vineyard views, pool, and spa. 4048 Sonoma Hwy., Napa, 707-299-4900 / 888-400-9000, thecarnerosinn.com

Meadowood Napa Valley Elegant Cape Cod–style resort on 250-acre grounds with all amenities including par-3 golf, tennis, pool and spa. 900 Meadowood Ln., St. Helena, 707-963-3646 / 800-458-8080, meadowood.com

Milliken Creek Inn An intimate and fabulously stylish 12-room inn on three landscaped acres above the banks of the Napa River. 1815 Silverado Tr., Napa, 707-255-1197 / 888-622-5775, millikencreekinn.com

Best Restaurants

Auberge du Soleil A hilltop retreat with a worldwide reputation as a luxurious, exclusive, and private escape; the renowned California-French restaurant by the same name is on site. 180 Rutherford Hill Rd., Rutherford, 707-963-1211 / 800-348-5406, aubergedusoleil.com

Bouchon Sit outside anytime of day, perch at the bar, indulge in a fantastic full meal, or just pop into their bakery next door. 6640 Washington St., Yountville, 707-944-8037, frenchlaundry.com/bouchon

The French Laundry Often touted as the best restaurant in the United States. 6534 Washington St., Yountville, 707-944-2380, frenchlaundry.com

Julia's Kitchen Named for chef Julia Child, this is Californian cuisine at its most sublime. 500 First St., Napa, 707-265-5700, copia.org

Martini House Fabulous fine dining in a California Craftsman bungalow renovated by famous restaurant designer Pat Kuleto; the busy Wine Cellar bar downstairs is Napa's place to see and be seen. 1245 Spring St., St. Helena, 707-963-2233, kuleto.com

Press It's all about steak at chic, modern Press. Perfectly aged meats are roasted on the enormous fireplace and served by a competent and knowledgeable staff. 587 St. Helena Hwy., St. Helena, 707-957-0550, pressthelena.com

Restaurant Budo Intimate, chic and modern, this multi-room restaurant with a beautiful patio serves a top-notch New American menu. 1650 Soscol Ave., Napa, 707-224-2330, restaurantbudo.com

Terra Intimate dining housed in a stunning century-old stone building. 1345 Railroad Ave., St. Helena, 707-963-8931, terrarestaurant.com

Tra Vigne Perhaps the closest thing to a scene in Napa Valley, this bustling and beautiful Italian restaurant continues to be a favorite. 1050 Charter Oak Ave., St. Helena, 707-963-4444, travignerestaurant.com

Contacts

Napa Valley Visitors Bureau 707-226-7459, napavalley.com

Getting There: From Hwy. 101 North, exit onto Hwy. 37, then take a left onto Hwy. 121 North. Stay on 121, following signs for Napa until you reach Hwy. 29, which runs the length of the valley.

Sonoma Valley and Healdsburg

45 miles N

Hot Tip: Spring and fall are ideal times to visit.

The Lowdown: As famous as neighboring Napa for its stellar vineyards, the legendary 17-mile-long Sonoma Valley nonetheless has its own distinctive identity. The tranquil back roads are still more often traveled by farm trucks than by rental limos, and the off-the-beaten-path wineries have an unforced charm (they allow picnics, too). The best place to start a visit is the town of Sonoma, steeped in the region's Spanish and Mexican heritage. A historic mission, established by Gen. Mariano Vallejo, the Mexican commander who established Sonoma in 1835, presides over the town's grassy central plaza lined with shops, restaurants, and outdoor cafes. Travel north from here on Sonoma's central wine road, Highway 12, to reach destinations like Kenwood and Glen Ellen, tiny little towns best known for the famous wineries and wine country inns they harbor. Around Glen Ellen, be sure to stop and enjoy the scenic beauty of Jack London State Park. The route to one of Sonoma's trendiest wine country destinations is not via Highway 12, however, but further north along Highway 101: Healdsburg, with its pretty tree-lined central plaza, and proximity to the premier wineries in Dry Creek Valley and Alexander Valley, has blossomed from a rural agricultural town into a sophisticated small-town getaway with luxury hotels and restaurants.

Best Attractions

Bartholomew Park Winery This historic, Spanish-colonial–style boutique winery is set in a beautiful 400-acre park with hiking trails and splendid picnic spots; view antique photographs documenting viticulture practices from the 19th century in the small museum on site. 1000 Vineyard Ln., Sonoma, 707-935-9511, bartholomewparkwinery.com

Gloria Ferrer Champagne Caves Tour the caves to learn about how fine champagne is created; then stay to sip some bubbly in the cozy parlor or on the vast outdoor veranda of this Spanish-style villa. 23555 Hwy. 121, Sonoma, 707-996-7256, gloriaferrer.com

Jack London State Historic Park Writer Jack London's estate is now maintained as a California historical park with beautiful grounds. 2400 London Ranch Rd., off Hwy. 12, 707-938-5216, jacklondonpark.com

Best Hotels

Fairmont Sonoma Mission Inn and Spa The sprawling, luxurious spa is the main draw at this 230-room pink stucco resort on perfectly groomed grounds. 100 Boyes Blvd., Sonoma, 707-938-9000 / 800-862-4945, fairmont.com/sonoma

Gaige House Inn Choose from this Italianate Victorian mansion's grand rooms or splurge on the freestanding luxury suites by the pool. 13540 Arnold Dr., Glen Ellen, 707-935-0237 / 800-935-0237, gaige.com

Hotel Healdsburg Chic, full-service luxury hotel on Healdsburg's central plaza has a see-and-be-seen vibe. 25 Matheson St., Healdsburg, 707-431-2800/ 800-889-7188, hotelhealdsburg.com

The Inn at Occidental This 16-room retreat in tiny, rural Occidental combines whimsical décor with wine country luxury. 3657 Church St., Occidental, 707-874-1047 / 800-522-6324, innatoccidental.com

Kenwood Inn and Spa Kenwood's stunning centerpiece villa appears to have been transplanted from a historic Mediterranean hillside; the 28 rooms and spa offer every possible modern luxury. 10400 Sonoma Hwy. (Hwy. 12), Kenwood, 707-833-1293 / 800-353-6966, kenwoodinn.com

Best Restaurants/Nightlife

Charlie Palmer's Dry Creek Kitchen at Hotel Healdsburg Sonoma's own celebrity chef restaurant with seasonal cuisine is the place to be seen in Healdsburg. 317 Healdsburg Ave., Healdsburg, 707-431-0330, hotelhealdsburg.com

Cyrus Expertise, innovation, and a knack for setting off luxury ingredients just so combine for unqualified excellence at Cyrus, the lavish dining experience that is giving the French Laundry some competition at last. 29 North St., Healdsburg, 707-433-3311, cyrusrestaurant.com

The Ledson Hotel's Harmony Club Located on the ground floor of the Ledson Hotel on the east side of Sonoma's central plaza, this elegant nightclub offers live jazz and, of course, wine tasting. 480 First St. E., Sonoma, 707-996-9779, ledson.com

Ravenous Popular California cuisine restaurant with warm Mediterranean-inspired décor and a casually sophisticated wine country crowd. 420 Center St., Healdsburg, 707-431-1302

Contacts

Sonoma Valley Visitors Bureau 707-996-1090, sonomavalley.com

Russian River Wine Road This association of wineries and lodgings in northern Sonoma County is a great resource. 707-433-4335, wineroad.com

Getting There: From Hwy. 101 North, exit onto Hwy. 37. Travel east on Hwy. 37 for about eight miles, then turn left onto Hwy. 121 North (Sears Point Raceway will be on your left). From 121, take Hwy. 12 North to reach the towns of Sonoma, Glen Ellen, and Kenwood. Other Sonoma County destinations such as Santa Rosa or Healdsburg are a straight shot on 101 North.

150 miles S

Big Sur

Hot Tip: Too far for a day trip on its own, a visit to Big Sur works best as an extension of a trip to Carmel (see p.194). Visit in late spring or early fall to avoid the summer fog, or in the winter for whale watching off the coast.

The Lowdown: Visiting Big Sur's 90-mile stretch of wild, rugged coastline is a quintessential California experience. Flanked by the Santa Lucia mountain range on one side and by the craggy Pacific Coast on the other, the area's protected and unspoiled nature makes it a mecca for hikers and bikers. Bring your binoculars—it's one of the best places to view wildlife in the state. The entire population of gray whales migrates past the Big Sur coastline twice a year, and it's a thrill to pull into a roadside turnout and see the creatures, up to 45 feet in length, heading south to Mexico (in late fall and early winter) or returning north to Alaska (in late winter and early spring). In December and January, hike to the end of the Overlook trail in Julia Pfeiffer Burns State Park (see below) for an especially good vantage point to see whales. Dress in layers for your visit; it's often chilly near the coast.

Best Attractions

Andrew Molera State Park The largest state park on the Big Sur Coast; flat one-mile trail leads to a protected sandy beach. 831-667-2315, parks.ca.gov

Julia Pfeiffer Burns State Park This park stretches from the Big Sur coastline into nearby 3,000-foot ridges covered with redwood, madrone, and chaparral; one popular trail leads to an 80-foot waterfall. 831-667-2315, parks.ca.gov

Pfeiffer Big Sur State Park Mountain bikers flock to the trails in summer at this park 12 miles north of Julia Pfeiffer Burns State Park. 831-667-2315, parks.ca.gov

Best Restaurants

Nepenthe This restaurant is something of an attraction in its own right, with its landscaped grounds with sculptures, gift shop, and unforgettable vantage point on the Pacific from the edge of an 800-foot cliff. Hwy. 1, Big Sur, 831-667-2345, nepenthebigsur.com

Contacts

Big Sur Chamber of Commerce 831-667-2100, bigsurcalifornia.org
National Forest Service's Big Sur Ranger Station Hwy. 1, Big Sur, 831-667-2315

Getting There: Big Sur is along Hwy. 1. The drive is slow but spectacular; located about 26 miles south of Carmel.

LEAVING SAN FRANCISCO • DAY TRIPS

East Bay

10 miles NE

Hot Tip: It's fun to visit year round, but come on weekends for cultural events, farmers markets, and the liveliest nightlife.

The Lowdown: An eclectic mix of sophistication and funkiness, the East Bay cities of Berkeley and Oakland offer distinct personalities and attractions. The University of California at Berkeley, an icon of radical liberalism in the 1960s, contributes to that town's laid-back identity; the neighborhood surrounding the pretty, sprawling campus is casual, artsy, and colorful, full of great music shops and bustling cafes. (Note that some areas around the campus can be a little rough edged.) More-polished Berkeley neighborhoods include the chic Fourth Street shopping district and the "Gourmet Ghetto" along Shattuck Avenue, which harbors Chez Panisse restaurant. Similarly, Oakland's destinations range from the upscale Rockridge neighborhood lined with shops and restaurants along College Avenue to the waterfront Jack London Square.

Best Attractions

Fourth Street Berkeley A chic shopping district with great restaurants, cafes, and eclectic boutiques. Exit I-80 N at University Avenue, 4thstreetshop.com
Jack London Square Oakland Oakland's premier tourist destination, with waterfront restaurants and shops. 866-295-9853, jacklondonsquare.com
Telegraph Avenue Berkeley The funky heart of old Berkeley, with great bookstores (Cody's, Black Oak), music shops (Amoeba, Rasputin), and street vendors selling tie-dye and silver jewelry. telegraphshop.com
Tilden Regional Park Berkeley 2,000 acres of forested trails, gardens, a golf course, and a splendid botanical garden. 510-562-7275, ebparks.org

Best Restaurants/Nightlife

A Côté French-inspired hot spot with a single long table shared by well-heeled patrons. 5478 College Ave., Oakland, 510-655-6469, citron-acote.com
César A see-and-be-seen tapas bar where Berkeley's beautiful people go to sip cocktails. 1515 Shattuck Ave., Berkeley, 510-883-0222, barcesar.com
Chez Panisse Northern California's most famous restaurant, with formal and informal dining, where Alice Waters jump started California cuisine in the 1970s. 1517 Shattuck Ave., Berkeley, 510-548-5525, chezpanisse.com
Yoshi's This famous jazz club and restaurant is a popular place for a night out. 510 Embarcadero Wy., Oakland, 510-238-9200, yoshis.com

Contacts

Berkeley Convention and Visitors Bureau 510-549-7040, visitberkeley.com
Oakland Convention and Visitors Bureau 510-839-9000, oaklandcvb.com

Getting There: For Berkeley, cross the Bay Bridge, take I-80, and exit at University Avenue. Access to Oakland is via the I-880 turnoff.

12 miles N

Muir Woods, Muir Beach, Stinson Beach

Hot Tip: Try March and April, when crowds are fewer; often, the best weather is in either spring or autumn, as summer can bring a chilly fog.

The Lowdown: Whether you visit the world-famous grove of mystical old-growth trees at Muir Woods, picnic at Muir Beach, or frolic in the waves at Stinson Beach, all of these well-loved day-trip destinations offer classic Northern California scenery. Proclaimed a National Monument in 1908 by President Theodore Roosevelt, Muir Woods is the most famous of the lot; approximately 1 million visitors tread its shady pathways each year. The six miles of trails that wind through this enchanted redwood forest afford views of thousands of old-growth coast redwoods—the tallest living things in the world—and range from flat and easy paved walkways to more difficult hiking paths. Parking space is limited, and in summer it's extremely crowded; for the best experience, arrive early or late (before 10am or after 4pm). Nearby, two beautiful beaches, Muir Beach and Stinson Beach, offer beachcombing and sunbathing.

Best Attractions

Muir Beach From this beach edged by high bluffs, climb the trail to the Muir Beach Overlook for spectacular panoramic ocean views and a glimpse of the Farallon Islands (when the weather's clear, of course). nps.gov/muwo/mube, muirbeach.com

Muir Woods Visit Cathedral Grove and Bohemian Grove to see the largest trees, some of which measure up to 260 feet tall and 14 feet wide. 415-388-2595, nps.gov/muwo

Stinson Beach At this popular and beautiful white sandy beach, lifeguards are on duty late May through mid-September (note that swimming is not advised at other times of the year). 415-868-1922 for recorded weather conditions, stinsonbeachonline.com

Best Restaurants

The Pelican Inn A cozy English-style pub just a short walk from the sandy stretch of Muir Beach. Ten Pacific Wy., Muir Beach, 415-383-6000, pelicaninn.com

Contacts

Muir Woods Visitor Center 415-388-2595, nps.gov/muwo
Stinson Beach Chamber of Commerce 415-868-1034, stinson-beach.org

Getting There: Exit Hwy. 101 North at Hwy. 1/Stinson Beach exit; follow signs to Muir Woods, approximately 12 miles north of the Golden Gate Bridge.

LEAVING SAN FRANCISCO · DAY TRIPS

60 miles N

Point Reyes

Hot Tip: Try to come for whale watching between January and April or when wildflowers peak in early spring.

The Lowdown: Point Reyes National Seashore is where San Franciscans come to get away from it all. Set between placid Tomales Bay and the Pacific Ocean, the region's hundreds of miles of trails through meadowlands, chaparral ridges, and California bay laurel valleys are a nature lover's dream come true. In addition, exquisite sandy beaches, rocky headlands, and sweeping views of the Pacific can be found all along the coast. Start at the centrally located Bear Valley Visitor Center for trail maps before embarking on a hike to the beach or visiting the scenic lighthouse. When you're ready for the comforts of civilization, explore the charming village of Point Reyes Station, home to Tomales Bay Foods, a converted barn that houses gourmet food purveyors and the Cowgirl Creamery. Overnight visitors often book far in advance to stay at the region's inns in blink-and-you'll-miss-it towns such as Olema or Inverness.

Best Attractions

Bear Valley Visitor Center With a selection of maps and brochures, and an informed staff, this is the best place to start your visit. Bear Valley Rd., Point Reyes Station, 415-464-5100, nps.gov/pore

Point Reyes Lighthouse Views go on forever from this lovely historic lighthouse, and it provides a fabulous vantage point for spotting California gray whales between mid-January and April. 415-669-1534

Best Restaurants

Manka's Inverness Lodge A luxury hunting lodge–style retreat with an elegant restaurant known for the wild game on the menu and its locally sourced ingredients. 30 Calendar Way, Inverness, 415-669-1034, mankas.com

Olema Inn Restaurant An upscale restaurant in a restored turn-of-the-century Victorian farmhouse. 10000 Sir Francis Drake Blvd., Olema, 415-663-9559, theolemainn.com

Pine Cone Diner Where locals and in-the-know visitors come for late breakfast or lunch. 60 4th St., Point Reyes Station, 415-663-1536

The Station House Café Casual dining; outdoor brick-terrace patio open in summer months. 11180 Shoreline Hwy., Point Reyes Station, 415-663-1515

Contacts

West Marin Chamber of Commerce 415-663-9232, pointreyes.org

Getting There: Exit Hwy. 101 North at Sir Francis Drake Blvd.; this will take you through West Marin to the town of Olema, where Hwy. 1 and Sir Francis Drake Boulevard intersect.

65 miles S

Santa Cruz

Hot Tip: The sun shines 300 days a year, but the fog can roll in and cool things off pretty quickly, so plan accordingly; if your destination is the beach boardwalk, visit in late spring and early fall to avoid the height of summer's tourist season.

The Lowdown: The reputed birthplace of American surfing, Santa Cruz has a thriving surf culture—and a charming offbeat personality thanks to its eco-friendly locals and liberal college-town mentality. Kick off a visit at the Santa Cruz Beach Boardwalk, the West Coast's last remaining seaside amusement park, and ride the park's old-fashioned wooden roller coaster, the Giant Dipper—the high point provides a fabulous bird's-eye view of the area. Nearby, bike or walk the pedestrian path along West Cliff Drive, a coastal road with outstanding views and beach access; or visit the quieter east side of town at Seabright Beach. The heart of town is the tree-lined Pacific Avenue. Here you'll find great bookstores, shops, and restaurants—and the occasional hippie drum circle. For a coastal getaway with beach access that's closer to San Francisco, check out the quaint, sleepy town of Half Moon Bay, located about halfway to Santa Cruz, 25 miles south of San Francisco along Highway 1.

Best Attractions

Lighthouse Field State Beach Check out the Santa Cruz Surfing Museum, housed in the landmark brick lighthouse here, or just come to watch surfers ride the famously big waves offshore. 831-420-5270, santacruzparksandrec.com

Natural Bridges State Beach This beautiful beach with its majestic sandstone sea arch is also a refuge for monarch butterflies; peak season to view their migration is mid-October through early February. 2531 West Cliff Dr., 831-423-4609, scparkfriends.org

Santa Cruz Beach Boardwalk It's fun to stroll this old-fashioned beachfront amusement park. 400 Beach St., Santa Cruz, 831-423-5590, beachboardwalk.com

Best Restaurants

El Palomar Great Mexican fare and fabulous margaritas on downtown's vibrant main drag. 1336 Pacific Ave., Santa Cruz, 831-425-7575

Oswald A spare, sophisticated bistro with elegant California-French cuisine. 1547 Pacific Ave., Santa Cruz, 831-423-7427

Contacts

Santa Cruz County Conference and Visitors Council 1211 Ocean St., Santa Cruz, 831-425-1234 / 800-833-3494, santacruz.org

Getting There: Hwy. 1 South leads directly to Santa Cruz, as does Hwy. 17 (via 280 South or 101 South).

LEAVING SAN FRANCISCO • DAY TRIPS

Sausalito and the Marin Headlands

1-2 miles N

Hot Tip: Marin is beautiful year-round, but is generally sunnier and warmer in the early afternoon once the morning fog lifts.

The Lowdown: The charming seaside town of Sausalito is reminiscent of a Mediterranean village, with beautiful homes on terraced hillsides and a scenic waterfront promenade. The only difference is that you're a stone's throw from the city—and the views of Angel Island, Alcatraz, and the city are right there to prove it. The ferry lands right in town, so consider leaving the car at home; Sausalito's main street, lined with souvenir shops, galleries, and restaurants, is easy and fun to explore on foot. Nearby, the Marin Headlands provide access to miles of trails and unspoiled nature—this is San Francisco's most easily accessed outdoor playground. Among the most popular trails are those off Tennessee Valley Road (call the Visitor Center for details). While fog can shroud the headlands in the morning, afternoons often turn sunny and hikers are rewarded with views of the Golden Gate Bridge and the city skyline.

Best Attractions

Marin Headlands Visitor Center Start here to get maps before embarking on a hike through the windswept ridges, protected valleys and secluded beaches. Come in spring to view the wildflowers. 415-331-1540, nps.gov/goga/mahe

Marine Mammal Center Wild Pacific harbor seals, sea lions, and other marine mammals are rescued, rehabilitated, and released back into nature at this popular nonprofit center. 415-289-7325, marinemammalcenter.org

Best Restaurants

Fish Excellent fish and chips and other fresh seafood served outside by the water. 350 Harbor Court Dr., Sausalito, 415-331-3474

Poggio An upscale Italian restaurant; the bar is a sophisticated spot for a nightcap. 777 Bridgeway, Sausalito, 415-332-7771, poggiotrattoria.com

Sushi Ran A famous destination for sushi; considered one of the best in the Bay Area. 107 Caledonia St., Sausalito, 415-332-3620, sushiran.com

Contacts

Marin County Visitors Bureau 415-925-2060, visitmarin.org
Sausalito Visitor Center 415-332-0505, sausalito.org

Getting There: From Hwy. 101 North, take the second exit after the Golden Gate Bridge to Alexander Avenue. For Sausalito, turn right off the exit to reach Bridgeway, Sausalito's main drag. For the Marin Headlands, turn left off the exit; follow signs to the Marin Headlands Visitor Center. Both the Golden Gate Transit System (415-455-2000, goldengate.org) and the Blue and Gold Fleet (Pier 41, Fisherman's Wharf, 415-705-5555, blueandgoldfleet.com) run daily ferries to and from Sausalito.

18 miles N

Tiburon and Angel Island

Hot Tip: For outdoor exploring or a scenic picnic, spring or fall usually bring the sunniest weather.

The Lowdown: Tiburon is a favorite weekend retreat from San Francisco, with its picturesque New England village–style downtown and great patio restaurants where urban refugees can sip drinks and soak up the Marin sunshine. Many visitors arrive by ferry—you avoid traffic, and the boat trip across the bay with fabulous views doubles the fun. If rugged outdoor exploration is more what you have in mind, opt for a different ferry ride—the one to Angel Island, the gem of San Francisco Bay. Thirteen miles of hiking trails and roadways criss-cross this 740-acre island where madrone trees, sagebrush, and manzanita punctuate scenic coastal views. To learn about the local history, take the one-hour, open-air tram tour with audio that recounts the island's military history and cultural past—it's a comfortable seat from which to relish the nonstop views of the Bay, city skyline, Sausalito, Tiburon, and the Golden Gate Bridge. You can also embark on the rugged climb to the top of 781-foot-high Mount Livermore. From the top, the 360-degree bird's-eye view across the Bay Area is spectacular.

Best Attractions

Angel Island To rent mountain bikes, embark on the tram tour, or sign up for a guided kayak tour around the island, contact Angel Island Tram Tours. 415-897-0715, parks.ca.gov/default.asp?page_id=468

Tiburon Audubon Center This 11-acre facility offers a hilltop hike leading to lovely views, a garden of native plants, a stretch of unspoiled shoreline, and bird-watching platforms. 376 Greenwood Beach Rd., Tiburon, 415-388-2524, tiburonaudubon.org

Best Restaurants

Guaymas Popular Mexican restaurant by the ferry with margaritas and an outdoor deck. Five Main St., Tiburon, 415-435-6300, guaymas.com

Sam's Anchor Café Seafood and burgers on an outdoor patio that gets downright rowdy on weekends. 27 Main St., Tiburon, 415-435-4827, samscafe.com

Contacts

Tiburon Chamber of Commerce 415-435-5633, tiburonchamber.org

Getting There: Cross the Golden Gate Bridge, exit at Tiburon Blvd., and follow signs into town. The Blue and Gold Fleet (Pier 41, Fisherman's Wharf, 415-705-5555, blueandgoldfleet.com) runs between downtown San Francisco and Tiburon. The Angel Island Ferry (415-435-2131, angelislandferry.com) runs between Tiburon and Angel Island.

SAN FRANCISCO BLACK BOOK

You're solo in the city—where's a singles-friendly place to eat? Is there a good lunch spot near the museum? Will the bar be too loud for easy conversation? Get the answers fast in the *Black Book*, a condensed version of every listing in our guide that puts all the essential information at your fingertips.

A quick glance down the page and you'll find the type of food, nightlife, or attractions you are looking for, the phone numbers, and which pages to turn to for more detailed information. How did you ever survive without this?

San Francisco Black Book By Neighborhood

Castro (CA)

R Bagdad Café	25	98
Catch		100
Home		102
Lime		102
Mecca		103
Tallula		105
N Café du Nord		109
Catch		109
Harvey's	30	
Home		111
Lime		112
Mecca		113
Pilsner Inn	23	114
SF Badlands	23	115
A Rolo		120
Twin Peaks		120

Downtown (DO)

H Campton Place Hotel		129
Clift Hotel		58
Commodore Hotel		95
Hotel des Arts		95
Hotel Diva		95
Hotel Monaco		59
Hotel Rex		96
Hotel Triton		96
The Phoenix Hotel		97
The Prescott Hotel		130
The Ritz-Carlton		131
Westin St. Francis Hotel		131
R Asia de Cuba		62
Bambuddha Lounge		63
Café Claude		134
Café de la Presse		135
Cortez		65
Farallon	38	65
First Crush		66
Fleur de Lys	36	136
Grand Cafe		137
Le Central		140
Le Colonial		140
Masa's	47	141
R Michael Mina	22	67
Postrio		142
The Rotunda at Neiman Marcus		142
Scala's Bistro		143
Sears Fine Food		143
The Terrace	17	144
N Azul Bar and Lounge		72
Bambuddha Lounge	44	72
Biscuits & Blues		146
Blue Cube		109
Café Claude		147
Cortez		74
First Crush	46	75
Harry Denton's Starlight Room	29	148
Le Colonial		149
Otis		78
Redwood Room	37	79
Ruby Skye	19	79
Rx Gallery		114
Scala's Bistro		150
Suite one8one	40	80
Swig		116
A Gimme Shoes		84
Glide Memorial United Methodist Church	31	118
Gump's		154
Kamalaspa		85
San Francisco Museum of Craft + Design		86
Wilkes Bashford		156

Embarcadero (EM)

H Harbor Court Hotel		58
Hotel Vitale		59
R Americano		62
Boulevard	36	134
Butterfly		64
Chaya Brasserie		65
La Suite		67
MarketBar		67
One Market	33	68
Pier 23 Cafe		69
Shanghai 1930		70

Code: H-Hotels; R-Restaurants; N-Nightlife; A-Attractions. Blue page numbers denote listings in 99 Best. Black page numbers denote listings in theme chapters. The San Francisco Neighborhoods Map is on p.232.

BLACK BOOK BY NEIGHBORHOOD

R	Slanted Door	18	70
N	Americano		72
	Chaya Brasserie		73
	La Suite		76
	MarketBar		77
	Pier 23 Cafe		79
	Shanghai 1930		80
	Slanted Door		80
A	Adventure Cat		82
	The Embarcadero Promenade		83
	Ferry Plaza Farmers Market		83
	The Gardener		84
	Signature Yacht Cruise		156

Financial District (FD)

H	Mandarin Oriental		60
R	Aqua	38	132
	B44		63
	Bix		133
	Bocadillos		64
	City View	20	
	Frisson	35	66
	Globe	25	66
	Kokkari Estiatorio		139
	Myth		67
	Rubicon	47	142
	Tadich Grill		144
N	B44		73
	Bix		147
	Bocadillos		73
	Bubble Lounge		147
	EZ5		111
	Frisson		75
	Myth		78
	Punch Line Comedy Club		150
	Voda		81
A	Equinox Fitness Club		83
	Tru Spa	41	87

Fisherman's Wharf (FW)

R	Ana Mandara	18	132
	The Buena Vista		134
	Gary Danko	22	137
N	The Buena Vista		147
	Suede	40	80
A	Alcatraz Island		152
	Blue and Gold Ferry		82

Haight (HA)

R	Eos		101
	RNM Restaurant	45	104
N	Eos		111
	Madrone Lounge		112
	Milk	21	113

Hayes Valley (HV)

R	Absinthe Brasserie and Bar		132
	Citizen Cake		101
	Hayes Street Grill	38	138
	Jardinière		139
	Soluna Cafe & Lounge		104
	Suppenküche		105
	Trader Vic's		145
	Zuni Café	16	107
N	Absinthe Brasserie and Bar		146
	CAV	46	73
	Hôtel Biron		111
	Jade Bar	30	75
	Jardinière		149
	Soluna Cafe & Lounge		115
	Trader Vic's	43	151
	Zuni Café		117
A	Asian Art Museum		82
	Minnie Wilde		119

Marina (MA)

R	A16	45	63
	Balboa Cafe		133
	Betelnut	18	63
	Boboquivari's		134
	Café Maritime		64
	Greens Restaurant	34	137
	Nectar		68
	PlumpJack Cafe		142
	Rose's Café		70
N	Balboa Cafe		146
	Betelnut		73
	MatrixFillmore	37	77
	Nectar	46	78
A	Palace of Fine Arts		155
	S Factor		86

Mission (MI)

R	Andalu	27	98
	Bar Tartine		98

209

Mission (MI) (cont.)

R	Bissap Baobab		99
	Blowfish Sushi		99
	Blue Plate		99
	Boogaloo's		99
	Chez Spencer		100
	Delfina		101
	Emmy's Spaghetti Shack		101
	Foreign Cinema	16	66
	Levende Lounge	35	67
	Limón	27	102
	Luna Park		102
	Medjool		103
	Range		103
	Slow Club		104
	Tartine		106
	Universal Cafe	17	106
	Walzwerk		106
	Woodward's Garden		107
N	Andalu		108
	Bar Tartine		108
	Beauty Bar		108
	Bissap Baobab		108
	DNA Lounge	26	74
	El Rio	30	110
	Elbo Room		110
	Emmy's Spaghetti Shack		110
	Laszlo		76
	Levende Lounge		76
	Lexington Club	23	111
	Little Baobab		112
	Martuni's		112
	Medjool		113
	Mighty		113
	Oxygen Bar		113
	Pink	21	114
	Power Exchange	39	
	Skylark		115
	12 Galaxies		116
A	Good Vibrations	39	118
	Mission Cliffs	48	119
	Mission Dolores		119
	Paxton Gate		120

Nob Hill (NH)

H	The Fairmont		129
	The Huntington Hotel		129
	InterContinental Mark Hopkins		130
R	Acquerello		132
	The Big 4 Restaurant		133
	Laurel Court Restaurant		140
	Swan Oyster Depot		144
N	The Big 4 Restaurant		146
	Element Lounge		110
	Tonga Room	43	150
	Top of the Mark	29	150
A	Nob Hill Spa	41	155

North Beach (NB)

R	Café Jacqueline	36	135
	Café Zoetrope		135
	Caffe Trieste		135
	El Raigon		136
	Iluna Basque		102
	Jazz at Pearl's		139
	Julius' Castle	34	139
	Mama's on Washington Square		141
	Moose's		141
	Piperade		69
N	*Beach Blanket Babylon*		146
	Bimbo's 365 Club	28	
	Café Zoetrope		147
	Dolce	40	74
	DragonBar		74
	Enrico's		148
	15 Romolo		148
	Jazz at Pearl's		149
	Julius' Castle		149
	Rosewood		114
	Sake Lab		79
	Tosca Café		150
	The Velvet Lounge		116
	Vesuvio		151
	Zebra Lounge		81
A	City Lights Bookstore		153
	Coit Tower		153

Pacific Heights (PH)

R	Elite Café		136
	Ella's	17	136
	Garibaldi's	16	137
	Harris' Restaurant		138
	Jackson-Fillmore		138
	Quince		69
N	Boom Boom Room		147
	G Bar		148

BLACK BOOK BY NEIGHBORHOOD

A	Audium	31	152
	International Orange Day Spa	41	84
	Kabuki Springs and Spa		119
	Sue Fisher King		156

Potrero Hill (PO)

R	Baraka		98
	Chez Papa Bistrot		100
	Circolo	35	65
N	Circolo		74
	Dogpatch Saloon		109
	Sublounge	21	115
	Whisper		116

Presidio (PR)

A	Baker Beach	39	118
	Crissy Field		154
	Golden Gate Bridge	32	154
	Presidio Golf Course & Clubhouse		156

Richmond (RI)

R	Park Chalet		141
	Sutro's at the Cliff House	34	143
	Ton Kiang	20	144
N	Park Chalet		149
A	Conservatory of Flowers		153
	de Young Museum		154
	Golden Gate Park	32	154
	Golden Gate Park—Skating		118
	Ocean Beach		155
	Palace of the Legion of Honor		155

SoMa (SM)

H	Four Seasons San Francisco		58
	Hotel Palomar		59
	The Palace Hotel		130
	St. Regis Hotel		60
	W San Francisco		61
R	Ame		62
	AsiaSF	31	133
	Azie		63
	Bacar	47	63
	Caffe Centro		100
	Coco500		65
	Fifth Floor	22	65
	Hawthorne Lane	33	138
	Kyo-Ya	42	140
	LuLu		140

R	Oola	25	68
	Ozumo	42	68
	The Public		103
	Roe		69
	Sneaky Tiki		104
	South Park Café		143
	supperclub San Francisco	45	70
	Sushi Groove South	42	105
	Town Hall	33	71
	Tres Agaves	27	71
	Yank Sing	20	145
	Zuppa		71
N	Anú		108
	AsiaSF		146
	Azie		72
	Bacar		72
	Bar at XYZ		73
	Club Six		109
	The EndUp	26	111
	Fluid Ultra Lounge	37	75
	House of Shields		149
	Le Duplex	26	76
	Loft 11	19	76
	Luna Lounge		112
	Mezzanine	19	77
	Mr. Smith's	44	77
	111 Minna Gallery	44	78
	Oola		78
	Ozumo		79
	The Public		114
	Roe		79
	Slim's	28	
	Sneaky Tiki	43	115
	supperclub San Francisco		81
	Tres Agaves		81
	View Lounge	29	151
	Wish		117
A	Club Sportiva		82
	It's Yoga	48	
	Jeremy's		84
	Limn		85
	Remède Spa		85
	SBC Park Tour		86
	SFMoMA		86
	SFMoMA Museum Store		87
	Sports Club/LA	48	87
	Vino Venue		87
	Yerba Buena Arts Center		120

San Francisco Black Book

Hotels

NAME TYPE (ROOMS)	ADDRESS (CROSS STREET) WEBSITE	AREA PRICE	PHONE 800 NUMBER	EXPERIENCE	PAGE
Campton Place Hotel Modern (117)	340 Stockton St. (Sutter St.) camptonplace.com	DO $$$$	415-781-5555 800-235-4300	Classic	129
Clift Hotel Trendy (363)	495 Geary St. (Taylor St.) clifthotel.com	DO $$$	415-775-4700 800-697-1791	Hot & Cool	58
Commodore Hotel Trendy (113)	825 Sutter St. (Leavenworth St.) thecommodorehotel.com	DO $	415-923-6800 800-338-6848	Hip	95
The Fairmont Timeless (591)	950 Mason St. (California St.) fairmont.com/sanfrancisco	NH $$$$	415-772-5000 800-257-7544	Classic	129
Four Seasons San Francisco Modern (277)	757 Market St. (Third St.) fourseasons.com/sanfrancisco	SM $$$$+	415-633-3000 800-819-5053	Hot & Cool	58
Harbor Court Hotel Modern (130)	165 Steuart St. (Howard St.) harborcourthotel.com	EM $$$	415-882-1300 866-792-6283	Hot & Cool	58
Hotel des Arts Trendy (51)	447 Bush St. (Grant Ave.) sfhoteldesarts.com	DO $	415-956-3232 866-285-4104	Hip	95
Hotel Diva Modern (115)	440 Geary St. (Mason St.) hoteldiva.com	DO $	415-885-0200 800-553-1900	Hip	95
Hotel Monaco Trendy (201)	501 Geary St. (Taylor St.) monaco-sf.com	DO $$$	415-292-0100 866-622-5284	Hot & Cool	59
Hotel Palomar Modern (198)	12 Fourth St. (Market St.) hotelpalomar.com	SM $$$	415-348-1111 866-373-4941	Hot & Cool	59
Hotel Rex Timeless (94)	562 Sutter St. (Mason St.) thehotelrex.com	DO $$	415-433-4434 800-433-4434	Hip	96
Hotel Triton Trendy (140)	342 Grant Ave. (Bush St.) hoteltriton.com	DO $$	415-394-0500 800-800-1299	Hip	96
Hotel Vitale Trendy (199)	Eight Mission St. (Steuart St.) hotelvitale.com	EM $$$	415-278-3700 888-890-8688	Hot & Cool	59
The Huntington Hotel Timeless (135)	1075 California St. (Taylor St.) huntingtonhotel.com	NH $$$	415-474-5400 800-227-4683	Classic	129
InterCont'l Mark Hopkins Timeless (380)	999 California St. (Mason St.) san-francisco.intercontinental.com	NH $$$	415-392-3434 888-303-1758	Classic	130
Mandarin Oriental Modern (154)	222 Sansome St. (California St.) mandarinoriental.com/sanfrancisco	FD $$$$+	415-276-9888 866-526-6567	Hot & Cool	60
The Palace Hotel Timeless (552)	2 New Montgomery St. (Market St.) sfpalace.com	SM $$$	415-512-1111 888-625-5144	Classic	130

Neighborhood (Area) Key

CA = Castro	HV = Hayes Valley	PH = Pacific Heights
DO = Downtown	MA = Marina	PO = Potrero Hill
EM = Embarcadero	MI = Mission	PR = Presidio
FD = Financial District	NB = North Beach	RI = Richmond
FW = Fisherman's Wharf	NH = Nob Hill	SM = SoMa
HA = Haight	NV = Noe Valley	VA = Various

Note regarding page numbers: Italic = itinerary listing; Roman = description in theme chapter listing.

SAN FRANCISCO BLACK BOOK

NAME TYPE	ADDRESS (CROSS STREET) WEBSITE	AREA PRICE	PHONE 800 NUMBER	EXPERIENCE	PAGE
The Phoenix Hotel Trendy (41)	601 Eddy St. (Larkin St.) thephoenixhotel.com	DO $	415-776-1380 800-248-9466	Hip	97
The Prescott Hotel Modern (164)	545 Post St. (Mason St.) prescotthotel.com	DO $$	415-563-0303 866-271-3632	Classic	130
The Ritz-Carlton Timeless (336)	600 Stockton St. (California St.) ritzcarlton.com/hotels/san_francisco	DO $$$$+	415-296-7465 800-241-3333	Classic	131
St. Regis Hotel Modern (260)	124 Third St. (Mission St.) stregis.com/sanfrancisco	SM $$$$+	415-284-4000 888-625-5144	Hot & Cool	60
W San Francisco Trendy (423)	181 Third St. (Howard St.) whotel.com/sanfrancisco	SM $$$$	415-777-5300 888-625-5144	Hot & Cool	61
Westin St. Francis Hotel Timeless (1,200)	335 Powell St. (Geary St.) westinstfrancis.com	DO $$$	415-397-7000 888-625-5144	Classic	131

Restaurants

NAME TYPE	ADDRESS (CROSS STREET) WEBSITE	AREA PRICE	PHONE SINGLES/NOISE	EXPERIENCE 99 BEST	PAGE PAGE
Absinthe Brasserie and Bar French Brasserie	398 Hayes St. (Gough St.) absinthe.com	HV $$	415-551-1590 [YF] [=]	Classic	132
Acquerello Italian (G)	1722 Sacramento St. (Polk St.) acquerello.com	NH $$$	415-567-5432 - [=]	Classic	132
Ame New American (G)	689 Mission St. (Third St.) amerestaurant.com	SM $$$	415-284-4040 [YB] [=]	Hot & Cool	52, 62
Americano Italian	Eight Mission St. (Steuart St.) americanorestaurant.com	EM $$	415-278-3777 [YF] [=]	Hot & Cool	62
Ana Mandara Vietnamese	891 Beach St. (Polk St.) anamandara.com	FW $$	415-771-6800 [YB] [=]	Classic Chic Asian	123, 132 18
Andalu Fusion/Tapas	3198 16th St. (Guerrero St.) andalusf.com	MI $$	415-621-2211 [YF] [=]	Hip Latin Restaurants	91, 98 27
Aqua Seafood (G)	252 California St. (Battery St.) aqua-sf.com	FD $$$	415-956-9662 - [=]	Classic Seafood	124, 132 38
Asia de Cuba Fusion	495 Geary St. (Taylor St.) (Clift Hotel) clifthotel.com	DO $$$	415-929-2300 [Q] [=]	Hot & Cool	62

Restaurant and Nightlife Symbols

Restaurants
Singles Friendly (eat and/or meet)
- [U] = Communal table
- [Y] = Bar scene
- [B] = Limited bar menu
- [F] = Full menu served at bar
- (G) = Gourmet Destination

Nightlife
Price Warning
- [C] = Cover or ticket charge
- Food served at bar or club
- [B] = Limited bar menu
- [F] = Full menu served at bar

Restaurant + Nightlife
Prime time noise levels
- [−] = Quiet
- [=] = A buzz, but still conversational
- [≡] = Loud

213

BLACK BOOK

Restaurants (cont.)

NAME / TYPE	ADDRESS (CROSS STREET) / WEBSITE	AREA / PRICE	PHONE / SINGLES/NOISE	EXPERIENCE / 99 BEST	PAGE / PAGE
AsiaSF / Tapas	201 Ninth St. (Howard St.) / asiasf.com	SM / $$	415-255-2742	Classic / Only-in-SF	133 / 31
A16 / Italian	2355 Chestnut St. (Divisadero St.) / a16sf.com	MA / $$	415-771-2216	Hot & Cool / Trendy Tables	53, 63 / 45
Azie / Asian	826 Folsom St. (Fifth St.) / azierestaurant.com	SM / $$	415-538-0918	Hot & Cool	63
Bacar / Mediterranean	448 Brannan St. (Third St.) / bacarsf.com	SM / $$$	415-904-4100	Hot & Cool / Wine Lists	63 / 47
Bagdad Café / Diner	2295 Market St. (16th St.)	CA / $–	415-621-4434	Hip / Late-Night Eats	98 / 25
Balboa Cafe / Traditional American	3199 Fillmore St. (Greenwich St.) / balboacafe.com	MA / $$	415-921-3944	Classic	125, 133
Bambuddha Lounge / Asian	601 Eddy St. (Larkin St.) / bambuddhalounge.com	DO / $$	415-885-5088	Hot & Cool	63
Bar Tartine / French	561 Valencia St. (16th St.) / tartinebakery.com/bar_tartine.htm	MI / $	415-487-1600	Hip	98
Baraka / North African	288 Connecticut St. (18th St.) / barakasf.net	PO / $	415-255-0387	Hip	90, 98
Betelnut / Asian	2030 Union St. (Buchanan St.) / betelnutrestaurant.com	MA / $	415-929-8855	Hot & Cool / Chic Asian	53, 63 / 18
B44 / Spanish	44 Belden Pl. (Bush St.)	FD / $$	415-986-6287	Hot & Cool	51, 63
The Big 4 Restaurant / Traditional American	1075 California St. (Taylor St.) / big4restaurant.com	NH / $$$	415-771-1140	Classic	133
Bissap Baobab / Senegalese	2323 Mission St. (19th St.) / bissapbaobab.com	MI / $	415-826-9287	Hip	99
Bix / Traditional American	56 Gold St. (Sansome St.) / bixrestaurant.com	FD / $$	415-433-6300	Classic	125, 133
Blowfish Sushi / Japanese	2170 Bryant St. (20th St.) / blowfishsushi.com	MI / $$	415-285-3848	Hip	99
Blue Plate / Californian	3218 Mission St. (Valencia St.) / blueplatesf.com	MI / $$	415-282-6777	Hip	99
Boboquivari's / Steak House	1450 Lombard St. (Van Ness Ave.) / boboquivaris.com	MA / $$$	415-441-8880	Classic	134
Bocadillos / Basque/Tapas	710 Montgomery St. (Washington) / bocasf.com	FD / $	415-982-2622	Hot & Cool	64
Boogaloo's / Diner	3296 22nd St. (Valencia St.)	MI / $–	415-824-4088	Hip	89, 99
Boulevard / Californian (G)	One Mission St. (Steuart St.) / boulevardrestaurant.com	EM / $$$	415-543-6084	Classic / Romantic Dining	124, 134 / 36
The Buena Vista / Traditional American	2765 Hyde St. (Beach St.) / thebuenavista.com	FW / $–	415-474-5044	Classic	123, 134
Butterfly / Asian	Pier 33 (Bay St.) / butterflysf.com	EM / $$	415-291-9482	Hot & Cool	64

SAN FRANCISCO BLACK BOOK

NAME / TYPE	ADDRESS (CROSS STREET) / WEBSITE	AREA PRICE	PHONE SINGLES/NOISE	EXPERIENCE 99 BEST	PAGE PAGE
Café Claude / French Bistro	Seven Claude Ln. (Bush St.) / cafeclaude.com	DO $	415-392-3515	Classic	134
Café de la Presse / French Bistro	352 Grant Ave. (Bush St.)	DO $	415-398-2680	Classic	135
Café Jacqueline / French	1454 Grant Ave. (Green St.)	NB $$	415-981-5565	Classic / Romantic Dining	135 / 36
Café Maritime / Seafood	2417 Lombard St. (Scott St.) / cafemaritimesf.com	MA $	415-885-2530	Hot & Cool	64
Café Zoetrope / Italian	916 Kearny St. (Columbus Ave.) / cafecoppola.com	NB $	415-291-1700	Classic	123, 135
Caffe Centro / Cafe	102 South Park (Second St.) / caffecentro.com	SM $–	415-882-1500	Hip	100
Caffe Trieste / Cafe	609 Vallejo St. (Grant Ave.) / caffetrieste.com	NB $–	415-392-6739	Classic	124, 135
Catch / Seafood	2362 Market St. (Castro St.) / catchsf.com	CA $	415-431-5000	Hip	100
Chaya Brasserie / Fusion	132 Embarcadero (Mission St.) / thechaya.com	EM $$	415-777-8688	Hot & Cool	65
Chez Papa Bistrot / French Bistro	1401 18th St. (Missouri St.) / chezpapasf.com	PO $$	415-255-0387	Hip	100
Chez Spencer / French	82 14th St. (Folsom St.)	MI $$	415-864-2191	Hip	100
Circolo / Asian	500 Florida St. (Mariposa St.) / circolosf.com	PO $$	415-553-8560	Hot & Cool / Restaurants w/Bars	65 / 35
Citizen Cake / Californian	399 Grove St. (Gough St.) / citizencake.com	HV $$	415-861-2228	Hip	91, 101
City View / Dim Sum	662 Commercial St. (Kearny St.)	FD $–	415-355-9991	Dim Sum	20
Coco500 / Californian	500 Brannan St. (Fourth St.) / coco500.com	SM $$	415-543-2222	Hot & Cool	65
Cortez / Mediterranean	550 Geary St. (Powell St.) / cortezrestaurant.com	DO $$	415-292-6360	Hot & Cool	65
Delfina / Italian	3621 18th St. (Guerrero St.) / delfinasf.com	MI $$	415-552-4055	Hip	91, 101
El Raigon / Steak House	510 Union St. (Grant Ave.) / elraigon.com	NB $$	415-291-0927	Classic	136
Elite Café / Cajun Creole	2049 Fillmore St. (California St.) / theelitecafe.com	PH $	415-346-8668	Classic	136
Ella's / Traditional American	500 Presidio Ave. (California St.) / ellassanfrancisco.com	PH $	415-441-5669	Classic / Brunches	136 / 17
Emmy's Spaghetti Shack / Comfort Food	18 Virginia St. (Mission St.)	MI $	415-206-2086	Hip	101
Eos / Fusion	901 Cole St. (Carl St.) / eossf.com	HA $	415-566-3063	Hip	92, 101

BLACK BOOK

215

Restaurants (cont.)

NAME TYPE	ADDRESS (CROSS STREET) WEBSITE	AREA PRICE	PHONE SINGLES/NOISE	EXPERIENCE 99 BEST	PAGE PAGE
Farallon Seafood (G)	450 Post St. (Powell St.) farallonrestaurant.com	DO $$$	415-956-6969 YF ≡	Hot & Cool Seafood	65 38
Fifth Floor French (G)	12 Fourth St. (Market St.) hotelpalomar.com	SM $$$	415-348-1111 YB —	Hot & Cool Fine Dining	53, 65 22
First Crush New American	101 Cyril Magnin St. (Ellis St.) firstcrush.com	DO $$	415-982-7874 F ≡		66
Fleur de Lys French (G)	777 Sutter St. (Jones St.) fleurdelyssf.com	DO $$$	415-673-7779 - —	Classic Romantic Dining	125, 136 36
Foreign Cinema Mediterranean	2534 Mission St. (21st St.) foreigncinema.com	MI $$	415-648-7600 YBO ≡	Hot & Cool Always Hot	53, 66 16
Frisson New American	244 Jackson St. (Sansome St.) frissonsf.com	FD $$	415-956-3004 YB —	Hot & Cool Restaurants w/Bars	54, 66 35
Garibaldi's Californian	347 Presidio Ave. (Sacramento St.) garibaldisrestaurant.com	PH $$	415-563-8841 F ≡	Classic Always Hot	126, 137 16
Gary Danko New American (G)	800 North Point St. (Hyde St.) garydanko.com	FW $$$	415-749-2060 - —	Classic Fine Dining	124, 137 22
Globe Californian	290 Pacific Ave. (Battery St.) 	FD $$	415-391-4132 F ≡	Hot & Cool Late-Night Eats	51, 66 25
Grand Cafe French Brasserie	501 Geary St. (Taylor St.) grandcafe-sf.com	DO $$	415-292-0101 YB —	Classic	137
Greens Restaurant Vegetarian	Fort Mason Center, Bldg. A greensrestaurant.com	MA $$	415-771-6222 - —	Classic Restaurants w/View	125, 137 34
Harris' Restaurant Steak House	2100 Van Ness Ave. (Pacific Ave.) harrisrestaurant.com	PH $$$	415-673-1888 - —	Classic	138
Hawthorne Lane Californian	22 Hawthorne Ln. (Howard St.) hawthornelane.com	SM $$$	415-777-9779 F —	Classic Power Lunch Spots	138 33
Hayes Street Grill Seafood	320 Hayes St. (Franklin St.) hayesstreetgrill.com	HV $$	415-863-5545 F —	Classic Seafood	138 38
Home Traditional American	2100 Market St. (Church St.) home-sf.com	CA $	415-503-0333 YF ≡	Hip	102
Iluna Basque Tapas	701 Union St. (Powell St.) ilunabasque.com	NB $	415-402-0011 O ≡	Hip	102
Jackson-Fillmore Italian	2506 Fillmore St. (Jackson St.)	PH $	415-346-5288 - ≡	Classic	138
Jardinière Californian (G)	300 Grove St. (Franklin St.) jardiniere.com	HV $$$	415-861-5555 YF —	Classic	126, 139
Jazz at Pearl's Spanish	256 Columbus Ave. (Broadway) jazzatpearls.com	NB $	415-291-8255 YF ≡	Classic	139
Julius' Castle Italian	1541 Montgomery St. (Union St.) juliuscastlerestaurant.com	NB $$$	415-392-2222 - —	Classic Restaurants w/View	139 34
Kokkari Estiatorio Greek	200 Jackson St. (Front St.) kokkari.com	FD $$	415-981-0983 - ≡	Classic	139
Kyo-Ya Japanese	Two New Montgomery St. (Jessie St.) kyo-ya-restaurant.com	SM $$	415-546-5090 - —	Classic Sushi	140 42

SAN FRANCISCO BLACK BOOK

NAME / TYPE	ADDRESS (CROSS STREET) / WEBSITE	AREA PRICE	PHONE SINGLES/NOISE	EXPERIENCE 99 BEST	PAGE PAGE
La Suite / French Brasserie	100 Brannan St. (Embarcadero) / lasuitesf.com	EM $$	415-593-5900	Hot & Cool	67
Laurel Court Restaurant / High Tea	950 Mason St. (California St.)	NH $$$	415-772-5260	Classic	125, 140
Le Central / French Bistro	453 Bush St. (Grant Ave.)	DO $$	415-391-2233	Classic	140
Le Colonial / Vietnamese	20 Cosmo Pl. (Taylor St.) / lecolonialsf.com	DO $$	415-931-3600	Classic	140
Levende Lounge / Fusion	1710 Mission St. (Duboce Ave.) / levendesf.com	MI $$	415-864-4585	Hot & Cool / Restaurants w/Bars	67 / 35
Lime / American/Tapas	2247 Market St. (Noe St.) / lime-sf.com	CA $	415-621-5256	Hip	102
Limón / Peruvian	524 Valencia St. (16th St.) / limon-sf.com	MI $$	415-252-0918	Hip / Latin Restaurants	90, 102 / 27
LuLu / Provençal	816 Folsom St. (Fourth St.) / restaurantlulu.com	SM $$	415-495-5775	Classic	140
Luna Park / Traditional American	694 Valencia St. (18th St.) / lunaparksf.com	MI $	415-553-8584	Hip	89, 102
Mama's on Washington Sq. / Traditional American	1701 Stockton St. (Filbert St.)	NB $–	415-362-6421	Classic	141
MarketBar / Californian	One Ferry Building (Market St.) / marketbar.com	EM $	415-434-1100	Hot & Cool	54, 67
Masa's / French (G)	648 Bush St. (Powell St.)	DO $$$	415-989-7154	Classic / Wine Lists	126, 141 / 47
Mecca / Californian	2029 Market St. (Dolores St.) / sfmecca.com	CA $$	415-621-7000	Hip	103
Medjool / Med./North African	2522 Mission St. (21st St.) / medjoolsf.com	MI $$	415-550-9055	Hip	103
Michael Mina / New American (G)	335 Powell St. (Geary St.) / michaelmina.net	DO $$$	415-397-9222	Hot & Cool / Fine Dining	54, 67 / 22
Moose's / Californian	1652 Stockton St. (Filbert St.) / mooses.com	NB $$$	415-989-7800	Classic	124, 141
Myth / New American	470 Pacific Ave. (Montgomery St.) / mythsf.com	FD $$	415-677-8986	Hot & Cool	51, 67
Nectar / Wine Bar	3330 Steiner St. (Chestnut St.) / nectarwinelounge.com	MA $	415-345-1377	Hot & Cool	68
One Market / Californian	One Market St. (Embarcadero) / onemarket.com	EM $$	415-777-5577	Hot & Cool / Power Lunch Spots	68 / 33
Oola / American	860 Folsom St. (Fourth St.) / oola-sf.com	SM $$	415-995-2061	Hot & Cool / Late-Night Eats	68 / 25
Ozumo / Japanese	161 Steuart St. (Mission St.) / ozumo.com	SM $$	415-882-1333	Hot & Cool / Sushi	52, 68 / 42
Park Chalet / Traditional American	1000 Great Hwy. (Fulton St.) / parkchalet.com	RI $	415-386-8439	Classic	141

217

Restaurants (cont.)

NAME TYPE	ADDRESS (CROSS STREET) WEBSITE	AREA PRICE	PHONE SINGLES/NOISE	EXPERIENCE 99 BEST	PAGE PAGE
Pier 23 Cafe Traditional American	Pier 23 (Lombard St.) pier23cafe.com	EM $	415-362-5125	Hot & Cool	54, 69
Piperade Basque	1015 Battery St. (Green St.) piperade.com	NB $$	415-391-2555	Hot & Cool	69
PlumpJack Cafe Californian	3127 Fillmore St. (Filbert St.) plumpjack.com/cafe_main.html	MA $$	415-563-4755	Classic	142
Postrio Californian	545 Post St. (Mason St.) postrio.com	DO $$$	415-776-7825	Classic	125, 142
The Public New American	1489 Folsom St. (11th St.) thepublicsf.com	SM $$	415-552-3065	Hip	103
Quince Californian (G)	1701 Octavia St. (Bush St.) quincerestaurant.com	PH $$	415-775-8500	Hot & Cool	69
Range New American	842 Valencia St. (20th St.) rangesf.com	MI $	415-282-8283	Hip	90, 103
RNM Restaurant New American/Tapas	598 Haight St. (Steiner St.) rnmrestaurant.com	HA $$	415-551-7900	Hip Trendy Tables	92, 104 45
Roe Asian	651 Howard St. (Third St.) roerestaurant.com	SM $$	415-227-0288	Hot & Cool	69
Rose's Cafe Comfort Food	2298 Union St. (Steiner St.)	MA $	415-775-2200	Hot & Cool	53, 70
The Rotunda at NM Californian	150 Stockton St. (Geary St.) rotundarestaurant.com	DO $$	415-362-4777	Classic	142
Rubicon Californian	558 Sacramento St. (Sansome St.) sfrubicon.com	FD $$	415-434-4100	Classic Wine Lists	142 47
Scala's Bistro French/Italian	432 Powell St. (Sutter St.) scalasbistro.com	DO $$	415-395-8555	Classic	143
Sears Fine Food Diner	439 Powell St. (Sutter St.) searsfinefood.com	DO $–	415-986-0700	Classic	124, 143
Shanghai 1930 Chinese	133 Steuart St. (Mission St.) shanghai1930.com	EM $$	415-896-5600	Hot & Cool	70
Slanted Door Vietnamese	One Ferry Building (Market St.) slanteddoor.com	EM $$	415-861-8032	Hot & Cool Chic Asian	52, 70 18
Slow Club Californian	2501 Mariposa St. (Hampshire St.) slowclub.com	MI $	415-241-9390	Hip	89, 104
Sneaky Tiki Polynesian	1582 Folsom St. (12th St.) sneakytiki-sf.com	SM $	415-701-8454	Hip	104
Soluna Cafe & Lounge American	272 McAllister St. (Larkin St.) solunasf.com	HV $$	415-621-2200	Hip	104
South Park Café French Bistro	108 South Park (Second St.)	SM $$	415-495-7275	Classic	143
Suppenküche German	525 Laguna St. (Hayes St.) suppenkuche.com	HV $	415-252-9289	Hip	91, 105
supperclub San Francisco French/Italian	657 Harrison St. (Third St.) supperclub.com	SM $$	415-348-0900	Hot & Cool Trendy Tables	53, 70 45

SAN FRANCISCO BLACK BOOK

NAME / TYPE	ADDRESS (CROSS STREET) / WEBSITE	AREA PRICE	PHONE SINGLES/NOISE	EXPERIENCE 99 BEST	PAGE PAGE
Sushi Groove South / Sushi	1516 Folsom St. (11th St.)	SM $$	415-503-1950	Hip / Sushi	91, 105 / 42
Sutro's at the Cliff House / Californian	1090 Pt. Lobos Ave. (Balboa Ave.) / cliffhouse.com	RI $$	415-386-3330	Classic / Restaurants w/View	126, 143 / 34
Swan Oyster Depot / Seafood	1517 Polk St. (California St.)	NH $	415-673-1101	Classic	144
Tablespoon / New American	2209 Polk St. (Vallejo St.) / tablespoonsf.com	VA $$	415-268-0140	Hip	105
Tadich Grill / Seafood	240 California St. (Front St.)	FD $$	415-391-1849	Classic	144
Tallula / Indian/Fusion/Tapas	4230 18th St. (Diamond St.) / tallulasf.com	CA $$	415-437-6722	Hip	92, 105
Tartine / Bakery/Cafe	600 Guerrero St. (18th St.) / tartinebakery.com	MI $–	415-487-2600	Hip	106
The Terrace / California	600 Stockton St. (California St.) / ritzcarlton.com/hotels/	DO $$$	415-773-6198	Classic / Brunches	144 / 17
Ton Kiang / Dim Sum	5821 Geary Blvd. (22nd Ave.) / tonkiang.net	RI $	415-387-8273	Classic / Dim Sum	126, 144 / 20
Town Hall / Traditional American	342 Howard St. (Fremont St.) / townhallsf.com	SM $$	415-908-3900	Hot & Cool / Power Lunch Spots	53, 71 / 33
Trader Vic's / Polynesian	555 Golden Gate Ave. (Van Ness Ave.) / tradervics.com/rest-sanfran.html	HV $$	415-775-6300	Classic	145
Tres Agaves / Mexican	130 Townsend St. (Second St.) / tresagaves.com	SM $	415-227-0500	Hot & Cool / Latin Restaurants	53, 71 / 27
Universal Cafe / Californian	2814 19th St. (Bryant St.) / universalcafe.net	MI $$	415-821-4608	Hip / Brunches	92, 106 / 17
Walzwerk / German	381 S. Van Ness Ave. (15th St.) / walzwerk.com	MI $	415-551-7181	Hip	106
Woodward's Garden / Californian	1700 Mission St. (Duboce Ave.) / woodwardsgarden.com	MI $$	415-621-7122	Hip	107
Yank Sing / Dim Sum	101 Spear St. (Mission St.) / yanksing.com	SM $	415-957-9300	Classic / Dim Sum	145 / 20
Zuni Café / Mediterranean	1658 Market St. (Franklin St.)	HV $$	415-552-2522	Hip / Always Hot	92, 107 / 16
Zuppa / Italian	564 Fourth St. (Brannan St.) / zuppa-sf.com	SM $	415-777-5900	Hot & Cool	71

Nightlife

NAME / TYPE	ADDRESS (CROSS STREET) / WEBSITE	AREA COVER	PHONE FOOD/NOISE	EXPERIENCE 99 BEST	PAGE PAGE
Absinthe Brasserie and Bar / Restaurant Bar	398 Hayes St. (Gough St.) / absinthe.com	HV -	415-551-1590 F ≡	Classic	146
Americano / Italian	Eight Mission St. (Steuart St.) / americanorestaurant.com	EM -	415-278-3777 F ≡	Hot & Cool	53, 72
Andalu / Restaurant Bar	3198 16th St. (Guerrero St.) / andalusf.com	MI -	415-621-2211 F ≡	Hip	108
Anú / Bar/Nightclub	43 Sixth St. (Market St.) / anu-bar.com	SM C	415-543-3505 B ≡	Hip	108
AsiaSF / Nightclub/Performance	201 Ninth St. (Howard St.) / asiasf.com	SM C	415-255-2742 F ≡	Classic / Only in SF	124, 146 / 31
Azie / Restaurant Bar	826 Folsom St. (Fifth St.) / azierestaurant.com	SM -	415-538-0918 F ≡	Hot & Cool	72
Azul Bar and Lounge / Jazz Club/DJ Bar	One Tillman Pl. (Grant St.) / azul-sf.com	DO -	415-362-9750 - ≡	Hot & Cool	72
Bacar / Lounge	448 Brannan St. (Third St.) / bacarsf.com	SM -	415-904-4100 F ≡	Hot & Cool	53, 72
Balboa Cafe / Restaurant Bar	3199 Fillmore St. (Greenwich St.) / balboacafe.com	MA -	415-921-3944 F _	Classic	146
Bambuddha Lounge / Hotel Bar/Lounge	601 Eddy St. (Larkin St.) / bambuddhalounge.com	DO C	415-885-5088 F ≡	Hot & Cool / Trendy Hangouts	53, 72 / 44
Bar at XYZ / Hotel Bar/Lounge	181 Third St. (Howard St.) / xyz-sf.com	SM -	415-817-7836 - ≡	Hot & Cool	52, 73
Bar Tartine / Wine Bar	561 Valencia St. (16th St.) / tartinebakery.com/bar_tartine.htm	MI -	415-487-1600 F ≡	Hip	108
Beach Blanket Babylon / Performance	678 Beach Blanket Babylon Blvd. / beachblanketbabylon.com	NB C	415-421-4222 - -	Classic	126, 146
Beauty Bar / Theme Bar	2299 Mission St. (19th St.) / beautybar.com	MI -	415-285-0323 - ≡	Hip	90, 108
Betelnut / Restaurant Bar	2030 Union St. (Buchanan St.) / betelnutrestaurant.com	MA -	415-929-8855 F ≡	Hot & Cool	73
B44 / Restaurant Bar	44 Belden Pl. (Bush St.)	FD -	415-986-6287 F ≡	Hot & Cool	73
The Big 4 Restaurant / Restaurant Bar	1075 California St. (Taylor St.) / big4restaurant.com	NH -	415-771-1140 F _	Classic	125, 146
Bimbo's 365 Club / Concert Hall	1025 Columbus Ave. (Chestnut St.) / bimbos365club.com	NB C	415-474-0365 - ≡	Live Music Venues	28
Biscuits & Blues / Blues Club	401 Mason St. (Geary St.) / biscuitsandblues.com	DO C	415-292-2583 F ≡	Classic	124, 146
Bissap Baobab / Restaurant Bar	2323 Mission St. (19th St.) / bissapbaobab.com	MI -	415-826-9287 B ≡	Hip	90, 108
Bix / Restaurant Bar	56 Gold St. (Sansome St.) / bixrestaurant.com	FD -	415-433-6300 F ≡	Classic	147
Blue Cube / Nightclub	34 Mason St. (Market St.) / bluecubesf.com	DO C	415-392-4833 B ≡	Hip	109

SAN FRANCISCO BLACK BOOK

NAME TYPE	ADDRESS (CROSS STREET) WEBSITE	AREA COVER	PHONE FOOD/NOISE	EXPERIENCE 99 BEST	PAGE PAGE
Bocadillos Restaurant Bar	710 Montgomery St. (Washington St.) bocasf.com	FD -	415-982-2622 F =	Hot & Cool	73
Boom Boom Room Blues Club	1601 Fillmore St. (Geary Blvd.) boomboomblues.com	PH C	415-673-8000 - =	Classic	126, 147
Bubble Lounge Lounge/Wine Bar	714 Montgomery St. (Washington St.) bubblelounge.com	FD -	415-434-4204 B =	Classic	124, 147
The Buena Vista Restaurant Bar	2765 Hyde St. (Beach St.) thebuenavista.com	FW -	415-474-5044 - =	Classic	147
Café Claude Restaurant Bar	Seven Claude Ln. (Bush St.) cafeclaude.com	DO -	415-392-3515 F =	Classic	147
Café du Nord Performance	2170 Market St. (15th St.) cafedunord.com	CA C	415-861-5016 F	Hip	92, 109
Café Zoetrope Restaurant Bar	916 Kearny St. (Columbus Ave.) cafecoppola.com	NB -	415-291-1700 F =	Classic	147
Catch Restaurant Bar	2362 Market St. (Castro St.) catchsf.com	CA -	415-431-5000 F =	Hip	109
CAV Wine Bar	1666 Market St. (Franklin St.) cavwinebar.com	HV -	415-437-1770 F =	Hot & Cool Wine Bars	73 46
Chaya Brasserie Restaurant Bar	132 Embarcadero (Mission St.) thechaya.com	EM -	415-777-8688 F =	Hot & Cool	52, 73
Circolo Restaurant Lounge	500 Florida St. (Mariposa St.) circolosf.com	PO -	415-553-8560 B =	Hot & Cool	74
Club Six DJ Bar/Nightclub	60 Sixth St. (Mission St.) clubsix1.com	SM C	415-863-1221 - =	Hip	90, 109
Cortez Hotel Bar/Lounge	550 Geary St. (Taylor St.) cortezrestaurant.com	DO -	415-292-6360 F =	Hot & Cool	54, 74
DNA Lounge Lounge/Nightclub	375 11th St. (Harrison St.) dnalounge.com	MI C	415-626-1409 - =	Hot & Cool Late-Night Hangouts	53, 74 26
Dogpatch Saloon Dive Bar/Jazz Club	2496 Third St. (22nd St.)	PO C	415-643-8592 B =	Hip	92, 109
Dolce Lounge	440 Broadway (Kearny St.) dolcesf.com	NB C	415-989-3434 - =	Hot & Cool Sexy Lounges	54, 74 40
DragonBar Nightclub	473 Broadway (Kearny St.) maximumproductions.com	NB C	415-834-9383 - =	Hot & Cool	74
El Rio Dive Bar/Performance	3158 Mission St. (César Chavez St.) elriosf.com	MI C	415-282-3325 B =	Hip Neighborhood Bars	92, 110 30
Elbo Room Dive Bar/Performance	647 Valencia St. (17th St.) elbo.com	MI C	415-552-7788 - =	Hip	92, 110
Element Lounge Lounge	1028 Geary St. (Polk St.) elementlounge.com	NH C	415-440-1125 - =	Hip	110
Emmy's Spaghetti Shack Restaurant Bar	18 Virginia St. (Mission St.)	MI C	415-206-2086 F =	Hip	90, 110
The EndUp Nightclub	401 Sixth St. (Harrison St.) theendup.com	SM C	415-646-0999 - =	Hip Late-Night Hangouts	91, 111 26

221

Nightlife (cont.)

NAME / TYPE	ADDRESS (CROSS STREET) / WEBSITE	AREA COVER	PHONE FOOD/NOISE	EXPERIENCE 99 BEST	PAGE
Enrico's / Restaurant Bar	504 Broadway (Kearny St.) / enricosidewalkcafe.com	NB / C	415-982-6223 / F	Classic	124, 148
Eos / Wine Bar	901 Cole St. (Carl St.) / eossf.com	HA / -	415-566-3063 / B	Hip	111
EZ5 / Bar/Nightclub	682 Commercial St. (Kearny St.) / ez5bar.com	FD / -	415-362-9321 / -	Hip	111
15 Romolo / DJ Bar	15 Romolo Pl. (Broadway)	NB / C	415-398-1359 / -	Classic	125, 148
The Fillmore Auditorium / Concert Hall	1805 Geary Blvd. (Fillmore St.) / thefillmore.com	PH / C	415-346-6000 / B	Live Music Venues	28
First Crush / Wine Bar	101 Cyril Magnin St. (Ellis St.) / firstcrush.com	DO / -	415-982-7874 / F	Hot & Cool / Wine Bars	75 / 46
Fluid Ultra Lounge / Lounge/Nightclub	662 Mission St. (New Montgomery) / fluidsf.com	SM / C	415-615-6888 / -	Hot & Cool / Scene Bars	52, 75 / 37
Frisson / Restaurant Lounge	244 Jackson St. (Sansome St.) / frissonsf.com	FD / -	415-956-3004 / B	Hot & Cool	75
G Bar / Hotel Bar/Lounge	488 Presidio Ave. (California St.) / gbarsf.com	PH / -	415-409-4227 / B	Classic	126, 148
Harry Denton's Starlight Rm. / Piano Bar	450 Powell St. (Sutter St.) / harrydenton.com	DO / C	415-395-8595 / -	Classic / Lounges with a View	125, 148 / 29
Harvey's / Bar	500 Castro St. (18th St.)	CA / -	415-431-4278 / F	Neighborhood Bars	30
Home / Restaurant Bar	2100 Market St. (Church St.) / home-sf.com	CA / -	415-503-0333 / F	Hip	111
Hôtel Biron / Wine Bar	45 Rose St. (Gough St.) / hotelbiron.com	HV / -	415-703-0403 / B	Hip	91, 111
House of Shields / Restaurant Bar	39 New Montgomery St. (Market St.)	SM / C	415-975-8651 / -	Classic	125, 149
Jade Bar / Bar	650 Gough St. (McAllister St.) / jadebar.com	HV / -	415-869-1900 / B	Hot & Cool / Neighborhood Bars	53, 75 / 30
Jardinière / Restaurant Bar	300 Grove St. (Franklin St.) / jardiniere.com	HV / -	415-861-5555 / F	Classic	149
Jazz at Pearl's / Jazz Club	256 Columbus Ave. (Broadway) / jazzatpearls.com	NB / C	415-291-8255 / F	Classic	126, 149
Julius' Castle / Restaurant Bar	1541 Montgomery St. (Union St.) / juliuscastlerestaurant.com	NB / -	415-392-2222 / -	Classic	149
La Suite / Restaurant Bar	100 Brannan St. (Embarcadero) / lasuitesf.com	EM / -	415-593-5900 / F	Hot & Cool	76
Laszlo / Bar/Nightclub	2534 Mission St. (21st St.) / foreigncinema.com/laszlo	MI / C	415-648-7600 / B	Hot & Cool	53, 76
Le Colonial / Restaurant Bar	20 Cosmo Pl. (Taylor St.) / lecolonialsf.com	DO / -	415-931-3600 / F	Classic	125, 149
Le Duplex / Lounge/Nightclub	1525 Mission St. (11th St.) / duplexsf.com	SM / C	415-355-1525 / -	Hot & Cool / Late-Night Hangouts	54, 76 / 26

SAN FRANCISCO BLACK BOOK

NAME / TYPE	ADDRESS (CROSS STREET) / WEBSITE	AREA / COVER	PHONE / FOOD/NOISE	EXPERIENCE / 99 BEST	PAGE / PAGE
Levende Lounge / Lounge	1710 Mission St. (Duboce Ave.) / levendesf.com	MI / C	415-864-5585 / F ≡	Hot & Cool / Restaurants w/Bars	54, 76 / 35
Lexington Club / Bar	3464 19th St. (Lexington St.) / lexingtonclub.com	MI / -	415-863-2052 / - ≡	Hip / Gay Bars and Clubs	111 / 23
Lime / Bar	2247 Market St. (Noe St.) / lime-sf.com	CA / -	415-621-5256 / F ≡	Hip	91, 112
Little Baobab / Nightclub	3388 19th St. (Mission St.) / bissapbaobab.com	MI / C	415-643-3558 / - ≡	Hip	112
Loft 11 / Lounge/Nightclub	316 11th St. (Folsom St.) / loft11sf.com	SM / C	415-701-8111 / - ≡	Hot & Cool / Club Scenes	52, 76 / 19
Luna Lounge / Lounge/Nighclub	1192 Folsom St. (Eighth St.) / lunaloungesf.org	SM / C	415-626-6043 / B ≡	Hip	112
Madrone Lounge / Bar/Art Gallery	500 Divisadero St. (Fell St.) / madronelounge.com	HA / C	415-241-0202 / F ≡	Hip	112
MarketBar / Restaurant Bar	One Ferry Building (Market St.) / marketbar.com	EM / -	415-434-1100 / F ≡	Hot & Cool	77
Martuni's / Piano Bar	Four Valencia St. (Market St.)	MI / -	415-241-0205 / - ≡	Hip	112
MatrixFillmore / Bar	3138 Fillmore St. (Greenwich St.) / matrixfillmore.com	MA / -	415-563-4180 / - ≡	Hot & Cool / Scene Bars	53, 77 / 37
Mecca / Restaurant Bar	2029 Market St. (Dolores St.) / sfmecca.com	CA / -	415-621-7000 / F ≡	Hip	92, 113
Medjool / Restaurant Bar	2522 Mission St. (21st St.) / medjoolsf.com	MI / -	415-550-9055 / F ≡	Hip	113
Mezzanine / Nightclub	444 Jessie St. (Fifth St.) / mezzaninesf.com	SM / C	415-625-8880 / - ≡	Hot & Cool / Club Scenes	52, 77 / 19
Mighty / Nightclub	119 Utah St. (15th St.) / mighty119.com	MI / C	415-626-7001 / - ≡	Hip	91, 113
Milk / Nightclub	1840 Haight St. (Stanyan St.) / milksf.com	HA / C	415-387-6455 / - ≡	Hip / DJ Bars	113 / 21
Mr. Smith's / Bar	34 Seventh St. (Mission St.) / maximumproductions.com	SM / -	415-355-9991 / - ≡	Hot & Cool / Trendy Hangouts	54, 77 / 44
Myth / Restaurant Bar	470 Pacific Ave. (Montgomery St.) / mythsf.com	FD / -	415-677-8986 / F ≡	Hot & Cool	78
Nectar / Wine Bar	3330 Steiner St. (Chestnut St.) / nectarwinelounge.com	MA / -	415-345-1377 / F ≡	Hot & Cool / Wine Bars	78 / 46
111 Minna Gallery / Bar/Art Gallery	111 Minna St. (Second St.) / 111minnagallery.com	SM / C	415-974-1719 / - ≡	Hot & Cool / Trendy Hangouts	52, 78 / 44
Oola / Restaurant Bar	860 Folsom St. (Fourth St.) / oola-sf.com	SM / -	415-995-2061 / - ≡	Hot & Cool	78
Otis / Lounge	25 Maiden Ln. (Kearny St.) / otissf.com	DO / -	no public phone / - ≡	Hot & Cool	78
Oxygen Bar / Theme Bar	795 Valencia St. (19th St.) / oxygensf.com	MI / -	415-255-2102 / F ≡	Hip	91, 113

223

BLACK BOOK

Nightlife (cont.)

NAME TYPE	ADDRESS (CROSS STREET) WEBSITE	AREA COVER	PHONE FOOD/NOISE	EXPERIENCE 99 BEST	PAGE PAGE
Ozumo Restaurant Bar	161 Steuart St. (Mission St.) ozumo.com	SM -	415-882-1333 F =	Hot & Cool	52, 79
Park Chalet Restaurant Bar	1000 Great Hwy. (Fulton St.) parkchalet.com	RI C	415-386-8439 F =	Classic	149
Pier 23 Cafe Restaurant Bar	Pier 23 (Lombard St.) pier23cafe.com	EM -	415-362-5125 F =	Hot & Cool	79
Pilsner Inn Bar	225 Church St. (Market St.)	CA -	415-621-7058 - =	Hip Gay Bars and Clubs	114 23
Pink DJ Bar/Theme Bar	2925 16th St. (S. Van Ness Ave.) pinksf.com	MI C	415-431-8889 - ≡	Hip DJ Bars	91, 114 21
Power Exchange Sex Club	74 Otis St. (Van Ness Ave.) powerexchange.com	MI C	415-487-9944 - =	Sex in the City	39
The Public Restaurant Bar	1489 Folsom St. (11th St.) thepublicsf.com	SM -	415-552-3065 - =	Hip	114
Punch Line Comedy Club Comedy Club	444 Battery St. (Washington St.) punchlinecomedyclub.com	FD C	415-397-0644 B =	Classic	125, 150
Redwood Room Hotel Bar	495 Geary St. (Taylor St.) clifthotel.com	DO -	415-929-2372 - ≡	Hot & Cool Scene Bars	54, 79 37
Roe Restaurant Lounge	651 Howard St. (Third St.) roerestaurant.com	SM C	415-227-0288 - =	Hot & Cool	79
Rosewood Bar/Lounge	732 Broadway (Stockton St.) rosewoodbar.com	NB -	415-951-4886 - =	Hip	114
Ruby Skye Nightclub	420 Mason St. (Geary St.) rubyskye.com	DO C	415-693-0777 - ≡	Hot & Cool Club Scenes	54, 79 19
Rx Gallery Bar/Art Gallery	132 Eddy St. (Mason St.) rxgallery.com	DO C	415-474-7973 - =	Hip	114
Sake Lab Bar	498 Broadway (Kearny St.) sakelab.com	NB -	415-837-0228 - =	Hot & Cool	79
Scala's Bistro Restaurant Bar	432 Powell St. (Sutter St.) scalasbistro.com	DO -	415-395-8555 F =	Classic	150
SF Badlands Nightclub	4121 18th St. (Castro St.) sfbadlands.com	CA C	415-626-9320 - =	Hip Gay Bars and Clubs	92, 115 23
Shanghai 1930 Restaurant Bar	133 Steuart St. (Mission St.) shanghai1930.com	EM -	415-896-5600 F ≡	Hot & Cool	80
Skylark Bar	3089 16th St. (Valencia St.) skylarkbar.com	MI -	415-621-9294 - ≡	Hip	115
Slanted Door Restaurant Bar	One Ferry Building (Market St.) slanteddoor.com	EM -	415-861-8032 F =	Hot & Cool	80
Slim's Concert Hall	333 11th St. (Folsom St.) slims-sf.com	SM C	415-255-0333 F ≡	Live Music Venues	28
Sneaky Tiki Restaurant Bar	1582 Folsom St. (12th St.) sneakytiki-sf.com	SM -	415-701-8454 F =	Hip Tiki Bars	115 43
Soluna Cafe & Lounge Restaurant Lounge	272 McAllister St. (Larkin St.) solunasf.com	HV -	415-621-2200 F =	Hip	115

224

SAN FRANCISCO BLACK BOOK

NAME / TYPE	ADDRESS (CROSS STREET) / WEBSITE	AREA / COVER	PHONE / FOOD/NOISE	EXPERIENCE / 99 BEST	PAGE / PAGE
Sublounge / DJ Bar	628 20th St. (Third St.) / sublounge.com	PO / C	415-552-3603 / - ≡	Hip / DJ Bars	90, 115 / 21
Suede / Lounge	383 Bay St. (Mason St.) / suedesf.com	FW / C	415-399-9555 / - ≡	Hot & Cool / Sexy Lounges	54, 80 / 40
Suite one8one / Lounge	181 Eddy St. (Taylor St.) / suite181.com	DO / C	415-345-9900 / - ≡	Hot & Cool / Sexy Lounges	53, 80 / 40
supperclub San Francisco / Restaurant Bar	657 Harrison St. (Third St.) / supperclub.com	SM / C	415-348-0900 / - ≡	Hot & Cool	81
Swig / Bar/Performance	561 Geary St. (Taylor St.) / swig-bar.com	DO / C	415-931-7292 / - ≡	Hip	92, 116
Tonga Room / Theme Bar	950 Mason St. (California St.) / tongaroom.com	NH / -	415-772-5278 / B ≡	Classic / Tiki Bars	125, 150 / 43
Top of the Mark / Hotel Bar	999 California St. (Mason St.) / sanfrancisco.intercontinental.com	NH / C	415-392-3434 / - —	Classic / Lounges with a View	126, 150 / 29
Tosca Café / Bar	242 Columbus Ave. (Broadway)	NB / -	415-986-9651 / - ≡	Classic	124, 150
Trader Vic's / Theme Bar	555 Golden Gate Ave. (Van Ness Ave.) / tradervics.com/rest-sanfran.html	HV / -	415-775-6300 / F —	Classic / Tiki Bars	126, 151 / 43
Tres Agaves / Restaurant Bar	130 Townsend St. (Second St.) / tresagaves.com	SM / -	415-227-0500 / F ≡	Hot & Cool	81
12 Galaxies / Nightclub/Performance	2565 Mission St. (21st St.) / 12galaxies.com	MI / C	415-970-9777 / B ≡	Hip	116
The Velvet Lounge / Bar/Nightclub	443 Broadway (Montgomery St.) / thevelvetlounge.com	NB / C	415-788-0228 / - ≡	Hip	91, 116
Vesuvio / Bar	255 Columbus Ave. (Broadway) / vesuvio.com	NB / -	415-362-3370 / - ≡	Classic	125, 151
View Lounge / Lounge	55 Fourth St. (Jessie St.)	SM / -	415-896-1600 / B —	Classic / Lounges with a View	151 / 29
Voda / Bar	56 Belden Pl. (Pine St.) / vodasf.com	FD / -	415-677-9242 / - ≡	Hot & Cool	81
Whisper / Bar/Nightclub	535 Florida St. (Mariposa St.) / whispersf.com	PO / C	415-252-9442 / F ≡	Hip	90, 116
Wish / Bar/Lounge	1539 Folsom St. (11th St.) / wishsf.com	SM / -	415-278-9474 / - ≡	Hip	117
Zebra Lounge / Lounge/Nightclub	447 Broadway (Kearny St.) / zebrasf.net	NB / C	415-788-0188 / - ≡	Hot & Cool	81
Zuni Café / Restaurant Bar	1658 Market St. (Franklin St.)	HV / -	415-552-2522 / F ≡	Hip	117

BLACK BOOK

Attractions

NAME / TYPE	ADDRESS (CROSS STREET) / WEBSITE	AREA / PRICE	PHONE	EXPERIENCE / 99 BEST	PAGE / PAGE
Adventure Cat / Sailing	J Dock, Pier 39 / adventurecat.com	EM / $$$	415-777-1630	Hot & Cool	54, 82
Alcatraz Island / Activity	Blue and Gold Ferry, Pier 39 / nps.gov/alcatraz and blueandgoldfleet.com	FW / $	415-705-5555	Classic	123, 152
Angel Island / Activity	Btw Alcatraz Island and Tiburon / parks.ca.gov/?page_id468	VA / $$		Outdoor Activity	32
Asian Art Museum / Art Museum	200 Larkin St. (Grove St.) / asianart.org	HV / $	415-581-3500	Hot & Cool	53, 82
Audium / Performance	1616 Bush St. (Franklin St.) / audium.org	PH / $$	415-771-1616	Classic / Only-in-SF	152 / 31
Baker Beach / Beach	Presidio National Park	PR / -		Hip / Sex in the City	90, 118 / 39
Blue and Gold Ferry / Tour	Pier 41 (Powell St.) / blueandgoldfleet.com	FW / $	415-705-5555	Hot & Cool	54, 82
Cable Cars / Scenic Route	Multiple stops / sfcablecar.com	VA / $—		Classic	123, 152
Chinatown: Wok Wiz Tour / Tour	654 Commercial St. (Kearny St.) / wokwiz.com	VA / $$$	212-209-3370	Classic	152
City Lights Bookstore / Shop	261 Columbus Ave. (Broadway) / citylights.com	NB / -	415-362-8193	Classic	153
Club Sportiva / Car Rental	840 Harrison St. (Fourth St.) / clubsportiva.com	SM / $$$$	415-978-9900	Hot & Cool	82
Coit Tower / Sight	One Telegraph Hill Blvd. / coittower.org	NB / $—	415-362-0808	Classic	124, 153
Conservatory of Flowers / Sight	John F. Kennedy Dr. (Golden Gate Pk.) / conservatoryofflowers.org	RI / $—	415-362-0808	Classic	126, 153
Crissy Field / Park	End of Marina Blvd. (Lyon St.) / crissyfield.org	PR / -	415-561-7690	Classic	125, 154
de Young Museum / Art Museum	50 Hagiwara Tea Garden Dr. / thinker.org/deyoung	RI / $	415-863-3330	Classic	126, 154
The Embarcadero Prom. / Waterfront Walk	King Street to Fisherman's Wharf	EM / -		Hot & Cool	83
Equinox Fitness Club / Health Club	301 Pine St. (Sansome St.) / equinoxfitness.com	FD / $$$$	415-593-4000	Hot & Cool	54, 83
Ferry Plaza Farmers Market / Shopping	One Ferry Building (Market St.) / ferrybuildingmarketplace.com	EM / -	415-291-3276	Hot & Cool	54, 83
The Gardener / Shop	One Ferry Building (Market St.) / thegardener.com	EM / -	415-981-8181	Hot	84
Gimme Shoes / Shop	50 Grant Ave. (Geary Blvd.) / gimmeshoes.com	DO / -	415-434-9242	Hot	84
Glide Memorial Church / Church	330 Ellis St. (Taylor St.) / glide.org	DO / -	415-674-6000	Hip / Only-in-SF	91, 118 / 31
Golden Gate Bridge / Sight	Hwy. 101 N. / goldengatebridge.org	PR / -	415-921-5858	Classic / Outdoor Activities	125, 154 / 32

226

SAN FRANCISCO BLACK BOOK

NAME	ADDRESS (CROSS STREET)	AREA	PHONE	EXPERIENCE	PAGE
TYPE	WEBSITE	PRICE		99 BEST	PAGE
Golden Gate Park	Bounded by Stanyan, Fulton, Lincoln, and Great Hwy.	RI	415-831-2700	Classic	*126*, 154
Park	parks.sfgov.org	-		Outdoor Activities	32
Golden Gate Park-Skating	Various	RI		Hip	*92*, 118
Activity		$$			
Good Vibrations	603 Valencia St. (17th St.)	MI	415-522-5460	Hip	118
Shopping	goodvibes.com	-		Sex in the City	39
Gump's	135 Post St. (Grant Ave.)	DO	415-982-1616	Classic	154
Shop	gumps.com	-			
Harding Park Golf Course	99 Harding Rd. (Skyline Blvd.)	VA	415-664-4690	Hot & Cool	*54*, 84
Golf Course	harding-park.com	$$$$			
International Orange Day Spa	2044 Fillmore St. (California St.)	PH	888-894-8811	Hot & Cool	84
Spa	internationalorange.com	$$$		Spas	41
It's Yoga	848 Folsom St. (Fifth St.)	SM	415-543-1970		
Health Club	itsyoga.com	$		Workouts	48
Jeremy's	2 South Park (Second St.)	SM	415-882-4929	Hot	84
Shop		-			
Kabuki Springs and Spa	1750 Geary Blvd. (Fillmore St.)	PH	415-922-6000	Hip	*91*, 119
Spa	kabukisprings.com	$$			
Kamalaspa	240 Stockton St. (Maiden Ln.)	DO	415-217-7700	Hot & Cool	85
Spa	kamalaspa.com	$$$$			
Limn	290 Townsend St. (Fourth St.)	SM	415-977-1300	Hot	85
Shop	limn.com	-			
Minnie Wilde	519 Laguna St. (Hayes St.)	HV	415-863-9453	Hip	119
Shop	minniewilde.com	-			
Mission Cliffs	2295 Harrison St. (19th St.)	MI	415-550-0515	Hip	*90*, 119
Health Club	touchstoneclimbing.com	$$		Workouts	48
Mission Dolores	3321 16th St. (Dolores St.)	MI	415-621-8203	Hip	*89*, 119
Church	missiondolores.org	$-			
Nob Hill Spa	1075 California St. (Taylor St.)	NH	415-474-5400	Classic	155
Spa	nobhillspa.com	$$$$		Spas	41
Ocean Beach	Great Highway (Balboa Ave.)	RI		Classic	*125*, 155
Beach		-			
Palace of Fine Arts	3301 Lyon St. (Marina Blvd.)	MA	415-567-6642	Classic	*125*, 155
Sight	palaceoffinearts.org	-			
Palace of the Legion of Honor	Lincoln Park, 100 34th Ave.	RI	415-863-3330	Classic	*124*, 155
Art Museum	thinker.org/legion	$			
Paxton Gate	824 Valencia St. (19th St.)	MI	415-824-1872	Hip	120
Shop	paxton-gate.com	-			
Presidio Golf Course & Clubhouse	300 Finley Rd. (Arguello Blvd.)	PR	415-561-4661	Classic	156
Golf Course	presidiogolf.com	$$$			
Remède Spa	125 Third St. (Mission St.)	SM	415-284-4000	Hot & Cool	85
Spa	remede.com	$$$$			
Rolo	2351 Market St. (Castro St.)	CA	415-431-4545	Hip	120
Shop	rolo.com	-			

BLACK BOOK

227

Attractions (Cont.)

NAME TYPE	ADDRESS (CROSS STREET) WEBSITE	AREA PRICE	PHONE	EXPERIENCE 99 BEST	PAGE PAGE
San Francisco Helicopter Tours Tour	sfhelicoptertours.com	VA $$$$	800-400-2404	Hot & Cool	85
SFMuseum Craft+Design Art Museum	550 Sutter St. (Mason St.) sfmcd.org	DO $–	415-773-0303	Hot & Cool	52, 86
S Factor Health Club	2159 Filbert St. (Fillmore St.) sfactor.com	MA $$	415-440-6420	Hot & Cool	86
SBC Park Tour Tour	24 Willie Mays Plaza (King St.) sbcpark.com	SM $$	415-972-2400	Hot & Cool	52, 86
SFMoMA Art Museum	151 Third St. (Howard St.) sfmoma.org	SM $	415-357-4000	Hot & Cool	52, 86
SFMoMA Museum Store Shop	151 Third St. (Mission St.) sfmoma.org	SM -	415-357-4000	Hot & Cool	87
Signature Yacht Cruise Sailing	Pier 9 (Embarcadero) signaturesf.com	EM $$$$	415-788-9100	Classic	156
Sports Club/LA Health Club	747 Market St. (Grant Ave.) thesportsclubla.com	SM $$$$	415-633-3900	Hot & Cool Workouts	87 48
Sue Fisher King Shop	3067 Sacramento St. (Baker St.) suefisherking.com	PH -	415-922-7276	Classic	156
Tru Spa Spa	750 Kearny St. (Washington St.) truspa.com	FD $$$$	415-399-9700	Hot & Cool Spas	54, 87 41
Twin Peaks Sight	Twin Peaks Blvd.	CA -		Hip	90, 120
Vino Venue Shop	686 Mission St. (Third St.) vinovenue.net	SM -	415-341-1930	Hot & Cool	87
West Coast Live Performance	various wcl.org	VA $$	415-664-9500	Hip	90, 120
Wilkes Bashford Shop	375 Sutter St. (Stockton St.) willkesbashford.com	DO -	415-986-4380	Classic	156
Yerba Buena Arts Center Arts Museum	701 Mission St. (Third St.) yerbabuenaarts.org	SM -	415-978-2787	Hip	91, 120

Notes

Notes

San Francisco Unique Shopping Index

NAME	(415) PHONE	AREA	PRODUCTS	PAGE
AB Fits	982-5726	NB	Men/Women's apparel	128
Abigail Morgan	567-1779	MA	Women's apparel	56
Alabaster	558-0482	HV	Home décor	94
Alla Prima Fine Lingerie	397-4077	NB	Fine European lingerie	128
The Bar	409-4901	PH	Women's apparel	128
Biordi Art Imports	392-8096	NB	Italian pottery	128
Blue Jeans Bar	346-4280	MA	Men/Women's jeans	56
Cielo	776-0641	PH	Women's apparel, cashmere	56
City Lights Bookstore	357-4000	NB	Legendary bookstore	128, 153
De Vera	788-0828	DO	Home décor, accessories	57
Flicka	292-2315	PH	Women's apparel, accessories	56
Friend	552-1717	HV	Accessories, furnishings	94
The Gardener	981-8181	EM	Home accessories	84
Gimme Shoes	864-0691	PH/DO	Men/Women's shoes	56, 57, 84
Good Vibrations	522-5460	MI	Sex toys, books	39, 94, 118
The Grocery Store	928-3615	PH	Women's apparel	128
Gumps	982-1616	DO	Jewels, linens, china, crystal	128, 154
Jeremy's	882-4929	SM	Discounted designer clothing	57, 84
Kiehl's	359-9260	PH	Beauty products	56
Laku	695-1462	MI	Women's apparel	94
Ligne Roset	777-1030	SM	French furnishings	57
Limn	977-1300	SM	Modern European furnishings	57, 85
Ma Maison	777-5370	SM	French home décor	57
Margaret O'Leary	929-0441	PH	Women's apparel	56
Metier	989-5395	DO	Women's apparel, jewelry	57
Mingle	674-8811	MA	Men/Women's apparel	56
Minnie Wilde	863-9453	HV/MI	Women's apparel	94, 119
Nest	292-6199	PH	Whimsical home accessories	56
Ooma	627-6963	NB	Women's apparel	128
Pamela Mills	474-8400	PH	Women's apparel	128
Paxton Gate	824-1872	MI	Unique plants, unusual objects	94, 120
Propeller	701-7767	HV	Accessories, furnishings	94
Rabat	929-8868	MA	Women's apparel, shoes	56
Rayon Vert	861-3516	MI	Gifts, accessories, flowers	94
Riley James	775-7956	MA	Men/Women's apparel	56
Rin	922-8040	MA	Women's apparel, accessories	57
Rolo	431-4545	CA	Men's apparel	120
Sarah Shaw	929-2990	PH	Women's apparel	128
SFMoMA Store	357-4000	SM	Jewelry, gifts, books	57, 87
Sue Fisher King	922-7276	PH	European linens, décor	128, 156
Sunhee Moon	355-1801	MI	Women's apparel	94
Toujours	346-3988	PH	Fine lingerie	56
Vino Venue	341-1930	SM	Wine shop	57, 87
Wilkes Bashford	986-4380	DO	Men's apparel	128, 156
X-21 Modern	647-4211	MI	Eclectic, unusual home items	94
Zinc Details	776-2100	PH	Modern home furnishings, décor	56
Zonal	255-9307	HV	Rustic home furnishings, décor	94

For Neighborhood (Area) Key, see p.212.

THE HEART OF SAN FRANCISCO

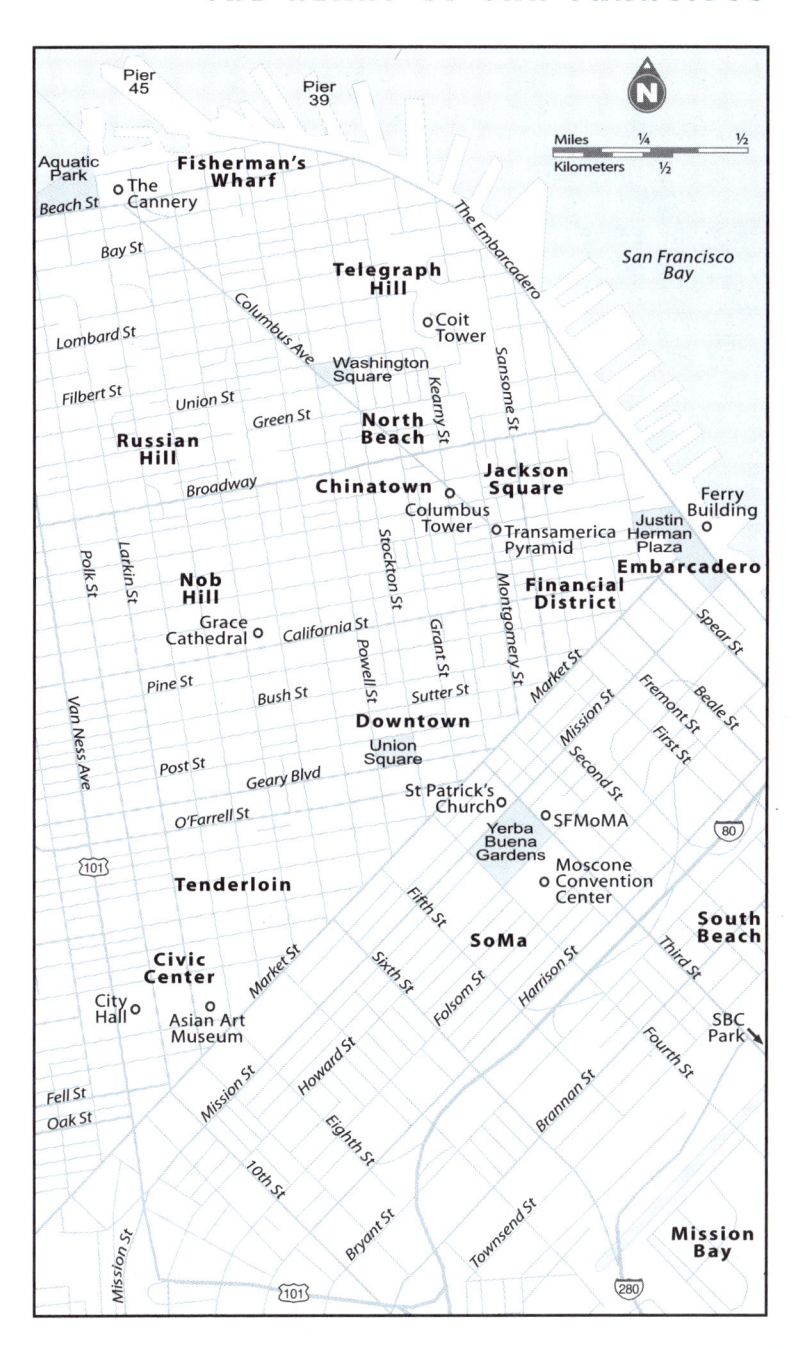

SAN FRANCISCO NEIGHBORHOODS

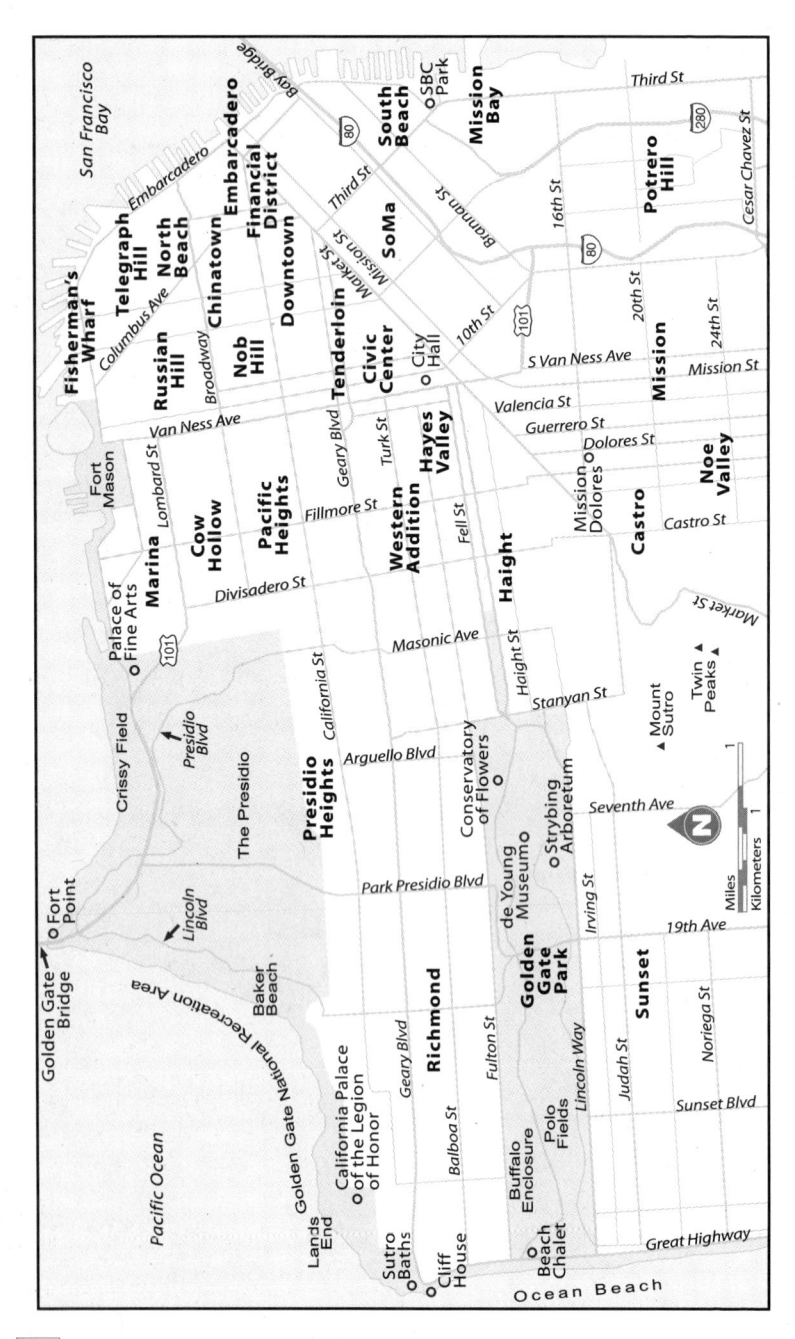